BUDAPEST

THE MINI ROUGH GUIDE

Rough Guide Credits

Text editor: Sophie Martin
Series editor: Mark Ellingham
Typesetting: Link Hall
Cartography: Nichola Goodliffe

Publishing Information

This first edition published August 1999 by
Rough Guides Ltd, 62–70 Shorts Gardens, London WC2H 9AB

Distributed by the Penguin Group:
Penguin Books Ltd, 27 Wrights Lane, London W8 5TZ
Penguin Books USA Inc., 375 Hudson Street, New York 10014, USA
Penguin Books Australia Ltd, 487 Maroondah Highway,
PO Box 257, Ringwood, Victoria 3134, Australia
Penguin Books Canada Ltd, 10 Alcorn Avenue,
Toronto, Ontario, Canada M4V 1E4
Penguin Books (NZ) Ltd, 182–190 Wairau Road,
Auckland 10, New Zealand

Typeset in Bembo and Helvetica to an original design by Henry Iles.
Printed in Spain by Graphy Cems.

304pp, includes index
A catalogue record for this book is available from the British Library.
ISBN 1-85828-431-7

BUDAPEST

THE MINI ROUGH GUIDE

Written and researched by
Charles Hebbert
and Dan Richardson

We set out to do something different when the first Rough Guide was published in 1982. Mark Ellingham, just out of university, was travelling in Greece. He brought along the popular guides of the day, but found they were all lacking in some way. They were either strong on ruins and museums but went on for pages without mentioning a beach or taverna. Or they were so conscious of the need to save money that they lost sight of Greece's cultural and historical significance. Also, none of the books told him anything about Greece's contemporary life – its politics, its culture, its people, and how they lived.

So with no job in prospect, Mark decided to write his own guidebook, one which aimed to provide practical information that was second to none, detailing the best beaches and the hottest clubs and restaurants, while also giving hard-hitting accounts of every sight, both famous and obscure, and providing up-to-the-minute information on contemporary culture. It was a guide that encouraged independent travellers to find the best of Greece, and was a great success, getting shortlisted for the Thomas Cook travel guide award, and encouraging Mark, along with three friends, to expand the series.

The Rough Guide list grew rapidly and the letters flooded in, indicating a much broader readership than had been anticipated, but one which uniformly appreciated the Rough Guide mix of practical detail and humour, irreverence and enthusiasm. Things haven't changed. The same four friends who began the series are still the caretakers of the Rough Guide mission today: to provide the most reliable, up-to-date and entertaining information to independent-minded travellers of all ages, on all budgets.

We now publish more than 100 titles and have offices in London and New York. The travel guides are written and researched by a dedicated team of more than 100 authors, based in Britain, Europe, the USA and Australia. We have also created a unique series of phrasebooks to accompany the travel series, along with an acclaimed series of music guides, and a best-selling pocket guide to the Internet and World Wide Web. We also publish comprehensive travel information on our Web site: **www.roughguides.com**

Help Us Update

A lot of effort has gone in to ensure that this first edition of *The Rough Guide to Budapest* is up to date and accurate. However, things can change fast: new restaurants and hotels appear, and prices and opening hours change. Any suggestions, comments, corrections or updates towards the next edition would be much appreciated. All contributions will be credited, and the best letters will be rewarded with a copy of the new book (or any other Rough Guide, if you prefer). Please mark all letters "Rough Guide to Budapest Update" and send to:

Rough Guides, 62–70 Shorts Gardens, London WC2H 9AB, or
Rough Guides, 375 Hudson St, New York NY 10014.

Or send email to: **mail@roughguides.co.uk**
Online updates about this book can be found on
Rough Guides' Web site (see opposite)

The Authors

Dan Richardson was born in England in 1958. Before joining the Rough Guides in 1984, he worked as a sailor on the Red Sea, and as a commodities dealer in Peru. Since then he has travelled extensively in Egypt and Eastern Europe. While in St Petersburg in 1992, he met his wife, Anna, and they now have a daughter, Sonia.

Charles Hebbert has been hanging around Hungary for seventeen years. He spent two years learning the language, supporting himself by starring in dreadful language-teaching videos and doing anything else that would bring in money, and then began a PhD on the position of women in Hungary. However in 1990, with research going everywhere and nowhere, he decided to try his hand as a journalist in Budapest. He returned to London in 1998, where he works as a freelance writer.

Acknowledgements

Thanks to all the many, many people, too many to name in this small space sadly, who made this work possible and worth doing.

CONTENTS

Listings

Contexts

Introduction

With its wonderful natural setting, straddling the River Danube, its beautiful architecture and excellent Magyar cuisine, **Budapest** is one of the most satisfying cities in Europe to visit. Its magnificent waterfront and boulevards invite comparisons with Paris, Prague and Vienna – as do many features of its cultural life such as its coffee houses, its love of opera and its wine-producing tradition. However, the city is also distinctively Hungarian, its inhabitants displaying fierce pride in their Magyar ancestry. Their language too, whose nearest European relatives are Finnish and Turkish, underlines the difference.

Ironically, provincial Hungarians have long regarded Budapest as a hotbed of alien values and loose morals – a charge that misses the point. Foreigners have played a major role in the city since its inception, and the Chinese and Arab communities established since the end of Communism simply bring it up to date as an international city for the next millennium. Even the sex trade that has earned it the reputation of the "Bangkok of Europe" is nothing new, having been a feature of life during Habsburg times. In politics, art and much else, Budapest is not only the capital but a catalyst for the country, without which Hungary would be a far duller place.

Budapest is divided into two halves, **Buda** and **Pest**, by the river Danube. Its compact centre located around the waterfront and its excellent public transport system make it an easy city for visitors to explore. **Várhegy** (Castle Hill) is the obvious starting point for an exploration of the city, where the **Mátyás Church**, **Fishermen's Bastion**, and Renaissance inns and cellars of **Buda Palace** evoke a proud and turbulent past. Nearby are two of Buda's famous **Turkish baths**, where you can wallow in the original Ottoman pools.

Várhegy and Gellért-hegy on the Buda side both offer stunning views over the bustling **Belváros** (Inner City) and central districts of Pest, where most of the restaurants, nightlife and other attractions are found. Encircled by the **Kiskörút** and **Nagykörút** (Small and Great Boulevards), these neighbourhoods form the heart of the city, and, though Pest contains such monumental sights as **Parliament** and **St Stephen's Basilica**, its social and cultural life is the prime attraction. The boulevards of **Váci utca** and **Vörösmarty tér** are synonymous with people-watching, café society, shopping and street entertainers, with concerts at the **Vigadó** concert hall. Around the corner is the *Gerbeaud* patisserie, the best-known of Budapest's **coffee houses**, whose Biedermeier elegance contrasts with the Art Nouveau opulence of the *New York* and *Astoria* coffee houses.

One of the great things about Budapest is that most of its pleasures are affordable for visitors on a tight budget. Delicious **meals** can be had all over the city, and discovering things for yourself can be half the fun. Though Hungarian cuisine is noted for its richly sauced meat and fish dishes, there are enough alternatives (Indian, Chinese, Italian, Middle Eastern) for vegetarians to enjoy themselves too.

Budapest's **nightlife** is also very affordable and, though small, it caters for a wide range of tastes. There isn't always much of a distinction between clubs and bars, as many bars play live music or have a disco; beer halls, however, usually serve full meals. Generally, the scene is trouble-free and welcoming, with a whole network of events that are surprisingly accessible. This is especially true of the **Táncház** (Dance House) scene, where Hungarians of all ages perform wild stamping dances to the rhythms of darkest Transylvania, and internationally renowned artists like Márta Sebestyén appear in an informal setting.

In the case of **classical music and opera**, world-class ensembles and soloists can be enjoyed in the palatial settings of the Vigadó and State Opera House, especially during the major **festivals** in spring, summer and autumn. You can also go to outdoor concerts on Margit sziget (Margit Island) over summer. For fans of pop, rock and world music, the two big events are the Budapesti Bucsú, first held to celebrate the departure of Soviet troops in 1991, and the Sziget Festival, which claims to be the largest in Europe.

When to visit

The best times to visit Budapest are **spring** (late March to the end of May) and **autumn** (Sept–Oct), when the weather is mild and there are fewer tourists, except during the Spring Festival (late March/early April). The majority of tourists come in the **summer**, when residents decamp to Lake Balaton and those who remain flock to the city's pools and parks to escape the heat and dust. Though many concert halls are closed over summer, there are all kinds of outdoor events to compensate – especially in August, when the Sziget Festival, the Formula-1 Grand Prix and the Opera and Ballet festival all take place around the middle of the month. **Winter** is cold and may be snowy, but you can still enjoy all the city's sights and cultural attractions (as well as trying roasted chestnuts from street vendors), while the thermal baths take on an extra allure. It's wise to book accommodation in advance for Christmas, New Year, the Spring Festival and Grand Prix.

Budapest's climate

Average daytime temperature

	Jan	Feb	Mar	Apr	May	June	July	Aug	Sept	Oct	Nov	Dec
°F	29	32	42	53	61	68	72	70	63	52	42	34
°C	-2	0	6	12	16	20	22	21	17	11	6	1

Average rainfall

mm	37	44	38	45	72	69	56	47	33	57	70	46

THE GUIDE

Introducing the city

The **River Danube** – which is seldom blue – separates **Buda** on the hilly west bank from **Pest** on the eastern plain, and is fundamental to the city's layout and history. **Várhegy** (Castle Hill) on the Buda side was for many centuries the seat of monarchs, and its palace, museums, churches and Baroque streets make it the obvious place to start sightseeing. Thereafter, you can wander through the **Víziváros** (Watertown) below the hill, before pushing on to **Gellért-hegy** (Gellért Hill), with its crags and towering Liberation Monument. The historic **Turkish baths** in the **Tabán** quarter between the two hills are also well worth experiencing.

Over in **Pest**, you're likely to spend most of your time enjoying the streetlife, bars and restaurants within the **Belváros** (Inner City) and the surrounding districts. In contrast to the medieval street plan of Várhegy and the Belváros, these surrounding districts are defined by two semicircular boulevards – the **Kiskörút** (Small Boulevard) and the **Nagykörút** (Great Boulevard) – and radial avenues such as Andrássy út and Rákóczi út. Exploring the area between them can easily occupy you for several days.

In the **Lipótváros**, the financial and government centre, the interest lies in **St Stephen's Basilica**, the monumental **Parliament** building rivalling the Várhegy across the

Danube, and some wonderful buildings around **Szabadság tér** (Liberty Square), including one by Ödön Lechner, whose work is often likened to Gaudí's in Barcelona. In the **Terézváros** one can hardly avoid making comparisons with Paris, as **Andrássy út** and the **Opera House** were clearly inspired by Haussmann's work for Napoleon III. Andrássy út terminates at **Hősök tere** (Heroes' Square), a magnificent imperial set piece that is Budapest's Les Invalides and Nelson's Column rolled into one.

Of the remaining inner-city districts, the **Erzsébetváros** and **Józsefváros** hold the most appeal. The former is traditionally Budapest's **Jewish quarter**, with a rich and tragic history that's still palpable in the backstreets, making them a wonderful place to explore. The great synagogue on Dohány utca provides more historical information. The adjacent Józsefváros is also fascinating but very seedy in parts, though there's nothing to fear in the vicinity of the **National Museum**, or even at **Kerepesi Cemetery**, out beyond the Nagykörút. In **Ferencváros**, the attractions are the great market hall on the Kiskörút, and the Applied Arts Museum further out, in an amazing building by Lechner.

Other parts of the city are also rewarding, but you need to be selective. **Óbuda** (Old Buda) really only lives up to its name in one locality, though its postwar sprawl harbours several Roman remains, with the ruins of Aquincum further out in **Római-Fürdő**. More alluringly, there are the **Buda Hills** that encircle the city to the west, with enjoyable **rides** on the Cogwheel and Children's railways, and intriguing **caves** to be visited. In fine weather people also flock to **Margit sziget** (Margit Island) to swim and sunbathe at two enormous lidos. The other Danube **islands** have less to write home about, unless you happen to attend the annual pop festival on **Óbudai sziget**, or have an interest in the militant history of working-class **Csepel**.

Further out, but still within the city limits, the **Statue Park** of redundant Communist monuments rates as a major attraction, as does the **Budakeszi Game Park**, while two romantic **cemeteries** might not be everyone's idea of fun, but can claim many admirers.

Providing you're willing to start out early, there's virtually no limit to the number of **excursions from the city** that are feasible, as most towns in Hungary are within three to four hours' journey from the capital. However, limiting yourself to under two hours' travel, the range narrows down to the scenic Danube Bend, where the historic towns of **Szentendre** and **Esztergom** get top billing, followed by **Visegrád**.

The telephone code for Budapest is ©1. To call Budapest from abroad, dial ©36, followed by the subscriber's number.

ARRIVAL

Other than the airport, all points of arrival are within walking distance or just a few stops by metro from downtown Pest, the major transport hub, where the three metro lines meet near the terminal for the airport shuttle bus and international buses.

For information on booking accommodation and details of the accommodation booking agencies listed below, see p.150.

By air

Ferihegy Airport, 20km from the centre of Pest, has two main terminals, 5km apart: Ferihegy 1 for charter flights and cargo; and Ferihegy 2 for scheduled flights, with Malév, the national carrier, using terminal 2A, and all other airlines 2B. Arriving at **terminal 2A or 2B**, you can change money easily before heading off into town. Outside the lower level of 2A and 2B you can board the **Airport-Centrum Minibusz** (every 30min 5.30am–9pm; 600Ft on board), which takes about forty minutes to reach Erzsébet tér in downtown Pest. This should not be confused with the **Airport Minibus**, a 24-hour service that takes clients directly to their destination. Tickets (1200Ft) for this service can be purchased in the baggage reclaim hall – give your address and wait until the driver calls your destination. Leaving Budapest, you can arrange to be collected from anywhere in the city and driven to the airport (©296-8555). Both services cost less than airport **taxis**, which are mafia-controlled and charge way above the odds; expect to pay 4000–5000Ft, though they often try to sting you for a lot more.

A cheaper, slower alternative is to use **public transport**. From outside arrivals, catch the red-numbered #93 bus (not to be confused with the black #93), which terminates in Kőbánya-Kispest, where you switch to metro M3 and alight ten stops later at Deák tér (160Ft for both tickets; about 55min in total). You will have to purchase a bus ticket from a machine by the stop before boarding.

By train

The Hungarian word *pályaudvar* (abbreviated to *pu.* in writing only) is used to designate Budapest's seven main-line **train stations**, only three of which are on the metro and of any use to visitors. Translated into English, their names refer to the general direction of services handled. Keleti is the most insalubrious of the stations, though all of them have pickpockets and beggars by day, and prostitutes, robbers and rough-sleepers at night; it's best not to hang around.

Nyugati Station, on the northern edge of Pest's Nagykörút, has a 24-hour left-luggage office near the waiting room by platform 10. You can change money or book rooms at Cooptourist (Mon–Fri 9am–4.30pm) or Budapest Tourist (Mon–Fri 9am–5.30pm, Sat 9am–noon) in the underpass in front of the station, near the metro entrance. For information, visit the Budapest Tourist Information Office by the police office (*rendőrség*) just inside the main station entrance (daily 7am–8pm; ©302-8580) – not to be confused with Budapest Tourist. To reach Deák tér, ride metro M3 two stops in the direction of Kőbánya-Kispest.

Trains from Vienna terminate at Pest's **Keleti Station** on Baross tér in the VIII district. Over the summer there are long queues at the 24-hour luggage office, and also at the tourist offices in the Lotz Hall, by the side exit on platform 6: Ibusz (Mon–Fri 8am–4pm) and Tourist Information Centre (daily: June–Aug 7.30am–9pm; Sept–May 7.30am–7pm; ©343-0748). For changing money it's easier to go to Budapest Tourist at Baross tér 3, beyond the overpass on the other side of the square (Mon–Fri 9am–4.30pm). Keleti Station is three stops from Deák tér by metro M2.

Déli Station is 500m behind the Várhegy in Buda. Rooms and exchange are handled by Budapest Tourist in the mall by the metro entrance (left-luggage is around the corner), or you can cross the park towards Várhegy to deal with Cooptourist at Attila út 107. Déli Station is four stops from Deák tér on metro M2.

By bus

International bus services invariably wind up at the **Erzsébet tér bus station**, just by Deák tér on the edge of downtown Pest. The station's left-luggage office is small but rarely busy, and there are several tourist offices in the vicinity – you'll find Dunatours and Cooptourist at

Bajcsy-Zsilinszky út 17, 150m north; and Ibusz at Dob utca 1, slightly further in the other direction. Tourinform (see opposite) is just around the corner and the 24-hour exchange bureau near the Pest embankment is less than ten minutes' walk away. The bus station is supposed to be moving after 2000, though its new location has yet to be decided.

Buses from some other parts of Hungary arrive at **Népstadion bus station** in the XIV district, or the **Árpád híd bus station** in the XIII district. Neither has any tourist facilities, but they're both just four or five metro stops from the centre of Pest.

By hydrofoil

Hydrofoils from Vienna (April–Oct) dock at the **international landing stage** on the Belgrád rakpart (embankment), near downtown Pest. Volántourist is just outside the terminal and there is an Ibusz office five minutes' walk north, on Ferenciek tere, inland of the Erzsébet Bridge.

By car

All things considered, **driving** in Budapest can't be recommended. Road manners are nonexistent, parking space is scarce and traffic jams are frequent. Careering trams, bumpy cobbles and unexpected one-way systems make things worse. If you do have a car, you might be better off parking it somewhere outside the centre and using public transport to get in and out. Don't leave it unattended for too long, though. Guarded **parking lots** exist at many suburban hotels and campsites, and in each district of the city.

If you want **to rent a car**, choose one of the Western models offered by most companies, which are in the region of $60 a day, with special weekly rates; old Russian Ladas should be avoided. With some agencies mileage and insurance are included in this price, and it's worth checking if there's going to be a surcharge or not. Most places accept a credit card as a deposit; if you don't have one, you can expect to pay upwards of $1000. See p.249 for agency addresses.

INFORMATION AND MAPS

The best source of unbiased information is **Tourinform** at V, Sütő utca 2, just around the corner from Deák tér metro (June–Aug daily 8am–8pm; May, Sept & Oct daily 9am–7pm; Nov–April Mon–Fri 9am–7pm, Sat & Sun 9am–4pm; ©317-9800). Their friendly polyglot staff can answer just about any question on Budapest, or travel elsewhere in Hungary. The tourist agencies in train stations provide a simple free map of Budapest and also book accommodation; for more information on this, see p.150.

Details of **what's on** can be found in the English-language magazines *Where Budapest* and *Panoráma* (both free from hotels) and the weeklies *Budapest Week* and *Budapest Sun* (around 150Ft). With a little knowledge of the language it is also possible to make use of the Hungarian listings weeklies *Pesti Est* (free in cinema foyers) and *Pesti Műsor* (available at newsagents for 70Ft).

The small free **map** supplied by tourist offices gives an idea of Budapest's layout and principal monuments, but lacks the detail of larger folding ones, sold all over the place, or the more conveniently sized *Budapest Atlasz*, available in bookshops for 1200Ft, which shows every street, bus and tram route, besides museums and suchlike. It also contains enlarged maps of Várhegy (Castle Hill), central Pest, Margit sziget (Margit Island) and the Városliget (City Park), plus a comprehensive index.

Budapest is divided into 23 districts (*kerület*), designated on maps and street signs by Roman numerals. Addresses begin with the number of the district – for example, V, Petőfi tér 3 – a system used throughout this guide.

Sightseeing tours

Although Budapest can easily be explored without a guide, visitors hard-pressed for time might appreciate a **city tour** (2–3hr). These range in price from 2400Ft to 2900Ft and can be arranged through Tourinform (see p.9), Budapest Tourist (leaving from their office at V, Roosevelt tér 5; ©118-6600) or Buda Tours (leaving from the same place; ©153-0558). Ibusz and Budapest Tourist also organize guided tours of the Parliament building, combined with visits to the Museum of Ethnography or the National Gallery.

If you are cramming in a lot of sightseeing and making plentiful use of public transport, you might consider investing in a **Budapest Card**. A three-day card, valid for one adult and one child under 14, costs 2950Ft, and gives you unlimited travel on public transport, free admission to a long list of museums, reductions on the airport minibus, car rental, certain sightseeing tours and cultural events, and discounts in some shops, restaurants and thermal baths. A small booklet comes with the pack to explain where you can use the card. There is also a two-day card for 2450Ft. Cards are available at tourist offices, hotels and major metro station ticket offices, such as Deák tér, Nyugati pu., Keleti pu., and Kálvin tér.

City transport

Budapest is an easy city to get around. The best way to see its historic quarters is on foot, and the cheap and efficient public transport system run by BKV ensures that few parts of the city are more than thirty minutes' journey from the centre, and many can be reached in half that time. The language and local geography may be unfamiliar, but it doesn't take long to pick up the basics, and it's much better value than taxis, which often take advantage of tourists.

The only drawback to public transport are **pickpockets**, especially on the M1 metro line. Gangs distract their victims by pushing them or blocking their way, while emptying their pockets and bags at the same time.

Tickets and passes

To avoid the hassle of buying tickets all the time you'd do well to invest in some kind of travel pass. **Tickets** valid for the metro, buses, trams, trolleybuses and suburban HÉV lines (see below) are sold at metro stations, newspaper kiosks and tobacconists, and currently cost 90Ft. You can also buy **day passes** (*napijegy*) costing 700Ft, valid for unlimited travel until midnight, or three-day passes for 1400Ft. **Season tickets** are available from metro stations, covering trams, trolleybuses, the metro, HÉV and cogwheel trains, and buses. They cost around 1750Ft for a week, 2250Ft for two weeks and 3400Ft for a month, including a photocard (bring a passport photo along), though you can get one without a photocard if you pay a bit more. **Metro tickets** (valid only on the metro) come in a variety of types, depending on how many lines you want to use, and how many stops you want to go. A metro section ticket (60Ft) takes you three stops on the same line; a metro transfer ticket (135Ft) is valid for as many stops as you like with one line change; a metro section transfer ticket (95Ft) takes you five stops with one line change. **Children** up to the age of six travel free.

There is a 1200Ft **fine** for travelling without a ticket – higher if you have a season ticket but were not carrying it, though most of it is refunded upon presentation of the ticket within three days at the Budapest Transport Company (BKV) office at VII, Akácfa utca 22, near Blaha Lujza tér metro.

The metro

The **metro** is by far the quickest way of getting around Budapest and serves most places you're likely to want to get to. Running at two- to fifteen-minute intervals between 4.30am and 11.10pm, its three colour-coded lines intersect at Deák tér in downtown Pest (see p.77). The yellow **M1** line runs from nearby Vörösmarty tér out beneath Andrássy út to Mexikoi út, beyond the Városliget; the red **M2** line connects Déli Station in Buda with Keleti Station and Örs vezér tere in Pest; and the blue **M3** line describes an arc from Kőbánya-Kispest to Újpest-Központ, via Ferenciek tere and Nyugati Station. There's little risk of going astray once you've learned to recognize the signs *bejárat* (entrance), *kijárat* (exit), *vonal* (line) and *felé* (towards). Drivers announce the next stop between stations and the train's direction is indicated by the name of the station at the end of the line.

See map 1 for a plan of the metro.

Buses, trams and trolleybuses

Buses (*autóbusz*) are useful for journeys that can't be made by metro – especially around Buda, where Moszkva tér (metro M2) and Móricz Zsigmond körtér (southwest of Gellért-hegy) are the main bus terminals. Bus stops are marked by a blue sign with a picture of a bus, which has a timetable underneath. Most buses run every five to twenty minutes from 5am to 11pm (*Utolsó kocsi indul . . .* means "the last one leaves . . ."). Regular services are numbered in black; buses with red numbers make fewer stops en route; and those with a red "E" suffix run nonstop between terminals. You punch your ticket on board; to get the bus to stop, push the button above the door or on the handrail beside the door. Busy routes are also served by **night buses** (1–4 an hour) with black numbers and an "É" suffix. After 8pm, you are required to show your ticket or pass to the driver as you board.

Yellow **trams** (*villamos*) are chiefly good for travelling around Nagykörút or along the embankments. Times are the same as for buses (above). Tram #2, along the Pest embankment, is ideal for seeing the city's splendid waterfront panorama.

As a tourist, you won't find much use for **trolleybuses** (*trolibusz*), since most of the thirteen routes take you along residential streets. However, they can be useful for getting to the Városliget (City Park), and provide a scenic route. Allegedly, route numbers start at 70 because the first trolleybus line was inaugurated on Stalin's seventieth birthday in 1949. Trolleybus #83 came into service in 1961, when Stalin would have been 83.

Taxis

Budapest has over 15,000 registered **taxis**, whose drivers have gained a reputation for ripping off foreigners. The best advice is to use one of the following established companies: Főtaxi (©222-2222) and Citytaxi (©211-1111), the most reliable. Taxis can be flagged down on the street or, to get a cheaper rate, ordered by phone. There are ranks throughout the city and you can hop into whichever cab you choose – don't feel you have to take the one at the front of the line.

Be sure your taxi has a meter that is visible, and that it is switched on when you get in; rates should also be clearly displayed. **Fares** begin at 100Ft, and the price per kilometre is

Useful routes

BUSES

#7 Bosnyák tér–Keleti Station–Móricz Zsigmond körtér (via Rákóczi út, Ferenciek tere, the *Gellért Hotel*, Rác and Rudas Baths). Red #7 continues on to Kelenföld Station.
#16 Erzsébet tér–Dísz tér (on Várhegy).
#22 Moszkva tér–Budakeszi Game Park.
#26 Nyugati tér–Szent István körút–Margit sziget–Árpád híd metro station.
#27 Móricz Zsigmond körtér–near the top of Gellért-hegy.
#56 Moszkva tér–Szilyági Erzsébet fasor–Hűvösvölgy.
#65 Kolosy tér–Pálvölgyi Cave–the foot of Hármashatár-hegy.
#86 Southern Buda–Gellért tér–the Víziváros–Flórián tér (Óbuda).
#105 Apor Vilmos tér–Lánchíd–Deák tér.
Várbusz Minibus Moszkva tér–Szentháromság tér–the Sikló terminal near Buda Palace.

NIGHT BUSES

#6É Moszkva tér–Margit sziget–Nyugati Station–Nagykörút–Móricz Zsigmond körtér.
#14É and **#50É** Kőbánya-Kispest metro station–Lehel tér and beyond along the route of metro M3.
#49É Moszkva tér–Erzsébet híd–*Gellért Hotel*–Móricz Zsigmond körtér.
#78É Örs vezér tere–Bosnyák tér–Keleti Station–Buda side of the Erzsébet híd.

TRAMS

#2 Margit híd–Petőfi híd along the Pest embankment.
#4 Moszkva tér–Margit sziget–Nyugati Station–Nagykörút–Boráros tér–Október 23 utca.

#6 Moszkva tér–Margit sziget–Nyugati Station–Nagykörút–Boráros tér–Móricz Zsigmond körtér.
#19 Batthyány tér–Víziváros–Kelenföld Station.
#47 Deák tér–Szabadság híd–*Gellért Hotel*–Móricz Zsigmond körtér–Budafok.
#49 Deák tér–Szabadság híd–*Gellért Hotel*–Móricz Zsigmond körtér–Kelenföld Station.
#56 Moszkva tér–Szilágyi Erzsébet fasor–Hűvösvölgy.

TROLLEYBUSES
#72 Petőfi Csarnok–Széchenyi Baths–Nyugati Station–Arany János utca metro.
#74 Dohány utca (outside the Synagogue)–Városliget.

around 150Ft (though this tends to go up with the price of fuel). The taxis to avoid are the unmarked private cars and those hanging around the stations and airport – be warned that the latter often charge six times the official metered fare from the airport into town. There are also fake Fő and City taxis sporting impersonations of the red and white chequerboard or yellow shield logos, who will charge you a vastly inflated price, so be sure to look carefully for the name.

Suburban trains

A network of suburban trains, running every ten to fifteen minutes between 6.30am and 11pm, provides easy access to several attractions. The most useful of the overground **HÉV trains** is the one from **Batthyány tér** (on metro M2) out to **Szentendre** (see p.134) north of Budapest, which passes through Óbuda, Aquincum and Római-Fürdő. A regular BKV ticket or pass is valid as far as the city limits, beyond which you must punch additional tickets according to the distance travelled. However, it's easier to purchase a ticket at the station where you board the train, or from the conductor on board, which covers the entire journey.

Ferries and other rides

Although **ferries** play little useful part in the transport system, they do offer an enjoyable ride. From May to September there are regular excursion boats from the **Vigadó tér pier** on the Pest embankment, south to Boráros tér and north to Jászai Mari tér – both brief (20 min), scenic routes (daily every 15–30min, 7am–7pm; 100–300Ft). From May to August there is also a boat from the Jászai Mari tér dock to Pünkösdfürdő in northern Buda (1hr; check times on the board at the main dock), though you might prefer to disembark at Margit sziget, before the boat reaches dismal Békásmegyer. Ferry tickets can be obtained from kiosks (where timetables are posted) or machines at the docks.

Other pleasure rides can be found in the Buda Hills, on the **Cogwheel Railway** (*Fogaskerekű vasút*), the **Children's Railway** (*Gyermekvasút*, largely staffed by kids) and the **Chairlift** (*Libegő*) between Zugliget and János-hegy, all of which are detailed on p.61. An experience not to be missed is a ride in the vintage **funicular** (*Sikló*) that ascends from Clark Ádám tér to the Buda Palace on Várhegy (see p.49).

Várhegy

Várhegy (Castle Hill) is Buda's most prominent feature. A mile-long plateau encrusted with bastions, mansions and a huge palace, it dominates both the Víziváros below and Pest, over the river, making this stretch of the river one of the grandest, loveliest urban waterfronts in Europe. The hill's striking location and its strategic utility have long gone hand in hand: Hungarian kings built their palaces here because it was easy to defend, a fact appreciated by the Turks, Habsburgs and other occupiers. **Buda Palace** serves as a reminder of this past, rising like a house of cards at the southern end of the hill, as proud yet insubstantial as those who ruled there while Hungary's fate was determined by mightier forces.

Várhegy's buildings have been almost wholly reconstructed from the rubble of 1945, when the Wehrmacht and the Red Army battled over the hill while Buda's inhabitants cowered underground. It was the eighty-sixth time that Várhegy had been ravaged and rebuilt over seven centuries, rivalling the devastation caused by the recapture of Buda from the Turks in 1686. It was this repeated destruction that caused the melange of styles that characterizes the hill. While the palace is a faithful postwar reconstruction of the Habsburg behemoth that bestrode the ruins of earlier palaces, the neo-Gothic **Mátyás Church** and **Fishermen's Bastion** are romantic nineteenth-century evocations of medieval glories, interweaving past and present national fixations.

However, the streets of the **Castle District** (*Várnegyed*), the residential area to the north of palace, still follow their medieval courses, with Gothic arches and stone carvings half-concealed in the courtyards and passages of eighteenth-century Baroque houses, whose facades are embellished with fancy ironwork grilles. For many centuries, residence here was a privilege granted to religious or ethnic groups, each occupying a specific street. This pattern persisted through the 145-year-long Turkish occupation, when Armenians, Circassians and Sephardic Jews established themselves under the relatively tolerant Ottomans. The liberation of Buda by a multinational Christian army under Habsburg command was followed by a pogrom and ordinances restricting the right of residence to Catholics and Germans, a law that remained in force for nearly a century. Almost every building here displays a *műemlék* (listed) plaque giving details of its history (in Hungarian), and a surprising number are still homes rather than embassies or boutiques – there are even a couple of schools and corner shops. At dusk, when most of the tourists have left, pensioners walk their dogs and toddlers play in the narrow streets.

Approaches to Várhegy

The simplest and most novel approach to Várhegy is to ride up to the palace by **Sikló** (see p.49), a renovated nineteenth-century funicular that runs from Clark Ádám tér by the Lánchíd (see p.47). From Moszkva tér (on metro line 2) you can either take the **Várbusz**, a minibus that leaves from the raised side of Moszkva tér and terminates by the palace, or walk uphill to the Vienna Gate at the northern end of the Castle District. Walking from Batthyány tér via the steep flights of steps (*lépcső*) off Fő utca involves more effort, and the stairway up to the Fishermen's Bastion is currently closed for repairs. The most direct approach **from Pest** is to ride bus #16 from Erzsébet tér.

SZENTHÁROMSÁG TÉR

Map 5, D3.

The obvious starting point is **Szentháromság tér** (Holy Trinity Square), the historic heart of the district, named after an ornate **Trinity Column** erected in 1713 in thanksgiving for the abatement of a plague; a scene showing people dying from the Black Death appears on the plinth. To the southwest stands the former **Town Hall** of Buda, which functioned as a municipality until the unification of Buda, Pest and Óbuda in 1873; notice the corner statue of Pallas Athene, bearing Buda's coat of arms on her shield. Down the road at Szentháromság utca 7, the tiny **Ruszwurm patisserie** has been a pastry shop and café since 1827, and was a gingerbread shop in the Middle Ages. Its Empire-style decor looks much the same as it would have done under Vilmos Ruszwurm, who ran the patisserie from 1884 for nearly four decades.

Mátyás Church

Map 5, D3. Daily: April–Sept 8.30am–8pm; Oct–March 7am–7pm; free, crypt and treasures 100Ft.

The square's most prominent feature is the neo-Gothic **Mátyás Church** (*Mátyás templom*), with its wildly asymmetrical diamond-patterned roofs and toothy spires. Officially dedicated to Our Lady but popularly named after "Good King Mátyás", the building is a late nineteenth-century re-creation by architect Frigyes Schulek, grafted onto those portions of the original thirteenth-century church that survived the siege of 1686.

As you enter the church through its twin-spired **Mary Portal**, the richness of the interior is overwhelming. Painted leaves and geometric motifs run up columns and under vaulting, while shafts of light fall through rose windows onto gilded altars and statues with stunning effect. Most of the **frescoes** were executed by Károly Lotz or Bertalan Székely, the foremost historical painters of the nineteenth century. The **coat of arms of King Mátyás** can be seen on the wall to your left, just inside; his family name, Corvinus, comes from the raven (*corvus* in Latin) that appeared on his heraldry and on every volume in the famous Corvin Library.

Around the corner, beneath the south tower, is the **Loreto Chapel**, containing a Baroque Madonna, while in the bay beneath the Béla Tower you can see two medieval capitals, one carved with monsters fighting a dragon, the other with two bearded figures reading a book. The tower is named after Béla IV, who founded the church, rather than his predecessor in the second chapel along, who shares a double sarcophagus with Anne of Chatillon. Originally located in the old capital, Székesfehérvár, the **tomb of Béla III** and his queen was moved here after its discovery in 1848. Although Hungary's medieval kings were crowned at Székesfehérvár, it was customary to make a prior appearance in Buda – hence the sobriquet, the "Coronation Church".

To the right of the pulpit is the entrance to the **crypt**, containing the red-marble tombstone of a nameless Árpád prince, and a small collection of **ecclesiastical treasures** and relics, including the right foot of St János. From here, stairs ascend to **St Stephen's Chapel**, decorated with a bust of the king as well as various scenes from his life, whence another staircase leads to the **Royal Oratory**, exhibiting the coronation thrones of emperors Franz Josef and Karl IV, and a **replica of the Hungarian Crown Jewels**. The originals are displayed in the Hungarian National Museum (see p.116), though the exhibition here is more informative about the provenance of St Stephen's Crown.

Mass is celebrated in the Mátyás Church every morning, and on Sunday at 7am, 8.30am, 10am, noon & 6pm. Its acoustics are superb, and evening organ recitals are regularly held throughout the year, with more concerts during the Spring Festival and summer season. Tickets are available on the spot or from any booking agency (see p.252).

FISHERMEN'S BASTION

Map 5, E3. 100Ft.

After the Mátyás Church, the most impressive sight in Várhegy is the **Fishermen's Bastion** (*Halászbástya*) just beyond, which frames the view of Pest across the river. Although fishermen from the Víziváros reputedly defended this part of the hill during the Middle Ages, the existing bastion is purely decorative. An undulating white rampart of cloisters and stairways intersecting at seven tent-like turrets (symbolizing the Magyar tribes that conquered the Carpathian Basin), it looks as though it was dreamt up by the illusionist artist Escher, but was actually designed by Schulek as a foil to the Mátyás Church. Since an admission charge was introduced, the upper level is no longer crowded with sightseers and vendors and has lost some of its charm as a result – but the view is as splendid as ever.

Between the bastion and the church, an equestrian **statue of King Stephen** honours the founder of the Hungarian nation, whose conversion to Christianity and coronation with a crown sent by the pope presaged the Magyars' integration into European civilization (see box overleaf). The relief at the back of the plinth depicts Schulek offering a model of the Mátyás Church to Stephen. Like the church and the bastion, his statue is reflected in the copper-glass facade of the **Budapest Hilton**, incorporating chunks of a medieval Dominican church and monastery on the side facing the river, and an eighteenth-century Jesuit college on the other, which bears a copy of the **Mátyás Relief** from Bautzen in Germany that's regarded as the only true likeness of Hungary's Renaissance monarch.

King Stephen

If you commit just one figure from Hungarian history to memory, make it **King Stephen**, for it was he who welded the tribal Magyar fiefdoms into a state and won recognition from Christendom. Born Vajk, son of Grand Duke Géza, he emulated his father's policy of trying to convert the pagan Magyars and develop Hungary with the help of foreign preachers, craftsmen and merchants. By marrying Gizella of Bavaria in 996, he was able to use her father's knights to crush a pagan revolt after Géza's death, and subsequently received an apostolic cross and crown from Pope Sylvester II for his coronation on Christmas Day, 1000 AD, when he took the name Stephen (István in Hungarian).

Though noted for his enlightened views (such as the need for tolerance and the desirability of multiracial nations), he could act ruthlessly when necessary. After his only son Imre died in an accident and a pagan seemed likely to inherit, Stephen had the man blinded and poured molten lead into his ears. Naming his successor, he symbolically offered his crown to the Virgin Mary rather than the Holy Roman Emperor or the pope; she has since been considered the Patroness of Hungary. Swiftly canonized after his death in 1038, **Saint Stephen** became a national talisman, his mummified right hand a holy relic, and his coronation regalia the symbol of statehood. Despite playing down his cult for decades, even the Communists eventually embraced it in a bid for some legitimacy, while nobody in post-Communist Hungary thinks it odd that the symbol of the republic should be the crown and cross of King Stephen.

MUSEUM OF COMMERCE AND CATERING

Map 5, D2. Tues–Fri 10am–5pm, Sat & Sun 10am–6pm; 100Ft.

Be sure to visit the fascinating **Museum of Commerce and Catering** (*Kereskedelmi és Vendéglátóipari Múzeum*) at Fortuna utca 4, where the *Fortuna Inn* was once located. The commerce section contains antique shopfronts and interiors and an early twentieth-century illuminated sign advertising beer, and, as a finale, its curator activates a model dog that raps on the glass with its paws, which was meant to attract passers-by into stores. The catering part pays homage to the restaurateur Károly Gundel, the confectioner Emil Gerbeaud, and Alfred Dobos, who became a celebrity when his *dobostorta*, a caramel-topped layered sponge cake, won a prize at the Vienna Exhibition. Another section called "Hospitable Budapest" covers tourism, nightlife and spas, featuring furnishings from old coffee houses and a reconstructed bedroom from the *Gellért Hotel.* Waiters used such specialized items of cutlery as asparagus clippers, produced by the Budapest instrument-makers Ignácz Dreher & Son, whose 25-bladed pocket knife (anticipating the Swiss Army version) is also on display.

THE MUSIC HISTORY MUSEUM

Map 5, E2. Tues–Sun: April–Oct 10am–6pm; Nov–March 10am–5pm; 100Ft.

The **Music History Museum** (*Zenetörténeti Múzeum*) at Táncsics Mihály utca 7 occupies the Erdödy Palace where Beethoven was a guest in 1800 and Bartók once had a workshop before he emigrated. Though its postwar interior is a letdown after the Baroque courtyard, it focuses attention on the splendid instruments that represent three centuries of music, from a Holczman harp made for Marie Antoinette and a unique tongue-shaped violin in the classical section to hurdy-gurdies, zithers, cowhorns and bagpipes in the folk part. You can also see the Schunda pedal-cimbalom, a factory product which began to replace home-made folk instruments by the 1900s. There's also an exhibition of Bartók's scores and jottings, including bits of *The Wooden Prince* and *Violin Rhapsody No. #2*. His former workshop, upstairs, is inaccessible.

On your way out, have a look at no. 9 next door, which was once the Joseph Barracks where the Habsburgs jailed Hungarian radicals such as Mihály Táncsics, after whom the street is named. In an earlier age the street was known as Zsidó utca (Jewish Street), when both Ashkenazi and Sephardic Jews lived here.

THE MEDIEVAL JEWISH PRAYER HOUSE

Map 5, D2. May–Oct Tues–Sun 10am–5pm; 100Ft.

Buda's Ashkenazi community was established in the reign of Béla IV and encouraged by King Mátyás, who let the Jews build a synagogue and appointed a Jewish council led by Jacobus Mendel. Part of Mendel's house survives in the entrance to Táncsics Mihály utca 26, which contains a **Medieval Jewish Prayer House** (*Középkori Zsidó Imaház*), once used by the Sephardis. All that remains of its original decor are two Cabbalistic symbols painted on a wall, and, though the museum does its best to flesh out the history of the community with maps and prints, all the real treasures are in the Jewish Museum in Pest (see p.110).

KAPISZTRÁN TÉR

At the end of Táncsics Mihály utca lies **Bécsi kapu tér**, named after the **Vienna Gate** (*Bécsi kapu*) that was erected on the 250th anniversary of the recapture of Buda. Beside it, the forbiddingly neo-Romanesque **National Archives** (no admission) guard the way to **Kapisztrán tér**, a larger square centred on the **Mary Magdalene Tower** (*Magdolna-torony*), whose accompanying church was wrecked in World War II. In medieval times this was where Hungarian residents worshipped; Germans used the Mátyás Church. Today the tower contains a private art gallery and boasts a peal of ornamental bells that jingles through a medley composed by the jazz pianist György Szabados that includes Hungarian folk tunes, Chopin *Études* and the theme from *Bridge Over the River Kwai*.

Beyond the tower is a **statue of Friar John Capistranus**, who exhorted the Hungarians to victory at the siege of Belgrade in 1456; the pope hailed it by ordering church bells to be rung at noon throughout Europe. It shows Capistranus bestriding a dead Turk and is aptly sited outside the Military History Museum.

The Military History Museum

Map 5, C1. April–Sept 10am–6pm; Oct–March 10am–4pm; closed Tues; 250Ft.

The **Military History Museum** (*Hadtörténeti Múzeum*), in a former barracks on the north side of the square, has gung-ho exhibitions on the history of hand weapons from ancient times till the advent of firearms, and the birth and campaigns of the Honvéd (national army) during the 1848–49 War of Independence. However, what sticks in the memory are the sections on the Hungarian Second Army that was decimated at Stalingrad, and the "Thirteen Days" of the 1956 Uprising (accompanied by newsreel footage at 11am & 2pm). In the courtyard are post-Communist memorials to the POWs who never returned from the Gulag.

The entrance to the museum is on the Tóth Árpád sétány, a promenade lined with cannons and chestnut trees, overlooking the Buda Hills, which leads past a giant **flag-**

pole striped in Hungarian colours to the symbolic **grave of Abdurrahman**, the last Turkish Pasha of Buda, who died on the walls in 1686 – a "valiant foe", according to the inscription.

ORSZÁGHÁZ UTCA

Heading back towards Szentháromság tér, there's more to be seen on **Országház utca**, which was the district's main thoroughfare in the Middle Ages and known as the "street of baths" during Turkish times. Its present name, Parliament Street, recalls the sessions of the Diet held in the 1790s in a former Poor Clares' cloister at no. 28, where the Gestapo imprisoned 350 Hungarians and foreigners in 1945. No. 17, over the road, consists of two medieval houses joined together and has a relief of a croissant on its keystone, from the time when it was a bakery. A few doors down from the old parliament building, Renaissance sgraffiti survives on the underside of the bay window of no. 22 and a Gothic trefoil-arched cornice on the house next door, while the one beyond has been rebuilt in its original fifteenth-century form.

ÚRI UTCA

Úri utca (Gentleman Street) also boasts historic associations, for it was at the former Franciscan monastery at no. 51 that the five Hungarian Jacobins were held before being beheaded on the "Blood Meadow" below the hill in 1795. Next door is a wing of the Poor Clares' cloister that served as a postwar telephone exhange before being turned into a **Telephone Museum** (*Telefónia Múzeum*; Tues–Sun 10am–6pm; 50Ft). More hands-on than most Hungarian museums, it lets visitors dial up a Magyar pop song or an English-speaking guide on a vintage bakelite phone, or send a fax to one other – something of a novelty when the museum opened in 1991. Further down the street, on either side, notice the statues of the four seasons in the first-floor niches at nos. 54–56, Gothic sedilia in the gateway of nos. 48–50, and three arched windows and two diamond-shaped ones from the fourteenth and fifteenth centuries at no. 31.

The Labyrinth of Buda Castle

Map 5, C4. Daily 9.30am–7.30pm.

An unusual attraction is the **Labyrinth of Buda Castle**, better known as the *Várbarlang* (Castle caves), whose main entrance is at Úri utca 9. Cavities formed by hot springs and cellars dug since medieval times form 10km of galleries that were converted into an air-raid shelter for up to 10,000 people in the 1930s and used as such in World War II. The labyrinth remained in military hands till the 1980s, when it opened as a waxworks; refurbished in 1997, it is now marketed as a New Age experience of shamanism and history. One section features copies of the cave paintings of Lascaux (Buda's caves also sheltered prehistoric hunters), while masked figures and a giant head sunken into the floor enliven other dank chambers. Their meaning is explained on guided tours (daily 9.30am–7.30pm; 600Ft), though these don't always run as scheduled. There's another entrance beyond the castle walls at Lovas út 4, which is wheelchair-accessible for some of the way.

THE GOLDEN EAGLE PHARMACY

Map 5, D4. Tues–Sun 10.30am–6.30pm; 60Ft.

Heading south from Szentháromság tér towards the palace, check out the **Golden Eagle Pharmacy Museum** (*Arany Sas Patikamúzeum*) at Tárnok utca 18. The Golden Eagle was the first pharmacy in Buda, established after the expulsion of the Turks, and moved to its present site in the eighteenth century. Its original murals and furnishings lend authenticity to dubious nostrums, including the skull of a mummy used to make "Mumia" powder to treat epilepsy, and a reconstruction of an alchemist's laboratory complete with dried bats and crocodiles. Notice the portrait of the Dominican nun who is also a pharmacist – common practice for nuns and monks in the Middle Ages. The *Tárnok* coffee house, next door but one, occupies a medieval building with a Renaissance sgraffiti facade of red and yellow checks and roundels, and, like the street, is named after the royal treasurers who once lived there.

DÍSZ TÉR

Map 5, D5.

Both Tárnok utca and Úri utca end in **Dísz tér** (Parade Square), whose cobbled expanses are guarded by a **statue of a hussar** (see box opposite). From here on ramparts and gateways buttress the hillside and control access to the palace grounds. Straight ahead lies the scarred hulk of the old **Ministry of Defence**, now at last undergoing restoration and slated to become a cultural centre, while to your left stands the **Castle Theatre** (*Várszínház*). A Carmelite church until the order was dissolved by Josef II, its conversion was supervised by Farkas Kempelen, inventor of a chess-playing automaton. It was here that the first-ever play in Hungarian was staged in 1790, and where Beethoven performed in 1808. The last building in the row is the **Sándor Palace** (*Sándor Palota*), formerly the prime minster's residence. Restored after the war, it now holds the **Panoptikum Waxworks** (March–Oct daily 10am–6pm; tours every 15min; 450Ft) that used to be housed in the Labyrinth – a lame romp through Hungarian history in all its gory glory.

The Turul statue

Next door to Sándor Palace, the upper terminal of the **Sikló** funicular is separated from the terrace of Buda Palace by stately railings and the ferocious-looking **Turul statue** – a giant bronze eagle clasping a sword in its talons, which is visible from across the river. In Magyar mythology the Turul sired the first dynasty of Hungarian kings by raping the grandmother of Árpád. She then led the tribes into the Carpathian Basin and accompanied their raids on Europe bearing the sword of Attila the Hun. During the nineteenth century it became a symbol of Hungarian identity in the face of Austrian culture, but wound up being co-opted by the Habsburgs, who cast Emperor Franz Josef as a latter-day Árpád, founder of the Dual Monarchy for the next millennium. Another Turul adorns the gates of Parliament, but the largest such statue is in Tatabánya, overlooking the railway line from Budapest to Vienna. Today, the Turul has been adopted as a symbol by Hungary's skinheads.

Hussars

Hussars were a Hungarian innovation later adopted by armies throughout Europe. The first such unit of light cavalry was organized by King Mátyás in 1480; armed with sabres, pikes and daggers, it excelled in surprise attacks and rapid manoeuvres. By the time of the Napoleonic Wars every national army fielded hussars and most infantry wore hussar-style cylindrical felt or leather hats (called *shako*, from the Magyar word for a peaked hat) instead of metal helmets. Although Hussar is one of the few Hungarian words to have entered the English language, it is thought to derive from the Latin *cursor* (runner) rather than the Magyar *húsz* (meaning twenty). In Hungary their romantic image endures, and costumed riders appear in Buda Palace as part of the national celebrations on March 15.

BUDA PALACE

Map 5, D7–D8. Sikló, Várbusz or bus #16.

As befits a former royal residence, the lineage of **Buda Palace** (*Budavári palota*) can be traced back to medieval times, the rise and fall of various palaces on the hill reflecting the changing fortunes of the Hungarian state. The first fortifications and dwellings, hastily erected by Béla IV after the Mongol invasion of 1241–42, were replaced by the grander palaces of the Angevin kings, who ruled in more prosperous and stable times. This process of rebuilding reached its zenith in the reign of Mátyás Corvinus (1458–90), whose palace was a Renaissance extravaganza to which artists and scholars from all over Europe were drawn by the blandishments of Queen Beatrice and the prospect of lavish hospitality. The rooms had hot and cold running water and during celebrations the fountains and gargoyles flowed with wine. After the Turkish occupation and the long siege that ended it, only ruins were left – which the Habsburgs, Hungary's new rulers, levelled to build a palace of their own.

From Empress Maria Theresa's modest beginnings (a mere 203 rooms, which she never saw completed), the palace expanded inexorably throughout the nineteenth century, though no monarch ever dwelt here, only the Habsburg Palatine (viceroy). After the collapse of the empire following World War I, Admiral Horthy inhabited the building with all the pomp of monarchy until he was deposed by a German coup in October 1944. The palace was left unoccupied, and it wasn't long before the siege of Buda once again resulted in total devastation. Reconstruction work began in the 1950s in tandem with excavations of the medieval sub-strata beneath the rubble. The medieval section was incorporated into the new building, whose interior is far less elegant than the prewar version, being designed to accommodate cultural institutions.

The complex houses the **Museum of Contemporary Art** (Wing A), the **Hungarian National Gallery** (Wings B, C and D), the **Budapest History Museum** (E) and the **National Széchényi Library** (F) – of which the first three are definitely worth seeing and could easily take an afternoon. There are separate entrances for each.

The Hungarian National Gallery

Map 5, D7. Daily: April–Nov 10am–6pm; Dec–March 10am–4pm; 300Ft, free Wed. Guided tours in English 1000Ft for up to five persons; ©224-3700 ext 423.

Most people's first port of call is the **Hungarian National Gallery** (*Magyar Nemzeti Galéria*), devoted to Hungarian art from the Middle Ages to the present. It contains much that's superb, but the vastness of the collection and the fusty layout and lighting can soon tire you out, so it's best to concentrate on what interests you most. The main **entrance** is on the eastern side of Wing C, overlooking the river, behind the statue of Eugene of Savoy. While art books and posters are sold in the foyer, no room-by-room guidebook nor audiotapes are available, though you can arrange a guided tour. Paintings are labelled in English, but other details are scanty, even in Hungarian.

Ground floor

Most of the ground floor is used for **temporary exhibitions** or not at all, and the **medieval and Renaissance lapidarium** makes a poor introduction to Wing D, its casts of stonecarvings from Ják and Esztergom dusty and unlabelled in English – though the two red marble reliefs of Beatrice and Mátyás from Buda Castle and a beautiful **wooden ceiling** from a sixteenth-century church, further in, are more interesting.

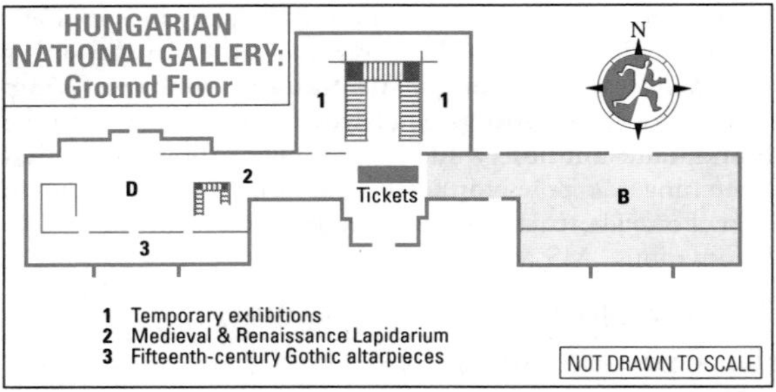

The real lure is a collection of fifteenth-century **Gothic altarpieces** and panels from churches great and small that escaped destruction by the Turks. Some are artful, others rustic, but all are full of character and detail. Notice the varied reactions to the *Death of the Virgin* from Kassa (a centre of altar-painting) and the gloating of the mob in the Jánosrét *Passion*. From the same church comes a *St Nicholas* altar as long as a limo and lurid as a comic strip, whose final scene shows cripples being cured by the saint's corpse. Also strange to modern eyes are *The Expulsion of St Adalbert*, who seems blithely oblivious to the burning of his church, and *St Anthony the Hermit*, carrying a hill upon his back. The pointed finials on the high altar from Liptószentmária anticipate the winged altarpieces of the sixteenth century on the floor above. To get there without returning to the foyer, use the small staircase nearby and turn left, left and left again at the top.

First floor

The first floor covers the widest range of art and is likely to engage you the longest. It picks up where the ground floor left off in the former Throne Room, where **late Gothic altarpieces** with soaring pinnacles and carved surrounds are displayed. Most of them come from churches that are now in Slovakia or Romania, such as the altarpiece of the Virgin from Csíkmenaság or the homely Kisszeben *Annunciation*, which looks like a medieval playgroup. On an altar from Berki, Mary Magdalene is raptured by angels as bishops are impaled, while another piece shows St Andrew clutching the poles for his crucifixion. Also look out for *The Visitation*, part of a recently restored altarpiece by the anonymous "MS Master".

Many of the works in the adjacent section on **Baroque art** once belonged to Prince Miklós Esterházy (including his portrait), or were confiscated from private owners in the 1950s. The prolific Austrian, **Anton Maulbertsch**, who executed scores of altars and murals reminiscent of Caravaggio, is represented here by smaller works such as *Christ Carrying His Cross*. Don't miss **Ádám Mányoki**'s portrait of Ferenc Rákóczi II from 1712, a sober study of a national hero that foreshadowed a new artistic genre of **National Historical art** in the nineteenth century, which can be seen in the central block.

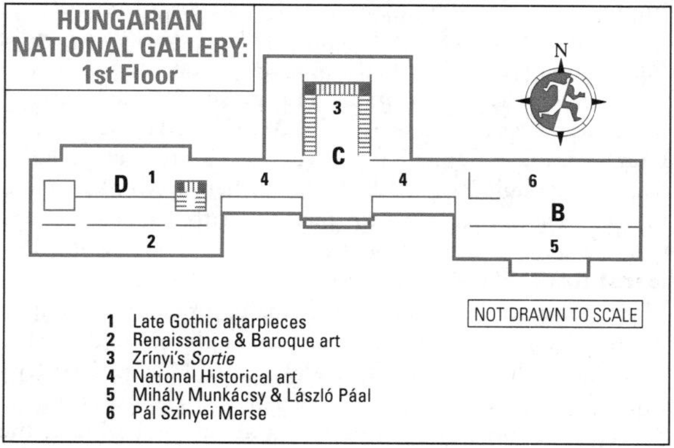

People coming up the staircase to the central block are confronted by *Zrínyi's Sortie*, a vast canvas by Peter Krafft depicting the suicidal sally by the defenders of Szigetvár against a Turkish army fifty times their number. Not a drop of blood spatters the melee, as Count Zrínyi leads the charge across the bridge. On the upper landing hangs **Gyula Benczúr**'s *Recapture of Buda Castle*, whose portrayal of Eugene of Savoy and Karl of Lotharingia suggests a mere exchange of Turkish rulers for Habsburg ones, while *The Mourning of László Hunyadi* by **Viktor Madarász**, in Wing D, would have been read as an allusion to the execution of Hungarian patriots after the War of Independence. In Wing B, notice Benczúr's *The Baptism of Vajk*, depicting the future St Stephen's conversion to Christianity, and two disparate battle scenes by **Bertalan Székely**: *Recovering the Corpse of the King* after the catastrophic Hungarian defeat at Mohács in 1526, and *The Women of Eger*, exalting their defiance of the Turks in 1552.

The rest of Wing B covers other trends in **nineteenth-century art**, namely genre painting, rural romanticism and Impressionism. Though best known as a historical painter, **Károly Lotz** also excelled at scenes like *Thunderstorm on the Puszta* and *Horses at the Watering Place*, evoking the hazy skies and manly world of the Hungarian "Wild West". A section is devoted to works by **Mihály Munkácsy** and **László Paál**, exhibited together since both painted landscapes – though Paál did little else, whereas Munkácsy was internationally renowned for pictures with a social message (*The Condemned Cell*, *Tramps of the Night*) and bravura historical works like *The Conquest* (in the Parliament building). Many canvases have suffered from his use of bitumen in mixing paint, which has caused them to darken and crack – a problem that hasn't affected **László Mednyánszky**'s heavily impasted *Fishing on the Tisza* and *Head of a Tramp*. Another section displays works by **Pál Szinyei Merse**, the "father of Hungarian Impressionism", whose models and subjects were cheerfully bourgeois, for example *A Picnic in May*.

Second and third floors

Walking upstairs to the second floor, you come face to face with three huge canvases by the visionary artist **Tivadar Kosztka Csontváry**, whose obsession with the Holy Land and the "path of the sun" inspired scenes like *Look Down on the Red Sea* and *Ruins of the Greek Theatre at Taormina*. When Picasso saw an exhibition of his works years later, he remarked: "And I thought I was the only great painter of our century." There are four more, smaller Csontvárys to be found amongst the **twentieth-century art** in Wing C, which is largely attributable to members of Hungary's Gödöllő and Nagybánya artists' colonies, and reflects influences as diverse as William Morris, Klimt and Cézanne.

Symbolism and **Art Nouveau** were so entwined in Hungary that any distinction is moot in the case of **Simon Hollósy** (*Dancing Girls at the Outskirts of the Forest*) or János Vaszary (*The Golden Age*), whose works are framed as decoratively as a Beardsley engraving. The chief exponent of Art Nouveau was **József Rippl-Rónai**, a pupil of Munkácsy's

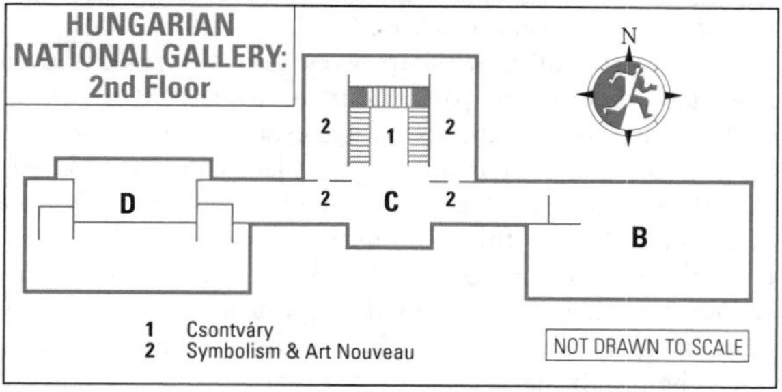

whose portraits went mostly unrecognized in his lifetime but are now regarded as Hungarian classics; applied artists like Miksa Róth, Károly Kernstok and the architect Ödön Lechner had more successful careers. Other trends such as Post-Impressionism are represented by works like Ödön Márffy's Cézannish *The Old Toll House at Vác*, but there's less abstract art than you'd expect from the 1930s and 40s, due to the risk of censure it entailed under the authoritarian regimes of the time.

In the Kádár years (1956-88) **contemporary art** was less shackled by ideology than in any other Communist state except Poland, but the regime naturally preferred to promote the work of safely dead socialist artists from the Group of Eight or still living ones like Béla Czóbel, rather than younger non-conformists. When Hungary ceased to be an avowedly socialist state such art lost its value overnight, leaving the National Gallery with a lot of rehanging to do, which expains why the third floor is closed more often than not. Meanwhile, it's being upstaged by a parvenu interloper with money for acquisitions, ensconced in Wing A of the palace (see below).

Museum of Contemporary Art

Map 5, D7. Tues–Sun 10am–6pm; 100Ft.

The **Museum of Contemporary Art** (*Kortárs Művészti Múzeum*) is a stylish joint venture by the Ministry of Culture and corporate sponsors, established in 1996 to build upon an earlier bequest by the late German industrialist Peter Ludwig, in the year of Hungary's transition to democracy. Before then, Wing A of the palace had contained the Museum of the Working Class Movement, whose staff made amends for decades of misinformation by organizing an exhibition on the Stalinist era before moving out – hence the lavish use of red marble in the cloistered atrium, which is now used for **temporary exhibitions**, usually of installation art.

The **Ludwig Collection** includes US pop art such as Warhol's silkscreen *Single Elvis*, Lichtenstein's *Vicky* and Rauschenberg's *Hedge*, and an instantly recognizable Hockney room-with-a-view from his Pointillist period. However, most of the museum's acquisitions are work by lesser-known Europeans, in veins from Hyper-Realism (Domenico Gnoli's *Trouser-Pocket*) to neo-Primitivism (Imre Butka's *Officers at a Pig-killing Feast*), plus the odd resinous sculpture (Toni Grand's *Two by Two*) or menacing installation (Miklós Erdély's *War Secrets*).

The museum has a pleasant **café** that's seldom crowded, with a view of the Buda Hills.

The Mátyás Fountain and Lion Courtyard

The square outside the museum is flanked on three sides by the palace and overlooks Buda to the west, though the **view** is marred by the high-tech MTI (Hungarian News Agency) building on Nap-hegy (Sun Hill). By the far wall stands the flamboyant **Mátyás Fountain**, whose bronze figures recall the legend of Szép Ilonka. This beautiful peasant girl met the king while he was hunting incognito, fell in love with him, and died of a broken heart after discovering his identity and realizing the futility of her hopes. The man with a falcon is the king's Italian chronicler, who recorded the story for posterity (it is also enshrined in a poem by Vörösmarty).

A gateway guarded by lions leads into the **Lion Courtyard**, totally enclosed by further wings. To your right is the **National Széchényi Library** (*Országos Széchényi Könyvtár*), occupying the nineteenth-century Ybl block, whose full size is only apparent from the far side of the hill, where it looms over Dózsa tér like a mountain. The library was founded in 1802 on the initiative of Count

Ferenc Széchényi, the father of István, who spearheaded the Reform era. A repository for publications in Hungarian and material relating to the country from around the world, by law it receives a copy of every book, newspaper and magazine that is published in Hungary. Its central reading room is open to the public (Mon 1–9pm, Tues–Sat 9am–9pm; free) and there are temporary exhibitions (150Ft) on diverse subjects. During library hours, a passenger **lift** (10Ft) beside the building provides direct access to and from Dózsa tér, at the foot of the hill.

The Budapest History Museum

Map 5, D8. Mid-May to mid-Sept daily 10am–6pm; Nov-Feb 10am–4pm, March & Oct 10am–6pm. Closed Tues; 250Ft, free Wed.

On the far side of the Lion Courtyard, the **Budapest History Museum** (*Budapest Történeti Múzeum*) covers two millennia of history on three floors, before descending into original vaulted, flagstoned halls from the Renaissance and medieval palaces unearthed during excavations. It's worth starting with **prehistory**, on the top floor, to find out about the ancient Magyars. Here you can see the artefacts of their nomadic precursors, who overran the Pannonian Plain after the Romans left, such as a gold bridle and stirrup fastenings in a zoomorphic style from Avar burial mounds. Due to the ravages inflicted by the Mongols and the Turks there's little to show from the time of the Conquest or Hungary's medieval civilization, so most of the second floor is occupied by "Budapest in Modern Times", an exhibition giving insight into urban planning, fashions, trade and vices, from 1686 onwards. At either end of the section, two lifesize replicas of the lions on the Lánchíd bracket the century, starting with the hopes of the Reform era and ending with the devastated city of 1945. Other items range from an 1880s barrel organ to one of the Swedish Red Cross notices affixed to Jewish safe houses by Wallenberg (see p.111).

The **remains of the medieval palace** are reached from the basement via an eighteenth-century cellar spanning two medieval yards on a lower level. A wing of the ground floor of King Sigismund's palace and the cellars beneath the Corvin Library form an intermediate stratum overlaying the cross-vaulted crypt of the **Royal Chapel** and a **Gothic Hall** displaying statues from later in the fourteenth century, which were found in 1974. In another chamber are portions of red marble fireplaces and a massive portal carved with cherubs and flowers from the palace of King Mátyás. Emerging into daylight, bear left and up the stairs to reach another imposing hall, with a view over the castle ramparts.

Gellért-hegy, Tabán and the Víziváros

Gellért-hegy is as much a feature of the city's waterfront panorama as Várhegy and the Parliament building: a craggy dolomite cliff rearing 130m above the embankment, offering a fabulous view of the city. At its foot, the *Gellért Hotel* is famous for its Art Nouveau thermal baths and summer terrace. This is one area you'd be foolish to miss.

North of Gellért-hegy, **Tabán**, once Buda's artisan quarter, now has more roads than buildings and makes an incongruous setting for two of Budapest's most historic and magical Turkish baths. Further north again, between the castle and the river, the **Víziváros** is something of a quiet residential backwater in the heart of Buda, with a distinctive atmosphere, but few specific sights other than the Parish Church on Batthyány tér, and the Lánchíd and Sikló, 800m south.

The area to the **north of Várhegy** has a few attractions in the backstreets off Margit körút, and is best approached from the transport hub of Moszkva tér. Its seedy streetlife and surprisingly wide range of eating and drinking places is a world apart from the affluent Rózsadomb, just uphill, while beyond are the Buda Hills.

GELLÉRT-HEGY

Map 3, G13. Bus #86 or tram #19 from Batthyány tér; tram #47 or #49 from the Kiskörút in Pest.

Surmounted by the Liberation Monument and the Citadella, **Gellért-hegy** makes a distinctive contribution to Budapest's skyline. The hill is named after the Italian missionary Ghirardus (Gellért in Hungarian), who converted pagan Magyars to Christianity at the behest of King Stephen. After his royal protector's demise, vengeful heathens strapped Gellért to a barrow and toppled him off the cliff, where a larger than life **statue of St Gellért** now stands astride an artificial waterfall facing the Erzsébet híd, his crucifix raised as if in admonition to motorists.

The Gellért Hotel and Baths

Pool: May–Sept daily 6am–7pm; Oct–April Mon–Fri 6am–7pm, Sat & Sun 6am–5pm; 1200Ft. Baths: May–Sept Mon–Fri 6am–7pm, Sat & Sun 6am–5pm, evening swimming Fri & Sat; Oct–April Mon–Fri 6am–5pm, Sat & Sun 6am–2pm; 1500Ft.

At the foot of the hill, the graceful wrought-iron **Szabadság híd** (Liberty Bridge) links the inner boulevard of Pest to Szent Gellért tér on the Buda side, dominated by the Art Nouveau **Gellért Hotel**. Opened in 1918, it was commandeered as a staff headquarters by the Reds, the Romanian army, and finally by Admiral Horthy, following his triumphal entry into "sinful Budapest" in 1920. During the 1930s and 40s, its balls were the highlight of Budapest's social calendar, when debutantes danced on a glass floor laid over its pool. The **Gellért Baths** (entered from Kelenhegyi út, on the right-hand side of the hotel) are magnificently appointed with majolica tiles and columns, and lion-headed spouts gushing into its mixed-sex thermal pool. Stairs at the far end descend to the Turkish baths, with ornate plunge pools and separate areas for men and women. There is also an outdoor summer pool with a wave-machine and terraces for nude sunbathing. Even if you don't plan on taking a dip, you should take a peek into the ornate and lofty foyer, entered via a portal carved with writhing figures.

The Cave Church

Map 3, H13. Daily 8am–9pm; free.

On the hillside opposite the hotel you'll find the **Cave Church** (*Sziklatemplom*), a series of chapels established in the 1930s by the Pauline order. The only order indigenous to Hungary, founded in 1256, its monks served as confessors to the Hungarian kings until Josef II dissolved the order in 1773, though it was re-established 150 years later. During the 1950s the Communists jailed the monks and blocked up the chapels, which weren't reopened until 1989. During mass (11am & 5pm), white-robed monks glide about to mournful organ music against the backdrop of a painting of the Hungarian flag between two bleeding hearts, giving the church a very eerie atmosphere. From here, you can follow one of the footpaths to the summit – about a twenty-minute climb. The hillside, which still bears fig trees planted by the Turks, was covered in vineyards until a phylloxera epidemic struck in the nineteenth century.

The Citadella and Liberation Monument

Map 3, G13. Tram #16 or #19 from Szent Gellért tér to Móricz Zsigmond körtér, then bus #27 to the end of the line.

Whether you walk up or get there by bus, the **summit** of Gellért-hegy affords a stunning **panoramic view**, drawing one's eye slowly along the curving river, past bridges and monumental landmarks, and then on to the Buda Hills and Pest's suburbs, merging hazily with the distant plain.

The best vantage point is the **Citadella**, a fortress built by the Habsburgs to dominate the city in the aftermath of the 1848–49 Revolution; ironically, both its architects were Hungarians. When the historic Compromise was reached in 1867, citizens breached the walls to affirm that it no longer posed a threat to them, and since World War II, when an SS regiment holed up in the fortress, nothing more sinister than fireworks has been launched from the citadel. Today it contains a casino and a tourist hostel, plus a small **museum** (100Ft) comprising a few archeological remains relating to the Celtic Eravisci, who lived on the hill two thousand years ago.

From the ramparts you get a fine view of the **Liberation Monument** (*Felszabadulási emlékmű*) beside the citadel – a female figure brandishing the palm of victory over 30m aloft – which is too large to be properly appreciated when you stand directly below it. There is a famous tale that the monument was originally commissioned by Admiral Horthy in memory of his son István (who was killed in a plane crash on the Eastern Front in 1942), but that, by substituting a palm branch for the propeller it was meant to hold and placing a statue of a Red Army soldier at the base, it was deftly recycled to commemorate the Soviet soldiers who died liberating Budapest from the Nazis. While the story may not be true, the monument's sculptor, Zsigmond Kisfaludi-Strobl, certainly succeeded in winning approval as a "Proletarian Artist", despite having previously specialized in busts of the aristocracy – and was henceforth known by his compatriots as "Kisfaludi-Strébel" (*strébel* meaning "to climb" or "step from side to side"). Following the end of Communism there were calls to demolish the monument, but it was finally agreed to settle for removing the Red

Army figure, which can now be seen in the Statue Park on the outskirts of Budapest (p.127).

TABÁN

The **Tabán** district, bordering the northern end of Gellért-hegy, chiefly consists of arterial roads built in Communist times on land left vacant by the prewar demolition of a quarter renowned for its drinking dens and open sewers. Traditionally this was inhabited by Serbs (*Rác* in Hungarian), who settled here en masse after the Turks were expelled, though, in a typically Balkan paradox, some were present earlier, working in the Ottoman gunpowder factories which may have been the origin of the name Tabán (from *tabahane*, the Turkish for "armoury"). The attractions here are two Turkish baths that retain their original Ottoman pools and the Semmelweis Medical Museum.

The Rudas Baths

Map 3, G12. Men only, Mon–Fri 6am–5pm, Sat 6am–noon; 450Ft.

The relaxing and curative effects of Buda's **mineral springs** have been appreciated for two thousand years. The Romans built splendid bathhouses at Aquincum and, while these declined with the empire, interest revived after the Knights of St John built a hospice on the site of the present Rudas Baths, near where St Elizabeth cured lepers in the springs below Gellért-hegy. However, it was the Turks who consolidated the habit of bathing (as Muslims, they were obliged to wash five times daily in preparation for prayer) and constructed proper bathhouses which function to this day – though their surroundings and exteriors give little clue to what's inside.

The **Rudas Baths** (*Rudas Gyógyfürdő*), in the shadow of Gellért-hegy, harbour a fanastic octagonal pool constructed in 1556 on the orders of Pasha Sokoli Mustapha. Bathers wallow amid shafts of light pouring in from the star-shaped apertures in the domed ceiling, surrounded by stone pillars with iron tie-beams and a nest of smaller pools for parboiling oneself or cooling down.

The Király Baths (p.51) to the north of Batthyány tér are just as atmospheric as the Rudas. See p.217 for a rundown of the city's bathhouses, their practices and etiquette, and the relevant Hungarian terms.

The Rác Baths

Map 3, F11. Women: Mon, Wed & Fri 6.30am–6pm; men Tues, Thurs & Sat 6.30am–6pm; 450Ft.

Heading on to the Rác Baths, you'll pass the **Water Hall** (*Ivócsarnok*; Mon, Wed & Fri 11am–6pm, Tues & Thurs 7am–2pm) beneath the road to the bridge, which sells mineral water from three nearby springs by the tumbler. Regular imbibers bring bottles or jerrycans to fill.

The **Rác Baths** (*Rác Gyógyfürdő*), in a yellow building dating from the 1830s, are tucked away beneath Hegyalja út, leading uphill away from the bridgehead of the Erzsébet híd. The Turkish pool is less impressive than the ones in the Rác and Király baths, and is frequented by those who find its sulphurous water at 40°C good for skin complaints and painful joints, or are attracted by the active gay scene.

The cuboid **memorial stone** outside the baths commemorates the 51st Esperanto Congress held in Budapest in 1966 – an event that would have been inconceivable in Stalin's day, when Esperanto was forbidden for conflicting with his thesis that the time for an international language had yet to come. Nearby, on one of the grassy areas that comprise Döbrentei tér, is a seated **statue of Empress**

Elizabeth (1837–98), who endeared herself to Hungarians by learning their language and refusing to be stifled by her crusty husband, Franz Josef. Assassinated by an anarchist in Switzerland, she was widely mourned in Hungary and is still fondly known by her nickname, "Sissy". The Erzsébet híd (Elizabeth Bridge) is named after her.

The Semmelweis Medical Museum

Map 3, F10. Tues–Sun 10am–6pm; 120Ft.

Often overlooked by tourists, the **Semmelweis Medical Museum** (*Semmelweis Orvostörténeti Múzeum*), at Apród utca 1–3, contains a fascinating collection of artefacts relating to the history of medicine, with mummified limbs from ancient Egypt and a shrunken head used by Borneo witch doctors giving an international dimension to the display. Other exhibits, including a medieval chastity belt, trepanning drills, a lifesize wax model of a dissected female cadaver, and a sewing machine for closing stomach incisions, all give an idea of the centuries of misconceptions and the slow progress of medicine through fatal errors.

The story of the museum's namesake, **Dr Ignác Semmelweis**, is also explained, though only in Hungarian. While serving in Vienna's public hospitals in the early nineteenth century, he discovered the cause of puerperal fever – a form of blood poisoning contracted in childbirth that was usually fatal. He noticed that deaths were ten times lower on the wards where only midwives worked than on the ones attended by doctors and students, who went from dissecting corpses to delivering babies with only a perfunctory wash. His solution was simply to sterilize hands, clothes and instruments between operations, earning him the title of "saviour of mothers".

The museum also contains the 1876 **Holy Ghost Pharmacy**, transplanted here from Király utca, and a collection of portraits including one of Vilma Hugonai,

Hungary's first woman doctor, and one of Kossuth's sister, Zsuzsanna, who founded the army medical corps during the War of Independence. The insignificant-looking stones in the park out back are actually Turkish gravestones.

The museum is just around the corner from **Szarvas tér** (Stag Square), named after the eighteenth-century *Stag House* inn at no. 1, which functions as a restaurant to this day.

THE VÍZIVÁROS

Inhabited by fishermen, craftsmen and their families in medieval times, the **Víziváros** or Watertown, between Várhegy and the Danube, became depopulated during the seventeenth century, and was resettled by Habsburg mercenaries and their camp followers after the Turks were driven out. The following century saw the neighbourhood gradually gentrified, with solid apartment blocks meeting at odd angles on the hillside, reached by alleys which mostly consist of steps rising from the main street, **Fő utca**. Some of these are still lit by gas lamps and look quite Dickensian on misty evenings. Although the Víziváros extends as far north as the Király Baths (see p.51), most visitors find the stretch between the Lánchíd and Batthyány tér quite sufficient.

The Széchenyi Lánchíd

Map 3, F8. Bus #86 or tram #19 from Szent Gellért tér; bus #2 or #16 from Erzsébet tér in Pest.

The majestic **Lánchíd** (Chain Bridge) has a special place in the history of Budapest and in the hearts of its citizens. As the first permanent link between Buda and Pest (replacing seasonal pontoon bridges and ferries), it was a tremendous spur to the country's economic growth and eventual unification, linking the rural hinterland to European civilization so that Budapest became a commercial centre and transport hub. The bridge symbolized the abolition of feudal privilege, as nobles, hitherto exempt from taxes, were obliged pay the toll to cross it. It also symbolized civic endurance, having been inaugurated only weeks after Hungary lost the 1849 War of Independence, when Austrian troops tried and failed to destroy it.

However, in 1945, the Wehrmacht dynamited all of Budapest's bridges in a bid to check the Red Army. Their reconstruction was one of the first tasks of the postwar era, and the reopening of the Lánchíd on the centenary of its inauguration (November 21) was heralded as proof that life was returning to normal, even as Hungary was becoming a Communist dictatorship. Today, the bridge is once again adorned with the national coat of arms, rather than Soviet symbols.

The idea for a bridge came to **Count István Széchenyi** (see box opposite) after he was late for his father's funeral in 1820 because bad weather had made the Danube uncrossable. Turning his idea into reality was to preoccupy him for two decades, and it became the centrepiece of a grand plan to modernize Hungary's communications. Due to Britain's industrial pre-eminence and Széchenyi's Anglophilia, the bridge was designed by **William Tierney Clark** (based on his earlier plan for Hammersmith Bridge) and constructed under the supervision of a Scottish engineer, **Adam Clark** (no relation), from components cast in Britain. Besides the technical problems of erecting what was then the longest bridge in Europe (nearly 380m), there was also an attempt by the Austrians to blow it up – which Adam Clark personally thwarted by flooding its chain-lockers. He also dissuaded a Hungarian general from setting it alight in 1849.

Whereas Széchenyi later died in an asylum, having witnessed the triumph and defeat of his *bête noire*, Kossuth, Clark settled happily in Budapest with his Hungarian wife. After his death, he was buried on the spot that now bears his name, though his remains were subsequently moved to Kerepesi Cemetery.

Count Széchenyi

Count István Széchenyi (1791–1860) was the outstanding figure of Hungary's Reform era. As a young aide-de-camp he cut a dash at the Congress of Vienna and did the rounds of stately homes across Europe. While in England, he steeplechased hell-for-leather, but still found time to examine factories and steam trains, providing Bernard Shaw with the inspiration for the "odious Zoltán Karpathy" of *Pygmalion* (and the musical *My Fair Lady*). Back in Hungary, he pondered solutions to his homeland's backwardness and offered a year's income from his estates towards the establishment of a Hungarian Academy. In 1830 he published *Hitel* (Credit), a hard-headed critique of the nation's feudal society.

Though politically conservative, Széchenyi was obsessed with **modernization**. A passionate convert to steam power after riding on the Manchester–Liverpool railway, he invited Britons to Hungary to build rail lines and the Lánchíd. He also imported steamships and dredgers, promoted horsebreeding and silk-making, and initiated the dredging of the River Tisza and the blasting of a road through the Iron Gates of the Danube. Alas, his achievements were rewarded by a melancholy end. The 1848 Revolution and the triumph of Kossuth triggered a nervous breakdown, and Széchenyi eventually shot himself.

The Sikló and Kilometre Zero

Map 3, F8. Daily 7.30am–10pm; closed second & fourth Mon of every month; 250Ft.

Clark also built the **tunnel** (*alagút*) under Várhegy, which Budapesters joked could be used to store the new bridge when it rained. Next to the tunnel entrance at the river end is the lower terminal of the **Sikló**, a nineteenth-century **funic-**

ular running up to the palace. Constructed on the initiative of Ödön, Széchenyi's son, it was only the second funicular in the world when it was inaugurated in 1870, and functioned without a hitch until wrecked by a shell in 1945. The yellow carriages are exact replicas of the originals, but are now lifted by an electric winch rather than a steam engine. In the small park at its foot stands **Kilometre Zero**, a zero-shaped monument from where all distances from Budapest are measured.

Szilágyi Desző tér

Map 3, F6.

Before you emerge right onto **Szilágyi Desző tér**, notice an old Capuchin church featuring Turkish window arches on the left-hand side, at no. 30. The square itself is famous for the events that occurred here in January 1945. When Eichmann and the SS had already fled, members of the Fascist Arrow Cross massacred hundreds of Budapest's Jews and dumped their bodies in the river by **Szilágyi Desző tér**. A plaque commemorates the victims, though the polychrome-tiled church and a floating hotel moored beside the embankment mark the spot more conspicuously.

A brief detour up Vám utca, just north of the square, leads you to the **Iron Block**, a replica of a wooden block into which itinerant apprentices once hammered nails for good luck; the original is in a museum.

Batthyány tér

Map 3, E5. Batthyány tér metro (M2); bus #16 from Erzsébet tér in Pest.

The main square and social hub of the Víziváros, **Batthyány tér** is named after the nineteenth-century prime minister, Lajos Batthyány, but started out as Bomba tér (Bomb Square), after an ammunition depot sited here for the defence of the Danube. Today it is busy with shoppers visiting the supermarket in an old market hall on the western side of the square, and commuters using the underground interchange between the metro and the HÉV suburban line to Szentendre. The sunken, two-storey building to the right of the market used to be the *White Cross Inn*, where Casanova reputedly once stayed. Many of the older buildings in this area are sunken in this way due to the ground level being raised several feet in the last century to combat flooding.

The twin-towered **Church of St Anne** (*Szent Anna templom*) on the corner of Fő utca is one of the finest Baroque buildings in Budapest. Commissioned by the Jesuits in 1740, it wasn't consecrated until 1805 due to financial problems, the abolition of the Jesuit order in 1773, and an earthquake. During Communist times there were plans to demolish it, as it was feared that the metro would undermine its foundations, but these, fortunately, came to nothing. Figures of Faith, Hope and Charity hover above the entrance, and in the middle of the facade St Anne cherishes the child Mary, while God's eye surmounts the Buda coat of arms on its tympanum. The interior is ornate yet homely, its high altar festooned with statues of St Anne presenting Mary to the Temple in Jerusalem, accompanied by a host of cherubim and angels, while chintzy bouquets and potted trees welcome shoppers dropping in to say their prayers.

In the northern corner of the square, the **Church of the St Elizabeth Nuns** is worth a look inside for its fresco of St Florian protecting the faithful during the 1810 Fire of Tabán.

The Király Baths

Map 3, E3. Men, Mon, Wed & Fri 6.30am–7pm; women, Tues & Thurs 6.30am–7pm, Sat 6.30am–noon; 450Ft.

You can identify the **Király Baths** (*Király gyógyfürdő*) by the four copper cupolas, shaped like tortoise shells, poking from its eighteenth-century facade. Together with the Rudas, this is the finest of Budapest's Turkish baths, whose octagonal pool, lit by star-shaped apertures in the dome, was built in 1570 for the Buda garrison. The baths' name, meaning "king", comes from that of the König family who owned them in the eighteenth century.

On the way to the baths you will pass the hulking Fascist-style **Military Court of Justice** at Fő utca 70–72, where Imre Nagy and other leaders of the 1956 Uprising were secretly tried and executed in 1958. The square outside has now been renamed after Nagy, whose body lay in an unmarked grave in the New Public Cemetery for over thirty years (see p.130).

Bem tér

Map 3, F3.

Fő utca terminates at **Bem tér**, named after the Polish general Joseph Bem, who fought for the Hungarians in the War of Independence, and was revered by his men as "Father". A **statue of Bem** with his arm in a sling recalls him leading them into battle at Piski, crying "I shall recapture the bridge or die! Forward Hungarians! If we do not have the bridge we do not have the country." Traditionally a site for demonstrations, it was here that the crowds assembled prior to marching on parliament at the beginning of the 1956 Uprising.

A century ago, the surrounding neighbourhood was dominated by a foundry established by the Swiss ironworker Abrahám Ganz, which grew into the mighty Ganz Machine Works. The original ironworks only ceased operation in 1964, when it was turned into a **Foundry Museum** (*Öntödei Múzeum*; Tues–Sun 9am–4pm; 100Ft). You can still see the old wooden structure and the huge ladles and jib-cranes *in situ*, together with a collection of cast-iron stoves, tram wheels, lampposts and other exhibits. The museum is located at Bem utca 20, 200m uphill from Bem tér, or barely a block from Margit körút.

MOSZKVA TÉR TO RÓZSADOMB

Map 3, B4. Moszkva tér metro (M2); tram #4 or #6 from the Nagykörút in Pest.

The area immediately north of Várhegy is defined by the transport hub of **Moszkva tér** (Moscow Square), which has kept its name in the post-Communist era because nobody cared to restore the prewar one, honouring a feeble politician. Once a quarry and subsequently an ice rink and tennis courts, its surrounding buildings were laid waste in the streetfighting of 1945, except for the castle-like one on the crest of the hill. Nowadays, the plaza outside the metro station functions as a flower market and an unofficial labour exchange, with a shifting crowd of commuters, casual workers and drunks.

By day, the reason for coming here is to catch a ride to somewhere else – either the Buda Hills (bus or tram #56) or the Budakeszi Game Park (bus #22), or tram #4 or #6 towards Margit sziget and Pest – which is also the way to reach Gül Baba's tomb and the Foundry Museum. At night, however, you're more likely to come to eat, drink or dance at various venues in the backstreets off the square (see "Listings").

Gül Baba's tomb and Rózsadomb

Map 3, D1. Tram #4 or #6 from Moszkva tér or the Nagykörút in Pest.

The smoggy arc of **Margit körút** underlines the gulf between the polluted inner city and the breeze-freshened heights of Budapest's most affluent neighbourhood, Rózsadomb (Rose Hill). The hill is named after the flowers that were reputedly introduced to Hungary by a revered Sufi dervish, Gül Baba, the "Father of the Roses", who participated in the Turkish capture of Buda but died during the thanksgiving service afterwards. The **Tomb of Gül Baba** (May–Oct Tues–Sun 10am–5pm; 100Ft) is fittingly located on Mecset utca (Mosque Street), a stiff five minutes' walk uphill from Margit körút. Having been restored with funds donated by the Turkish government, it is surrounded by a colonnaded parapet with fine views, set in a pristine park with rosebushes and marble fountains decorated with ceramic tiles. The octagonal shrine is adorned with Arabic calligraphy and Turkish carpets; at one time visitors had to remove their shoes before entering, but now they're allowed to clump in as they are.

The **Rózsadomb** itself is as much a social category as a neighbourhood, for a list of residents would read like a Hungarian *Who's Who*. During the Communist era this included the top Party *funcionárusok*, whose homes featured secret exits that enabled several ÁVO chiefs to escape lynching during the Uprising. Nowadays, wealthy film directors and entrepreneurs predominate, and the sloping streets are lined with spacious villas and flashy cars.

Óbuda, Romai-Fürdő and Margit sziget

Óbuda is the oldest part of Budapest, though that's hardly the impression given by the factories and high-rises that dominate the district today, hiding such ancient ruins as remain. Nonetheless, it was here that the Romans built a legionary camp and a civilian town, later taken over by the Huns. Under the Hungarian Árpád dynasty this developed into an important town, but in the fifteenth century it was eclipsed by Várhegy. The original settlement became known as Óbuda (Old Buda) and was incorporated into the newly formed Budapest in 1873. The old town centre is as pretty as Várhegy, but to find the best-preserved Roman ruins you'll have to go to the **Római-Fürdő** district, further out. Both are accessible by HÉV train from Batthyány tér or the Margit híd.

ÓBUDA

Map 7. HÉV train to the Árpád híd stop.

After its incorporation within the city, **Óbuda** became a popular place to eat, drink and make merry, with dozens of garden restaurants and taverns serving fish and wine from the locality. Some of the most famous establishments still exist around **Fő tér**, the heart of eighteenth-century Óbuda, but, while there's no denying the charm of their Baroque facades and wrought-iron lamps, in many cases they are simply trading on past glories and you'd do better eating elsewhere (see p.163).

There's more to enjoy from a cultural standpoint, with three museums in the vicinity. Directly opposite the HÉV exit at Szentlélek tér 1, the **Vasarely Museum** (Map 7, H2; Tues–Sun 10am–6pm; 100Ft) displays eyeball-throbbing Op Art works by Viktor Vasarely, one of the founders of the genre, who was born in Pécs in southern Hungary and emigrated to Paris in 1930.

Just around the corner from the museum, at Fő tér 1, the Baroque Zichy mansion contains the **Kassák Museum** (Map 7, H2; Tues–Sun 10am–6pm; 100Ft) dedicated to the Hungarian constructionist Lajos Kassák, and a **Local History Exhibition** (Tues–Fri 2–6pm, Sat & Sun 10am–6pm; 50Ft), with rooms in the Sváb (German) and Art Nouveau styles, and a cute collection of antique toys. The mansion's courtyard seems unchanged since Habsburg times.

Whatever the weather, you'll see several figures sheltering beneath umbrellas on Fő tér: life-sized sculptures by Imre Varga, whose *oeuvre* is the subject of the **Varga Museum** at Laktanya utca 7 (Map 7, H1; Tues–Sun 10am–6pm; 100Ft). While a sense of humour pervades his sheet-metal, iron and bronze effigies of famous personages (including the one of Béla Kun addressing a crowd that's now in the Statue Park), Varga was also responsible for the sobering Holocaust Memorial in Pest.

Óbuda's Roman remains

Map 7. Bus #86 from Batthyány tér or Flórián tér.

Although the largest site lies further out in Római-Fürdő

district (see overleaf), Óbuda does have several excavated ruins to show for its past. On modern-day Flórián tér, 500m west of Fő tér, graceful columns stand amid a shopping plaza, while the old **military baths** and other finds lurk beneath the Szentendrei út flyover, running off Flórián tér. Relics of the 6000-strong legionary garrison that once existed here can be seen in the **Camp Museum** at Pacsirtamező utca 63, ten minutes' walk south of Flórián tér (Map 7, G3; *Táborvárosi Múzeum*; May–Oct Tues–Fri 10am–2pm, Sat & Sun 10am–6pm; 150Ft), together with fragmented murals and the interior of an officers' bathhouse that was discovered beneath a postwar block.

The largest ruin is the weed-choked, crumbling **amphitheatre** (*amfiteátrum*) at the junction of Pacsirtamező and Nagyszombat utca, 800m further south, which can be reached by bus #86 or by walking 400m north from Kolosy tér, near the Szépvölgyi út HÉV stop. The ampitheatre once covered a greater area than the Colosseum in Rome, seating up to 16,000 spectators. While you're in the area, check out a couple of good patisseries renowned for their ice creams: the *Veress*, on the corner of Bok utca, leading south from the amphitheatre, and the *Daubner*, up on Szépvölgyi út, leading towards the caves in the Buda Hills (see Chapter 5).

The most intriguing relic, however, is fifteen minutes' walk northwest of Flórián tér, where three canopies behind the high-rise block at Meggyfa utca 19–21 shelter the remains of the **Hercules Villa** (April–Oct Tues–Fri 10am–2pm, Sat & Sun 10am–6pm; 150Ft), whose name derives from the third-century AD **mosaic floor** beneath the largest canopy. This mosaic, originally composed of 60,000 stones carefully selected and arranged in Alexandria, depicts Hercules about to vomit at a wine festival. Another mosaic portrays the centaur Nessus abducting Deianeira, whom Hercules had to rescue as one of his twelve labours.

RÓMAI-FÜRDŐ

Map 2, E3. Access by HÉV to Aquincum for the ruins, or Római-Fürdő for the campsite and lido.

North of Óbuda, the riverside factory belt merges into the **Római-Fürdő** (Roman Bath) district, a prelude to the leafy suburb of Csillaghegy that could be ignored but for its **campsite** and **lido** and the ruins of Aquincum. Originally a settlement of camp followers spawned by the legionary garrison, Aquincum eventually became a *municipium* and then a *colonia*, the provincial capital of Pannonia Inferior. The **ruins of Aquincum** (Map 2, E3; May–Oct Tues–Sun 10am–6pm; 200Ft) are visible from the Aquincum HÉV stop, as is a small ampitheatre on the other side of the tracks. Enough foundation walls and underground piping survive to give a fair idea of Aquincum's layout, although you'll need to pay a visit to the museum and use considerable imagination to envisage the town during its heyday in the second to third centuries. A great concourse of people would have filled the main street, doing business in the forum and law courts, near the site entrance. Herbs and wine were burned before altars in sanctuaries holy to the goddesses Epona and Fortuna Augusta, while fraternal societies met in the collegiums and bathhouses further east. The **museum** (same hours and price) contains statues of deities and oddments of the imperium – cake moulds, a bronze military diploma, and buttons used as admission tickets to the theatre.

MARGIT SZIGET

Bus #26 from Nyugati tér or the Árpád híd metro in Pest runs the length of the island; trams #4 and #6 from Moszkva tér or the Nagykörút stop halfway across the Margit híd, at the southern end of the island.

There's a saying that "love begins and ends on **Margit sziget**", for this verdant island has been a favourite meeting place for lovers since the nineteenth century (though before 1945 a stiff admission charge deterred the poor). It remains one of Budapest's most popular parks, with two public baths fed by thermal springs, an outdoor theatre and other amenities. At a refreshing distance from the noise and pollution of the city centre, it's still sufficiently close to feature in its waterfront panorama.

Motorists can only approach from the north of the island, via the Árpád híd, at which point they must leave their vehicles at a paying car park. Trams stop at the southern entrance to the island, where one can rent **bikes** on the left-hand side; they tend to be rather battered, but are good enough to get you around the five-kilometre circuit from one end to the other.

A royal game reserve under the Árpáds and a monastic colony until the Turkish conquest, the island was named at the end of the nineteenth century after Princess **Margit** (Margaret), the daughter of Béla IV. Legend has it that he vowed to bring her up as a nun if Hungary survived the Mongol invasion, and duly confined the 9-year-old in a convent when it did. She apparently made the best of it, acquiring a reputation for curing lepers and other saintly deeds, as well as for never washing above her ankles. Beatification came after her death in 1271, and a belated canonization in 1943. Her name had already been bestowed on the **Margit híd**, which was built by a French company in the 1870s and linked Margit sziget to Buda and Pest. It is an unusual bridge in the form of a splayed-out V, with a short arm joined to the southern tip of the island. In November 1944 it was blown up by the Nazis, killing hundreds of people including the German sappers who had detonated the explosives by mistake. Photos of the result can be seen in the underpass at the Pest end.

The southern part of the island features a huge circular concrete fountain, a millennial monument and the **Hajós Alfréd** swimming pools (popularly known as the "Sport"), named after the winner of the 100m and 1200m swimming races at the 1896 Olympics. Hajós was also an architect and designed the indoor pool, but the main attractions here are the all-season outdoor 50m pool and the fresh pastries at the buffet. Two hundred metres further north lies the **Palatinus Strand** (daily May–Sept), which can hold as many as ten thousand people at a time in seven open-air thermal pools, complete with a water chute, wave machine and segregated terraces for nude sunbathing.

Off to the east of the road between the two pools are the **ruins of a Franciscan church** from the late thirteenth century, while a **ruined Dominican church and convent** stands in the vicinity of the **Outdoor Theatre** (*Szabadtéri Színpad*) further north along the main road, which hosts plays, operas, fashion shows and concerts during summer. The café here makes a convenient stop for a beer and a snack, being easily located by the **water tower** that rises above the complex.

A short way northeast of the tower is a **Premonstratensian Chapel**, whose Romanesque tower dates back to the twelfth century when the order first established a monastery on the island. The tower's fifteenth-century bell is one of the oldest in Hungary. Further north lie two luxury **spa hotels**, the *fin-de-siècle Danubius Grand* and the modern *Thermal*, the latter beside a rock garden with warm springs that sustain tropical fish and giant water lilies.

If it's sport you're after, the **Euro Gym**, to the east of the two hotels, offers aerobics classes, tennis courts and a sauna, while the pleasant *Europa Beer Garden* next door serves wood-grilled meats, Austrian lager and imported Kentish bitter.

The Buda Hills

The **Buda Hills** are as close to nature as you can get within the city limits: a densely wooded arc around a sixth of Budapest's circumference. It's a favourite place for walking in all seasons, with many trails all marked with the distance or the duration (*ó* stands for hour; *p* for minutes). While some parts can be crowded with walkers and mountain-bikers at the weekend, during the week it's possible to ramble for hours and see hardly a soul. If your time is limited, the most rewarding destinations are the "**railway circuit**" using the Cogwheel and Children's railways and the chairlift, or a visit to the **caves** near the valley of Szépvölgy, perhaps followed by the Kiscelli Museum or Bartók's house. You could also combine the railway circuit with a visit to Budakeszi Game Park, on the city limits (see Chapter 12).

THE "RAILWAY CIRCUIT"

Map 2.

This is an easy and enjoyable way to visit the hills that will especially appeal to kids. The whole return trip can take under two hours if connections click and you don't dawdle, or an afternoon if the opposite applies. You begin at Moszkva tér (see p.53) by boarding tram #18 or #56 or bus

#56, and alighting opposite the cylindrical *Budapest Hotel*, beside the lower terminal of the **Cogwheel Railway** (*Fogaskerekűvasút*). The third such railway in the world when it was inaugurated in 1874, the system was steam-powered until 1929 when it was electrified. Trains run every ten minutes or so, rising slowly through the villa-suburb of Svábhegy; for the best view take a window seat on the right-hand side, facing backwards.

From the upper terminal on **Széchenyi-hegy** it's a minute's walk to the **Children's Railway** (*Gyermekvasút*). A narrow-gauge line built by youth brigades in 1948, it's almost entirely run by 13- to 17-year-olds, enabling them to get hands-on experience if they fancy a career with MÁV, the Hungarian Railways company. Watching them wave flags, collect tickets and salute departures with great solemnity, you can see why it appealed to the Communists. Until a few years ago, it was known as the Pioneers' Railway after the organization that replaced the disbanded Scouts and Guides movements (now re-formed). Having been through lean times, when for a while it operated at weekends only, trains now run as frequently as they used to (every 45–60min; June–Aug daily 9am–5pm; Sept–May Tues–Sun same hours), stopping at various points en route to Hűvösvölgy (Cool Valley). The eleven-kilometre journey takes about 45 minutes.

The first stop, **Normafa**, is a popular excursion centre with a modest **ski-run**. Its name comes from a performance of the aria from Bellini's *Norma* given here by the actress Rozália Klein in 1840. In a wooden hut near the stop, the *Rétes büfé* serves delicious strudel and coffee every day of the year including holidays. Three stops on, **János-hegy** is the highest point in Budapest. On the 527-metre-high summit, fifteen minutes' climb from the station, the **Erzsébet lookout tower** offers a panoramic view of the city and the Buda Hills. By the buffet below the summit is the upper terminal of the **chairlift** or *Libegő*, meaning "floater" in Hungarian (May–Sept 9.30am–5pm; Oct–April 9.30am–4pm; closed every other Mon; 150Ft), down to **Zugliget**, from where #158 buses return to Moszkva tér.

From the main road by **Szépjuhászné**, the next stop after János-hegy, you can catch bus #22 to the Budakeszi Game Park. Wild boar, which prefer to roam during the evening and sleep by day, are occasionally sighted in the forests above **Hárshegy**, one stop before Hűvösvölgy, both in the Buda Hills. Also linked directly to Moszkva tér by #56 and #56E (nonstop) buses, **Hűvösvölgy** is the site of the popular *Náncsi Néni* restaurant (see p.169).

THE CAVES

Map 7, A5 & E7.

In the hills to the north of Hűvösvölgy are caves that are unique for having been formed by thermal waters rising up from below, rather than by rain water. Two of the sites have been accessible to the public since the 1980s, with guided tours (in Hungarian only) every hour on the hour. In both cases the starting point is Kolosy tér in Óbuda (accessible by bus #86 from Flórián tér or Batthyány tér, or bus #6 from Nyugati tér in Pest), from where you catch bus #65 five stops to the Pálvölgy Cave, or bus #29 four stops to the Szemlő-hegy Cave. As the two caves are ten minutes' walk apart, it's possible to dash from one to the other and catch both tours within two hours; if you're planning to do this, it's worth buying a combined ticket.

The **Pálvölgy Stalactite Cave** (*Pálvölgyi cseppkőbarlang*; Tues–Sun guided tours 10am–4pm; 160Ft), at Szépvölgyi út 162, is the larger and more spectacular labyrinth. Tours of the stalactites and stalagmites last about half an hour and involve lots of steps and constricted passages. Discovered in the 1900s, the Pálvölgy is the longest of the cave systems in the Buda Hills and is still being explored by speleologists.

The **Szemlő-hegy Cave** (*Szemlőhegyi barlang*; April–Oct Mon & Wed–Fri 10am–3pm, Sat & Sun 10am–4pm; 160Ft), at Pusztaszeri út 35, is quite different, with less convoluted and claustrophic passages and no stalactites. Instead, the walls are encrusted with cauliflower- or popcorn-textured precipitates formed by warm water dissolving mineral salts. The air is exceptionally clean and the lowest level of the cave is used as a respiratory sanatorium, though this isn't featured on the tour. Afterwards you can view a museum of cave finds and plans from all over Hungary.

If you're into caving, the Hungarian Association of Speleologists in Budapest (©201-9493) can put you in touch with groups exploring caves in the Buda Hills and elsewhere in Hungary.

THE KISCELLI MUSEUM

Map 7, D3. Bus #165 from Kolosy tér and a short walk. April–Oct Tues–Sun 10am–6pm; Nov–March Tues–Sun 10am–4pm; 150Ft.

Fifteen minutes' walk from the Szemlő-hegy Cave, the **Kiscelli Museum**, on a hilltop to the northwest of the caves, occupies a former Trinitarian monastery in a beautiful wooded setting at Kiscelli utca 108. A bombed-out Gothic church makes a dramatic backdrop for operas, fashion shows and performances, while the museum's collection includes paintings such as Rippl-Rónai's *My Parents after Forty Years of Marriage* and János Kmetty's Cubist *Városliget*, and engravings of eighteenth- and nineteenth-century Budapest showing such innovations as the Lánchíd. On the ground floor you can inspect the 1830 Biedermeier furnishings of the Golden Lion pharmacy, which used to stand on Kálvin tér, and have a copy of Petőfi's *National Song* run off on an antique printing press as a souvenir.

THE BARTÓK MEMORIAL HOUSE

Map 2, C4. Bus #29 from the Szemlő-hegy Cave to the Nagybányai út stop, or bus #5 from Moszkva tér to the Pasaréti stop, followed by a short walk. Tues–Sun 10am–5pm; 100Ft. ©376-2100 for concert information.

Secluded by trees, the **Bartók Memorial House** (*Bartók Béla Emlékház*) at Csalán utca 29, is in the leafy suburb below Láto-hegy, off the road to Hűvösvölgy. The villa was the residence of Béla Bartók, his wife and two sons from 1932 until their emigration to America in 1940, by which time Bartók despaired of Hungary's right-wing regime. Besides an extensive range of Bartók memorabilia you can see some of his original furniture and possessions, including folk handicrafts collected during his ethno-musical research trips to Transylvania with Zoltán Kodály. Music lovers may be drawn to the **concerts** of chamber music which are often held here on Fridays. To return to the centre of town, walk down to Pasaréti tér (5 mins) and catch a #5 bus back to Moszkva tér.

The Belváros

A buzz with pavement cafés, street artists, vendors, boutiques and nightclubs, the Belváros, or Inner City, is the hub of Pest and, for tourists at least, the epicentre of what's happening. Commerce and pleasure have been its lifeblood as long as Pest has existed, first as a medieval market town and later as the kernel of a city whose *belle époque* rivalled Vienna's. Since their fates diverged, the Belváros has lagged far behind Vienna's Centrum in prosperity, though the last decade has narrowed the gap, at least superficially. It's now increasingly like any Western city in its consumer culture, but you can still get a sense of the old atmosphere, especially in the quieter back-streets south of Kossuth utca.

The **Kiskörút** (Small Boulevard) that surrounds the Belváros follows the course of the medieval walls of Pest, showing how compact it was before the phenomenal expansion of the nineteenth century. However, little remains from further back than the eighteenth century, as the "liberation" of Pest by the Habsburgs in 1686 left the town in ruins. Some Baroque churches and the former Greek and Serbian quarters attest to its revival by settlers from other parts of the Habsburg empire, but most of the **architecture** dates from the era when Budapest asserted its right to be an imperial capital, roughly between 1860 and

Approaches to the Belváros

Most people walk into the Belváros from Deák tér (see p.77), whose metro station is near the terminus of trams #47 and #49 from Buda, and the Erzsébet tér bus station. Any of the side-streets to the west will bring you to Váci utca or Vörösmarty tér in a few minutes. Two other approaches by metro are M1 to Vörösmarty tér, exiting outside the *Gerbeaud* patisserie, or M3 to Ferenciek tere, midway down Váci utca.

1918. Today, first-time visitors are struck by the statues, domes and mosaics on the Neoclassical and Art Nouveau piles, which are reflected in the mirrored banks and luxury hotels that symbolize the new order.

After a stroll along **Váci utca** from **Vörösmarty tér** and a look at the splendid view of Várhegy from the **embankment**, the best way to appreciate the Belváros is by simply wandering around. People-watching and window-shopping are the most enjoyable activities, and though prices are above average any visitor should be able to afford to sample the **cafés**. Shops are another matter – there are few bargains – and nightclubs a trap for the unwary, but there's nothing to stop you from enjoying the **cultural life**, from jazz musicians and violinists on Vörösmarty tér to world-class conductors and soloists at the **Vigadó** concert hall, around the corner.

VÖRÖSMARTY TÉR

Map 6, C3. Vörösmarty tér metro (M1).

Vörösmarty tér, the leafy centre of the Belváros, is a good starting point for exploring the area. Crowds eddy around the portraitists, conjurers and saxophonists, and the craft stalls that are set up over summer, Christmas and the wine festival. While children play in the fountains, teenagers lounge around the **statue of Mihály Vörösmarty** (1800–50), a poet and translator whose hymn to Magyar identity, *Szózat* (Appeal), is publicly declaimed at moments of national crisis. Its opening line "Be faithful to your land forever, Oh Hungarians" is carved on the statue's pedestal. Made of Carrara marble, the statue has to be wrapped in plastic sheeting each winter to prevent it from cracking. The black spot above the inscription is reputedly a "lucky" coin donated by a beggar towards the cost of the monument.

On the north side of the square is the **Gerbeaud patisserie**, Budapest's most famous confectioners. Founded in 1858 by Henrik Kugler, it was bought in 1884 by the Swiss confectioner Emile Gerbeaud, who invented the *konyakos meggy* (cognac-cherry bonbon). He sold top-class cakes at reasonable prices, making *Gerbeaud* a popular rendezvous for the middle classes. His portrait hangs in one of the rooms, whose gilded ceilings and china recall the *belle époque*. The smaller *Kis-Gerbeaud* salon is no longer a haunt of octogenarian "Gerbeaud ladies" wearing furs and lace gloves, having been turned into a cake shop.

From the terrace outside you can observe the entrance to the **Underground Railway** (*Földalatti Vasút*), whose vaguely Art Nouveau cast-iron fixtures and elegant tile-work stamp it as decades older than the other metro lines. Indeed, it was the first on the European continent and the second in the world (after London's Metropolitan line) when it was inaugurated in 1896, and ran from Vörösmarty tér to the Millennial Exhibition grounds at Hősök tere. For its centenary, the line was equipped with the latest technology and its stations restored to their original decor. If you're curious to know more about its history, visit the Underground Railway Museum at Deák tér (see p.78).

The Underground Railway's route along Andrássy út is covered in Chapter 8, with Hősök tere described in Chapter 9.

At the lower end of the square, the **Bank Palace** was built between 1913 and 1915, in the heyday of Hungarian self-confidence, by Ignác Alpár, who also designed the prewar Stock Exchange on Szabadság tér (see p.83). It now houses the **Budapest Stock Exchange**, which was reborn in 1990, 42 years after the Communists suppressed its predecessor, and allows visitors to observe its trading floor (Mon–Fri 10.30am–1.30pm; free). Count Mihály Károlyi, the radical liberal who became Prime Minister in 1918, had an office in the building across the street and used to address crowds from its balcony.

VÁCI UTCA

Deák tér, Vörösmarty tér or Ferenciek tere metro.

When people refer to **Váci utca** they usually mean the stretch from Vörösmarty tér to Szabadsajtó út, which has been famous for its shops and **korzó** (promenade) since the eighteenth century. Though the shopfronts and fashions have changed, the parade of dressed-to-kill babes and their monied escorts would be familiar to anyone who can remember prewar Budapest. During the 1980s, its vivid **streetlife** became a symbol of the "consumer socialism" that distinguished Hungary from other Eastern Bloc states. Dreadlocked rollerbladers heralded its assimilation into the global village a year before the Wall came down, and its nightclubs were among the first to be taken over by foreign Mafia gangs, whose turf wars were blamed for a car bomb that killed four bystanders just off Váci utca in 1998. Normally, however, the worst hazard is being accosted by an evangelist in daytime or a prostitute late at night.

Heading south from Vörösmarty tér, down Váci utca, you'll pass **Kristóf tér** (Map 6, C3) immediately to your right, a small plaza adorned by the **fisher-girl statue**, whose scanty attire aroused criticism when it was originally erected by a fish market on the embankment. Near the corner of what is now Türr István utca, the northern Vác Gate formed part of the medieval walls of Pest until it was pulled down in the 1870s; an outline marks the spot. Like Váci utca, its name came from the town of Vác on the Danube Bend, to which they led.

Today's **Pest Theatre** at Váci utca 9 occupies the site of the *Inn of the Seven Electors*, where the 12-year-old Liszt performed in 1823. No. 13 is the oldest building on the street, dating from about 1805, and the *McDonald's* around the corner on Régiposta utca was the first in Hungary when it opened in 1988. During the 1930s, what is now the **Folkart Centrum** (no. 14) was a furriers, whose owner hired models to play mini-golf in the windows, wearing his coats.

Every other shop down to Ferenciek tere sells souvenirs, clothes or jewellery, and the ones that don't are bureaux de change. Besides designer clothes stores, there are all kinds of small **shops** in the yards off the street, some of them in delightful buildings with spiral staircases. On Váci utca itself, you'll see lines of women selling embroidered quilts and tablecloths; the ones in country dress are from Szék (in red skirts and white headscarves) or the Kalotaszeg (in green vests and skirts and yellow scarves), two ethnically Hungarian regions of Romania.

Beyond Ferenciek tere, Váci utca becomes quieter, and the stretch between here and Fővám tér has become an **alternative korzó** since it was pedestrianized in 1997, with smart boutiques and cafés ousting the old-fashioned specialist shops that used to predominate. There are also lots of restaurants and bars around here, making it an excellent spot for a night out. As you're walking around here, notice the beautifully restored prewar **Officers' Casino** on the corner of Irányi utca (now a bank's headquarters), and the pictorial **plaque** on the wall of no. 47, commemorating the fact that the Swedish King Carl XII stayed here during his lightning fourteen-day horse-ride from Turkey to Sweden, in 1714. Further down at nos. 62–64 is the **Old Budapest City Hall**, a dramatic nineteenth-century hulk.

PETŐFI SÁNDOR UTCA

Petőfi Sándor utca, running parallel to Váci utca between Vörösmarty tér and Ferenciek tere, has none of the glamour of Váci utca and a lot of traffic, but you may be lured by its array of **music shops** or need to visit the **MATÁV** phone, fax and email centre (no. 17) or the **central post office** (no. 13). Next to the modernist MATÁV building is the eighteenth-century **Servite Church**, which lends its name to the small square beside it, Szervita tér. The church's facade bears a relief of an angel craddling a dying horseman, in memory of the VII Kaiser Wilhelm Hussars killed in World War I. If the church is open, its Baroque interior and massive altar are worth a look.

Don't miss the pair of buildings on the left-hand side of Szervita tér – especially no. 3, its gable aglow with a superb **Secessionist mosaic** of *Patrona Hungariae* (Our Lady of Hungary) flanked by shepherds and angels, one of the finest works of Miksa Róth. The **Rózsavölgyi Building**, next door, was built a few years later between 1910 and 1913 by the "father" of Hungarian Modernism, Béla Lajta, whose earlier association with the National Romantic school is evident from the majolica decorations on its upper storeys, which are typical of the style. On the ground floor is the

Rózsavölgyi music shop, one of the oldest and best in the city.

FERENCIEK TERE

Map 6, C6. Ferenciek tere (M3) or Astoria (M2) metro.

Ferenciek tere is named after the **Franciscan Church** on the corner of Kossuth utca, whose facade bears a relief recalling the great flood of 1838, in which over four hundred citizens were killed. The death toll would have been higher had it not been for the efforts of Baron Miklós Wesselényi, who personally rescued scores of people in his boat; his efforts are depicted on a plaque outside the church. To the north of the square, a little way along Kigyó utca, the *Apostolok* restaurant is decorated with murals of the apostles and of towns lost to Hungary after World War I.

However, the square is chiefly notable for the **Párisi Udvar**, a flamboyantly eclectic shopping arcade. Completed by Henrik Schmal in 1915, its fifty naked statues above the third floor were deemed incompatible with its intended role as a savings bank, symbolized by images of bees throughout the building. The old deposit hall now houses an IBUSZ office, while the arcade is as dark as an Andalucian mosque and twice as ornate, but contains little more than a map shop and a bar, due to the risk of falling stained glass from Miksa Róth's dome.

As Ferenciek tere runs on towards the Kiskörút, it is known as Kossuth Lajos utca, which is the main east-west axis of the city, connecting Buda with the hinterland of Pest. Its junction with the Kiskörút is named after the **Astoria Hotel** on the corner, a prewar haunt of spies and journalists that was commandeered as an HQ by the Nazis in 1944 and the Soviets after the 1956 Uprising. Now restored to its prewar elegance, the *Astoria* is renowned for its magnificent coffee lounge.

KÁROLYI MIHÁLY UTCA

Károlyi Mihály utca is named after Count Mihály Károlyi, whose birthplace at no. 16 houses the **Petőfi Literary Museum** (*Petőfi Irodalmi Múzeum*; Tues–Sun: April–Oct 10am–6pm; Nov–March 10am–4pm; 80Ft), showcasing the personal effects of Petőfi and several other Hungarian writers, but with little text in English.

The street is subsequently called Kecskeméti utca, as it once led to a gate in the walls and thence to Kecskemét. Today, its junction with the Kiskörút is bridged by the **Korona Hotel**, a wild pink postmodernist creation of Finta's, with plain-clothes guards lurking outside its shopping arcade and a sex bar with dancers in the windows across the road.

The Serbian Orthodox Church

Map 6, C8.

Heading on along Kecskeméti utca, it's worth exploring the narrow streets off to the right. Down Szerb utca is the **Serbian Orthodox Church**, built by the Serbian artisans and merchants who settled here after the Turks were driven out. Secluded in a high-walled garden, it is only open for High Mass on Sunday (10.30–11.45am), when the singing of the liturgy, the clouds of incense and flickering candles create an atmosphere that's quite unearthly. Some of the worshippers are descendants of the original settlers, while others are refugees from former Yugoslavia. A block or so south, part of the **medieval wall of Pest** can be seen on the corner of Bástya utca and Veres Pálné utca.

ALONG THE EMBANKMENT

Ferenciek tere metro (M3) or tram #2.

The **Belgrád rakpart** (Belgrade Embankment) bore the

brunt of the fighting in 1944–45, when the Nazis and the Red Army exchanged salvos across the Danube and laid waste to the smart hotels here. As in the Várhegy in Buda, postwar clearances exposed historic sites and provided an opportunity to integrate them into the environment. Sadly, however, the planners took a brutalist approach, so that although the **view** of Buda Palace and Gellért-hegy is magnificent, the Pest side is disfigured by two colossal hotel blocks. While such historic architecture as remains can be seen in a fifteen-minute stroll between the Erzsébet híd and the Lánchíd, **tram #2** enables you to see a longer stretch of the waterfront between Fővám tér and Kossuth tér and admire the view. The tunnel interrupting this stretch is the first to be flooded if the Danube rises sufficiently to overflow its embankments, as sometimes happens in the summer.

The bold white pylons and cables of the newly cleaned **Erzsébet híd** (Elizabeth Bridge) are as cherished a feature of the panorama as the stone Lánchíd or the wrought-iron Szabadság híd. Of all the Danube bridges blown up by the Germans as they retreated to Buda in January 1945, this was the only one not rebuilt in its original form. Its approach ramp starts beyond twin *fin-de-siècle* office buildings known as the **Klotild Palaces**, built at the same time as the old bridge.

Belváros Parish Church

Map 6, B5. Mon–Sat 9am–12.30pm & 6–7pm, Sun 10am–noon.

In the shadow of the approach ramp, the grimy facade of the **Belváros Parish Church** masks its origins as the oldest church in Pest. Founded in 1046 as the burial place of St Gellért (see p.41), it was rebuilt as a Gothic hall church in the fifteenth century, turned into a mosque by the Turks and then reconstructed as a church in the eighteenth century. This history is reflected in the church's interior, and by coming after Latin Mass on Sunday you can see the Gothic sedilia and Turkish *mihrab* (prayer niche) behind the high altar, which are otherwise out of bounds. The vaulted nave and side chapels are Baroque.

MÁRCIUS 15 TÉR AND PETŐFI TÉR

On the square beside the Belváros Parish church, a sunken enclosure exposes the remains of **Contra-Aquincum**, a Roman fort that was an outpost of the settlement at Óbuda at the end of the third century. More pertinently to Hungarian history, the name of the square, **Március 15 tér**, refers to March 15, 1848, when the anti-Habsburg Revolution began, while the adjacent **Petőfi tér** is named after Sándor Petőfi, whose *National Song,* the anthem of 1848, and romantic death in battle the following year made him a patriotic icon (see box overleaf). Erected in 1882, the square's **Petőfi statue** has long been a focus for demonstrations (against Fascism in 1942 and Communism in 1956 and the 1980s) as well as patriotic displays – especially on March 15, when the statue is bedecked with flags and flowers. Behind the statue, the Baroque **Greek Orthodox Church** is the largest in Hungary, reflecting the importance of the Greek community when it was built in the 1790s. Services, on Saturday at 6pm and Sunday at 10am, are usually in Hungarian, not Greek, but are still accompanied by singing in the Orthodox fashion. The building is otherwise open from spring to autumn (daily 10am–6pm).

Just north of Petőfi tér, the gigantic **Marriott Hotel** is situated between the embankment and the street running parallel, Apáczai Csere János utca. Inaugurated as the *Duna Intercontinental* in 1969, it was the first hotel in the Eastern Bloc managed in partnership with a Western firm and the model for others on the rakpart. Its architect József Finta has since built a dozen hotels and business centres in Pest. On the

Sándor Petőfi

Born on New Year's Eve, 1822, of a Slovak mother and a Southern Slav butcher-innkeeper father, **Sándor Petőfi** was to become obsessed by acting and by poetry, which he started to write at the age of fifteen. As a strolling player, soldier and labourer, he absorbed the language of working people and composed his lyrical poetry in the vernacular, to the outrage of critics. Moving to Budapest in 1844, he fell in with the young radical intellectuals who met at the *Pilvax Café* and embarked on his career as a revolutionary hero. He declaimed his *National Song* from the steps of the National Museum on the first day of the 1848 Revolution, and fought in the War of Independence with General Bem in Transylvania, where he disappeared during the battle of Segesvár in 1849. Though he was most likely trampled beyond recognition by the Cossacks' horses (as predicted in one of his poems), Petőfi was long rumoured to have survived as a prisoner. In 1990, a Hungarian entrepreneur sponsored an expedition to Siberia to uncover the putative grave, but it turned out to be that of a woman.

Danube side of the *Marriott*, the concrete esplanade is a sterile attempt at recreating the prewar *Duna-korzó*, the most informal of Budapest's promenades, where it was socially acceptable for strangers to approach celebrities and stroll beside them. Since the 1960s it has been a **gay cruising** area – not that you'd notice if you're not in the market. The outdoor cafés here charge premium rate for the wonderful view.

THE VIGADÓ

Vigadó tér is an elegant square full of stalls and buskers, named after the **Vigadó** (concert hall), whose name translates as "having a ball" or "making merry". Inaugurated in

1865, this splendidly Romantic pile by Frigyes Feszl has hosted performances by Liszt, Mahler, Wagner, von Karajan and other renowned artists. Badly damaged in World War II, it didn't reopen until 1980, such was the care taken to recreate its sumptuous facade and interior, down to the last bust and gilded motif. The acoustics in the Large Hall were also improved, though, like the grand staircase, this can only be seen by concert-goers. The foyer, however, is accessible from 1pm, when the box office opens. The modern building on the right occupies the site of the *Angol királynő* (English Queen) hotel, where the likes of the Shah of Persia and Emperor Dom Pedro of Brazil used to stay during the city's *belle époque*.

From Vigadó tér, the *Duna-korzó* along the embankment continues past the *Inter-Continental Hotel* to end in a swirl of traffic at Roosevelt tér, on the edge of the Kiskörút (József Attila utca) and the Lipótváros, described in Chapter 7.

DEÁK TÉR AND ERZSÉBET TÉR

Map 6, E3. Deák tér metro (M1/M2/M3).

Three metro lines, two segments of the Kiskörút and several important avenues meet at **Deák tér** and **Erzsébet tér** – two squares that merge into one another (making local addresses extremely confusing) to form a jumping-off point for the Belváros and Lipótváros. You'll recognize the area by two landmarks: the enormous mustard-coloured **Anker Palace** on the Kiskörút, and the **Lutheran Church** by the metro pavilion on the edge of the Belváros, which hosts some excellent concerts, including Bach's *St John Passion* over the fortnight before Easter. Next door, the **Lutheran Museum** (*Evangélikus Múzeum*; Tues–Sun 10am–6pm; 200Ft) displays a facsimile of Martin Luther's last will and testament, and a copy of the first book printed in Hungarian, a New Testament from 1541. Across the way is a Porsche showroom, occupying what used to be a propaganda bureau for the old German Democratic Republic – one of those jokes played by history that Marx was keen on.

Underground Railway Museum

Map 6, E3. Tues–Sun 10am–6pm. 90Ft or one BKV ticket.

Accessible via the upper sub-level of Deák tér metro, the **Underground Railway Museum** (*Földalattivasút Múzeum*) extols the history of Budapest's original metro. Its genesis was a treatise by Mór Balazs, proposing a steam-driven tram network starting with a route along Andrássy út, an underground line being suggested as a fallback in case the overground option was rejected. Completed in under two years, in time for the Millennial Exhibition, the metro was inaugurated by Emperor Franz Josef, who agreed to allow it to bear his name, which it kept until 1918. The exhibits include two elegant wooden carriages (one used up until 1973) and period fixtures and posters, which enhance the museum's nostalgic appeal. At intervals you can hear the rumbling of today's trains, passing under Deák tér.

The Tourinform office (see p.9) is conveniently located just off Deák tér, on Sütő utca.

The Lipótváros

The **Lipótváros** (Leopold Town), lying to the north of the Belváros, started to develop in the late eighteenth century, first as a financial centre and later as the seat of government and bureaucracy. Several institutions of national significance are found here, including Parliament, St Stephen's Basilica, the National Bank and the Television headquarters. Though part of the V district, its ambience is quite different from that of the Belváros, with sombre streets of Neoclassical buildings interrupted by squares flanked by monumental Art Nouveau or neo-Renaissance piles. Busy with office workers by day, it was dead in the evenings and at weekends until a few years ago when new restaurants like *Gandhi* and *Lou Lou* started to bring some life to the area after dark. Another new source of vitality is the Central European University, funded by the Hungarian-born billionaire financier George Soros.

Depending on where you're coming from, it makes sense to start either with Roosevelt tér, just inland of the Lánchíd, or St Stephen's Basilica, two minutes' walk from Erzsébet tér. Most of the streets between them lead towards the set-piece expanse of Szabadság tér, whence you can head on towards Parliament – though the Kossuth metro station or tram #2 from the Belgrád rakpart will provide quicker access.

ROOSEVELT TÉR

Map 4, A8. Kossuth tér (M2) or Arany János utca (M3) metro.

At the Pest end of the Lánchíd, **Roosevelt tér** is blitzed by traffic, making it difficult to stand back and get a good view of the **Gresham Palace** on the eastern side of the square. This splendid but decrepit example of Art Nouveau was commissioned by a British insurance company in 1904. High up on the facade is a relief of a man in a ruff representing Sir Thomas Gresham, the originator of Gresham's law that bad money drives out good. Through the tall wrought-iron gates patterned with peacocks is a T-shaped, glass-roofed arcade with three staircases leading to stained-glass windows of Hungarian heroes, designed by the Art Nouveau master Miksa Róth.

Statues of Count Széchenyi and Ferenc Deák stand at opposite ends of the square, the former not far from the **Hungarian Academy of Sciences** (*Magyar Tudományos Akadémia*; free) that was founded after Széchenyi pledged a year's income from his estates towards its establishment in 1825 – as depicted on a relief on the wall facing Akadémia utca. The Nobel Prize-winning scientist György Hevesy, discoverer of the element hafnium, was born at Akadémia utca 3, across the road.

While the Academy and the Lánchíd are tangible reminders of Széchenyi's enterprise, there is, unfortunately, nothing to remind us of Deák's achievement in forging an *Ausgleich* (Compromise) with the Habsburgs. This was symbolized by the crowning of Emperor Franz Josef as King of Hungary in 1867, when soil from every corner of the nation was piled into a Coronation Hill, on the site of the present square. Here the emperor flourished the sword of St Stephen and promised to defend Hungary against all its enemies – a pledge that proved almost as ephemeral as the hill itself. Eighty years later, the square was renamed

Roosevelt tér in honour of the late US president – a rare example of Cold War courtesy that was never revoked.

ST STEPHEN'S BASILICA

Map 4, C7. Arany János utca (M3) or Bajcsy-Zsilinszky út (M1) metro. Daily 10am–6pm; free.

Looming above the rooftops, the bronze dome of **St Stephen's Basilica** (*Szent István-bazilika*), just off Bajcsy-Zsilinszky út, betrays the existence of a colossal edifice whose ugly mass is otherwise obscured by neighbouring buildings. Eroded and blackened by acid rain and soot, its restoration is proceeding almost as slowly as its construction did, and is set to continue for years yet. Building began in 1851 under the supervision of József Hild, continued after his death under Miklós Ybl, and was finally completed by Joseph Krauser in 1905. At the inaugural ceremony Franz Josef was seen to glance anxiously at the dome, whose collapse during a storm in 1868 had naturally set progress back. At 96m, it is exactly the same height as the dome of the Parliament building – both allude to the putative date of the Magyars' arrival in Hungary (896 AD).

The Basilica's glory lies in its interior carvings, frescoes and chapels, the variegated marble, gilded stucco and bronze mouldings, and the splendid organ above the doorway. On weekdays it is often closed, with only a limited view to be had through an open portal, so it's best to visit at the weekend.

In the second chapel to the right is a painting of King Stephen offering the Crown of Hungary to the Virgin (see p.22), while a statue of him haloed as a saint (but with a sword at his side) forms the centrepiece of the altar. To the left at the back, a separate **chapel** (April–Sept Mon–Sat 9am–5pm, Sun 1–5pm; Oct–March Mon–Sat 10am–4pm, Sun 1–5pm) harbours Hungary's holiest relic, the **mummified hand of St Stephen** (called the *Szent Jobb*, or "holy right"), which is paraded through the streets on August 20, the anniversary of his death. Its custodian collects 100Ft coins from visitors to drop into a cabinet, thereby illuminating the relic, which resembles a fossilized branch draped with jewelled bracelets.

While the display of chalices and monstrances in the one-room **treasury** (same hours as chapel; 100Ft) is nothing like the treasures kept in the Basilica at Esztergom, you shouldn't miss the so-called **Panorama Tower** (daily: April & May 10am–5pm; June–Aug 10am–7pm; Sept & Oct 10am–6pm; 300Ft); save the 302 steps for the return and take the lift up. Besides offering a grand **view** over Pest, you can also see the framework of girders and ladders inside the cupola, which is 25m higher than the Basilica's inner, acoustic dome.

BAJCSY-ZSILINSZKY ÚT

While Stephen is revered as the founder and patron saint of Hungary, the pantheon of national heroes includes a niche for Endre Bajcsy-Zsilinszky (1866–1944), after whom the avenue that runs past the Basilica is named. Originally a right-winger, he ended up an outspoken critic of Fascism, was arrested in Parliament (a statue on Deák tér captures the moment) and shot as the Russians approached. **Bajcsy-Zsilinszky út** runs northwards to **Nyugati tér**, where the glassy Skála-Metró department store faces **Nyugati Station**, an elegant, iron-beamed terminal built in 1874–77 by the Eiffel Company of Paris, and housing probably the ritziest *McDonald's* in the world. The avenue is also the demarcation line between the V (Lipótváros) and VI (Terézváros) districts.

SZABADSÁG TÉR

Map 4, B6. Arany János utca metro (M3).

For over a century the Lipótváros was dominated by a gigantic barracks where scores of Hungarians were imprisoned or executed, until this symbol of Habsburg tyranny was demolished in 1897 and the site redeveloped as **Szabadság tér** (Liberty Square). Invested with significance from the outset, it became a kind of record of the vicissitudes of modern Hungarian history, where each regime added or removed monuments, according to their political complexion.

The Stock Exchange and National Bank

In the early years of this century, Hungary's burgeoning prosperity was expressed by two monumental temples to capitalism on opposite sides of the square. To the west stood the **Stock Exchange**, one of the grandest buildings in Budapest. Designed by Ignác Alpár, it has blended motifs from Greek and Assyrian architecture and is crowned with twin towers resembling Khmer temples. After the Communists closed down the Stock Exchange in 1948, it became the headquarters of Hungarian Television (*Magyar Televizio*, or *MTV*), when its interior was subdivided into a warren of studios, though its former grandeur is still evident from the massive entrance hall.

Alpár also designed the **National Bank** (Map 4, B6; *Nemzeti Bank*), which still functions as such and is notable for the reliefs on its exterior, representing such diverse aspects of wealth creation as Magyars ploughing and herding, ancient Egyptians harvesting wheat, and Vikings loading their longships with loot. The building, to which access is via Bank utca, contains a small **Museum of Banknotes** (Thurs 9am–2pm; free) featuring curiosities like the "Kossuth" banknotes that were issued in America during the politician's exile after the failed War of Independence, and notes denominated in billions of forints from the period of hyper-inflation in 1946. Today's capitalists have commissioned the **International Bank Centre**, a huge postmodernist structure by Finta that stands across the road.

Szabadság tér's monuments

Turning from money to politics, notice the **statue of General Harry Bandholtz** of the US Army, who intervened with a dogwhip to stop Romanian troops from looting the Hungarian National Museum in 1919. The statue was erected in the 1930s, when Hungary was still smarting from the 1920 Treaty of Trianon that gave away two-thirds of its territory and a third of its Magyar population to the "Successor States" of Romania, Czechoslovakia and Yugoslavia. This deeply felt injustice inspired several other monuments on Szabadság ter, namely the Monument to Hungarian Grief – featuring a flag at half-mast and a quotation from Lord Rothermere (the proprietor of the *Daily Mail*, whose campaign against Trianon was so appreciated that he was offered the Hungarian crown) – and four statues called North, South, East and West, whose inauguration in 1921 was attended by 50,000 people.

At the end of World War II all of these monuments were removed by the Communists, who converted the base of the Monument to Hungarian Grief into the **Soviet Army Memorial**, commemorating the liberation of Budapest from the Nazis, with reliefs of Red Army troops and tanks advancing on Ferenciek tere and Parliament. When the Socialists got the boot in 1990, there were calls to remove the Soviet memorial and restore all the old nationalist ones (the Communists had already reinstated Bandholtz prior to President Bush's visit in 1989), but wiser counsels prevailed.

To compound the irony, the Soviet memorial stands near the former headquarters of the Fascist Arrow Cross, and directly in front of the **US Embassy**, which for fifteen years gave shelter to Cardinal Mindszenty, the Primate of Hungary's Catholic Church, in the aftermath of the 1956

Uprising. Later, however, the US became embarrassed by his presence, as did the Vatican, who finally persuaded him to leave for Austria in 1971 (see box on p.143).

THE FORMER POST OFFICE SAVINGS BANK

Map 4, B6.

Behind the US Embassy, the **former Post Office Savings Bank** on Hold utca is a classic example of Hungarian Art Nouveau – its facade patterned like a quilt, with swarms of bees (symbolizing savings) ascending to the polychromatic roof, which is the wildest part of the building. Its architect, Ödön Lechner, once asked why birds shouldn't enjoy his buildings too, and amazing roofs are also a feature of his other masterpieces in Budapest, the Applied Arts Museum and Geological Institute. The bank's interior is open to the public on only one day a year – European Heritage Day, in September (ask Tourinform for details; see p.9). Across the street is a wrought-iron **market hall**, one of five opened on a single day in 1896, which continue to serve the centre of Budapest to this day.

THE BATTHYÁNY AND NAGY MONUMENTS

At the junction of Hold and Báthory utca, a lantern on a plinth flickers with an **Eternal Flame** commemorating Count Lajos Batthyány, the Prime Minister of the short-lived republic declared after the 1848 War of Independence, whom the Habsburgs executed on this spot on October 6, 1849. As a staunch patriot – but not a revolutionary – Batthyány is a hero for conservative nationalists, and his monument the destination of annual marches on October 6 and public holidays.

The refrains and paradoxes of Hungarian history are echoed on Vértanuk tér (Martyrs' Square), between

Szabadság tér and Kossuth tér, where a **statue of Imre Nagy** – the reform Communist who became Prime Minister during the 1956 Uprising and was shot in secret two years afterwards – stands on a footbridge, gazing towards Parliament. With his raincoat, trilby and umbrella hooked over his arm, Nagy cuts an all-too-human, flawed figure – and is scorned by those who pay homage to Batthyány.

KOSSUTH TÉR

Map 4, A4. Kossuth tér metro (M2).

The apotheosis of the government district and Hungary's romantic self-image comes at **Kossuth tér**, with its colossal Parliament building and memorials to national heroes and epic moments in Hungarian history. The square is named after Lajos Kossuth, the leader of the 1848 Revolution against the Habsburgs (see box opposite), who was originally represented by a sculptural tableau showing him and his ministers downcast by their defeat in 1849. However, the Communists replaced it with a more "heroic" one of Kossuth rousing the nation to arms, by Kisfaludy-Strobl. The other main statue is of Prince Ferenc Rákóczi II, an earlier hero of the struggle for Hungarian independence, whose plinth is inscribed "The wounds of the noble Hungarian nation burst open!" This is a reference to the anti-Habsburg war of 1703–11, but also perfectly describes the evening of October 23, 1956, when crowds filled the square, chanting anti-Stalinist slogans at Parliament – the prelude to the Uprising that night. In the middle of the square is a memorial to the Uprising and all who died on Kossuth tér on October 25, when the peaceful demonstration was fired upon by snipers from the rooftop of the Ministry of Agriculture, even as the crews of Soviet tanks were fraternizing with the crowd.

Lajos Kossuth

Lajos Kossuth was the incarnation of post-Napoleonic bourgeois nationalism. Born into landless gentry in 1802, he began his career as a lawyer, representing absentee magnates in Parliament. His Parliamentary reports, which advocated greater liberalism than the Habsburgs would tolerate, became widely influential during the Reform era, and he was jailed for sedition. While in prison, Kossuth taught himself English by reading Shakespeare. Released in 1840, he became editor of the radical *Pesti Hírlap*, was elected to Parliament and took the helm during the 1848 Revolution.

After Serbs, Croats and Romanians rebelled against Magyar rule and the Habsburgs invaded Hungary, the Debrecen Parliament proclaimed a republic with Kossuth as de facto dictator. However, after the Hungarians surrendered in August 1849, Kossuth escaped to Turkey, later touring Britain and America, espousing liberty. So eloquent were his denunciations of Habsburg tyranny that London brewery workers attacked General Haynau, the "Butcher of Vienna", when he visited the city. Karl Marx loathed Kossuth as a bourgeois radical, and tried to undermine his reputation with articles published in the New York *Herald Tribune* and the London *Times*. As a friend of the Italian patriot Mazzini, Kossuth spent his last years in Turin, where he died in 1894. His remains now lie in the Kerepesi Cemetery (p.120).

PARLIAMENT

Map 4, A5. Kossuth tér metro (M2). Guided tours in English: July–Sept Mon–Fri 10am & 2pm from Gate XII, Sat & Sun 10am from Gate VI; Oct–June Wed–Fri 10am from Gate XII, Sat & Sun 10am from Gate VI. Tickets from Gate X. 750Ft.

The Hungarian **Parliament** building *(Országház)* makes the Houses of Parliament in London look humble, its architect Imre Steindl having larded Pugin's Gothic Revival style with Renaissance and Baroque flourishes. Sprawling for 268m along the embankment, its symmetrical wings bristle with finials and 88 statues of Hungarian rulers, surmounted by a dome 96m high (alluding to the date of the Magyar conquest, see p.256). Though most people are impressed by the building, the writer Gyula Illyés once famously dismissed it as "no more than a Turkish bath crossed with a Gothic chapel".

For centuries Hungarian assemblies convened wherever they could, and it wasn't until 1843 that the Diet of Pozsony resolved to build a permanent "House of the Motherland" in Pest-Buda (as it was then called). By the time work began in 1885, the concept of Parliament had changed insofar as the middle classes were now represented as well, though over ninety percent of the population still lacked the right to vote. Though gains were made in 1918, they were soon curtailed under the Horthy regime, just as the attainment of universal adult suffrage in 1945 was rendered meaningless after 1948 by a Communist dictatorship. Happily, the wheel turned full circle eventually, as creeping liberalization in the late 1980s paved the way for the introduction of a multi-party democracy in 1990 – a watershed symbolized by the removal of the red star from Parliament's dome and the replacement of Communist emblems by the traditional coat of arms featuring the double cross of King Stephen.

The interior

How much you see on the **tours** of the interior depends on Parliament's activities, but you can be sure of seeing the main staircase, the Dome Hall and the Lords Chamber, if nothing else. Statues, carvings, gilding and mosaics are ten a penny, lit by lamps worthy of the Winter Palace – but there are also cosy touches such as the individually numbered brass ashtrays where peers left their cigars smouldering in the lounge while they popped back into the chamber to hear someone speak; a good speaker was said to be "worth a Havana". If you're lucky, you might also see the Chamber of Deputies (the only chamber used for debates today) and even the reception rooms of the President of the Republic. Alas, the public are seldom shown the Munkácsy Room with its famous painting *The Conquest*, which originally offended many deputies who thought that Munkácsy's depiction of Árpád and his chiefs encountering the inhabitants of the Carpathian basin was lacking in militaristic glory and humble submission.

MUSEUM OF ETHNOGRAPHY

Map 4, A4. Kossuth tér metro (M2). Tues–Sun 10am–6pm; 200Ft, free on Tues. Photo permit 200Ft, video 1000Ft; pre-arranged guided tours 3000Ft (©312-4878).

Across the road from Kossuth's statue stands a neo-Renaissance building housing the **Museum of Ethnography** (*Néprajzi Múzeum*), one of the finest museums in Budapest, though it's little visited by tourists. Originally built as the Palace of the Supreme Court, petitioners would have been overawed by its lofty, gilded main hall, whose ceiling bears a fresco of the goddess Justitia surrounded by allegories of Justice, Peace, Revenge and Sin.

The museum's permanent exhibition on **Hungarian folk culture** occupies thirteen rooms on the second floor (off the left-hand staircase) and is fully captioned in English; there's also an excellent catalogue. Habsburg-ruled Hungary comprised a dozen ethnic groups, represented by exhibits arranged under headings such as "Institutions" and "Peasant Work"; the only groups not represented are the Jews and the gypsies. Though the beautiful costumes and objects on display are no longer part of everyday life in Hungary, you can still see them in parts of Romania, such as Maramureş and the Kalotaszeg, which belonged to Hungary before 1920.

Temporary exhibitions (on the first and third floors) cover anything from Bedouin life to Hindu rituals, while over Easter and Christmas there are **concerts** of Hungarian folk music and dancing, and **craft fairs**.

The Terézváros

The **Terézváros** (Theresa Town), or VI district, is home to the State Opera House, the Academy of Music and the Hungarian equivalent of Broadway, making it one of the most vibrant parts of the city. Trams and buses circle the Nagykörút (Great Boulevard) 24-hourly, making it especially popular at night. Laid out in the late nineteenth century, this district was heavily influenced by Haussmann's redevelopment of Paris. At that time it was one of the smartest districts in the city, but today much of the area is run-down and shabby.

Andrássy út, the main thoroughfare, is Budapest's longest, grandest avenue, marking the border between the Lipótváros and Terézváros. It runs in a perfect straight line for two and a half kilometres up to Hősök tere on the edge of the Városliget (City Park) – both of which are covered in the next chapter. Inaugurated in 1884 as the Sugár (Radial) út, it was soon renamed Andrássy út after the statesman Count Gyula Andrássy – the name that stayed in popular use throughout the years when this was officially Stalin Avenue (1949–56) or the Avenue of the People's Republic (1957–89), until it was formally restored in 1990. With its greystone edifices laden with dryads, its Opera House and coffee houses, the avenue retains something of the style that made it so fashionable in the 1890s, when "Bertie" the Prince of Wales drove its length in a landau, offering flowers to women as he passed.

The initial stretch up to the Oktogon is within walking distance of Erzsébet tér, but if you're going any further it's best to travel from sight to sight by the metro beneath the avenue, or bus #4.

THE POST OFFICE MUSEUM

Map 4, C7. Tues–Sun 10am–6pm; 150Ft.

At Andrássy út 3 the **Post Office Museum** (*Posta Múzeum*) occupies a fabulous old apartment complete with parquet floors, marble fireplaces, Venetian mirrors and frescoes by Károly Lotz. Exhibits include a compressed-air mail tube, vintage delivery vehicles, and a display on the inventor Tivadar Puskás, a colleague of Thomas Edison who set up the world's first switchboard and telephonic news service in Budapest in the early 1900s.

THE STATE OPERA HOUSE

Map 4, D6. Tours daily at 3 & 4pm; 100Ft.

The **State Opera** (*Állami Operaház*) was founded by Ferenc Erkel, the composer of Hungary's national anthem, and occupies a magnificent neo-Renaissance pile built in 1875–84 by Miklós Ybl. It can boast of being directed by Mahler (who complained about the anti-Semitism in the city), hosting performances conducted by Otto Klemperer and Antal Doráti, and sheltering hundreds of local residents in its huge cellars during the siege of Budapest. Tours of the grand interior leave from the side entrances, performances permitting. The productions can often be dated and patchy, but it's still a good night out at the opera and at that price it's worth it for the decor alone.

"BROADWAY"

Map 4, D6.

One block north of the Opera, Andrássy út is crossed by **Nagymező utca** – nicknamed "**Broadway**" because of the clubs and theatres on either side of the street. During the interwar years the most famous club was the *Arizona,* run by Sándor Rozsnyai and his wife Miss Arizona, which inspired Pal Sándor's film of the same name, starring Hanna Schygulla and Marcello Mastroianni. The Rozsnyais were murdered by the Arrow Cross in 1944, and the building in which the club was sited, at Nagymező utca 20, is now the home of the **Mai Manó Photography Museum**, on the first floor (Mon–Fri 2–6pm), displaying temporary exhibitions.

THE OKTOGON AND BEYOND

Map 4, E5.

Two squares with pavement cafés provide a leafy interlude before Andrássy út meets the Nagykörút at the **Oktogon**, an eight-sided square flanked by Eclectic buildings. With 24-hour fast-food chains ensconced in three of them, and trams and taxis running along the Nagykörút through to the small hours, the Oktogon never sleeps. During the Horthy period it rejoiced in the name of Mussolini tér, while under the Communists it was called November 7 tér after the date of the Bolshevik revolution.

A minute's walk past the Oktogon on the left-hand side, Andrássy út 60 was once the most terrifying address in Budapest – the **headquarters of the secret police**. Jews and other victims of the Arrow Cross were tortured here during World War II, after which the ÁVO (see box overleaf) commandeered the building and used it for the same purposes. Prisoners were brought in by the side entrance on

The ÁVO

The **Communist secret police** began as the party's private security section during the Horthy era, when its chief, **Gábor Péter**, betrayed Trotskyites to the police to take the heat off their Stalinist comrades. After World War II it became the *Államvédelmi Osztály* or **ÁVO** (State Security Department), its growing power implicit in a change of name in 1948 – to the State Security Authority or **ÁVH** (though the old acronym stuck). Ex-Nazi torturers were easily persuaded to apply their skills on its behalf, and its network of spies permeated society. So hated was the ÁVO that any members caught during the Uprising were summarily killed, and their mouths stuffed with banknotes (secret policemen earned more than anyone else).

Csengery utca. When it was captured by insurgents in 1956, no trace was found of the giant meat-grinder rumoured to have been used to dispose of corpses.

A little further on the opposite side, the Old Music Academy at no. 67 harbours the **Liszt Memorial Museum** (*Liszt Ferenc Emlékmúzeum*; Mon–Fri 10am–6pm, Sat 9am–5pm; 100Ft), where the composer – who was the first president of the Academy – lived from 1881 until his death in 1886. His glass piano and travelling keyboard are the highlights of an extensive collection of memorabilia and scores. Concerts are performed here by young pianists every Saturday at 11am (free with admission to museum).

KODÁLY KÖRÖND TO HŐSÖK TERE

Kodály körönd, named after the composer, is one of Budapest's most elegant squares, flanked by four neo-Renaissance mansions (one with gilt sgraffiti). At no. 1, the flat where Kodály lived until his death in 1967, is a **Kodály**

Memorial Museum (Wed 10am–4pm, Thurs–Sat 10am–6pm, Sun 10am–2pm; 80Ft), preserving his library, salon, dining room and folk art collection. During World War II the körönd was named Hitler tér, prompting the émigré Bartók to vow that he would not be buried in Hungary so long as anywhere in the country was named after Hitler or Mussolini.

Just beyond the körönd are two fine collections of Asian art. The **György Ráth Museum**, in an Art Nouveau villa at Városligeti fasor 12 (Tues–Sun April–Oct 10am–6pm; Nov-March 10am–5pm; 100Ft, free Tues), is an art historian's bequest of Chinese snuff bottles and painted scrolls, Samurai armour and lacquer combs, while the nearby **Museum of Eastern Asiatic Art** at Andrássy út 103 (*Kelet-ázsiai Múzeum*; same hours & prices) exhibits Tibetan scrolls and Indian sculptures trawled by businessman Ferenc Hopp on five voyages to the Far East.

The final stretch of Andrássy út up to Hősök tere is lined by large villas, set back from the avenue.

Hősök tere and the Városliget

Andrássy út culminates in Budapest's two grandest public spaces, **Hősök tere** (Heroes' Square) and the **Városliget** (City Park). Both were created for the nationwide celebrations of the millennium of the Magyar conquest of Hungary, but as neither was ready on time the anniversary was rescheduled for the following year; historians revised the date of the conquest accordingly and have stuck to 896 ever since. The millennial celebrations were unashamedly nationalistic, but full of contradictions, as the Dual Monarchy tried to flatter Hungarians without alienating other ethnic groups that resented Magyar chauvinism, so each was represented at the exhibition.

Today, the chief attractions are the **Museum of Fine Arts** and the romantic **Vajdahunyad Castle**, followed by a wallow in the **Széchenyi Baths**. Budapest's **zoo**, **circus** and amusement park are also located in the vicinity, together with two of the city's classiest restaurants, and a handful of other museums.

HŐSÖK TERE

Map 4, H2. Hősök tere metro (M1) or bus #4.

The enormous ceremonial plaza of **Hősök tere** is flanked by two galleries resembling Greek temples, while at its centre is the **Millenary Monument** – Budapest's answer to Nelson's Column in London. It consists of a 36-metre-high column topped by the figure of Archangel Gabriel who, according to legend, appeared to Stephen in a dream and offered him the crown of Hungary. Around the base are figures of Prince Árpád and his chieftains, who led the seven Magyar tribes into the Carpathian Basin. They look like a wild bunch; Huba even has stag's antlers strapped to his horse's head. As a backdrop to this, a semicircular colonnade displays statues of Hungary's most illustrious leaders, from King Stephen to Kossuth.

During the brief Republic of Councils in 1919, when the country was governed by revolutionary Soviets, the square was decked out in red banners and the column enclosed in a red obelisk bearing a relief of Marx. More recently, it was the setting for the ceremonial reburial of Imre Nagy and other murdered leaders of the Uprising (plus an empty coffin representing the "unknown insurgent") on June 16, 1989 – an event which symbolized the dawning of a new era in Hungary. Today it's more likely to be filled with coach parties of tourists, and rollerbladers and skateboarders, for whom the smooth surface is ideal. The square was originally laid out as a garden, but paved over for the Eucharistic Congress of 1932.

Museum of Fine Arts

Map 4, H1. Tues–Sun 10am–5.30pm; 500Ft, guide tape 500Ft.

To the left of the square stands the **Museum of Fine Arts** (*Szépművészeti Múzeum*), the international equivalent of the

Hungarian National Gallery (see p.31), housed in an imposing Neoclassical building completed in 1906. After years of financial constraints, most of the collections have recently been reorganized, freeing additional rooms for further displays from its holdings. However, the floor plan printed on the tickets is out of date. Almost all the exhibits are captioned in English.

In addition to its exhibition halls, the modernized lower ground floor contains a fine **shop** for art books, posters and contemporary ceramics, a decent **café**, and the most stylish toilets in Budapest.

Lower ground floor: the Egyptian and twentieth-century art collections

To the right of the stairs is a small but choice **Egyptian Collection**, chiefly from the Late Period and Greco-Roman eras of Egyptian civilization. The highlights of the first room are four huge painted coffins and a child-sized one from Gamhud in Middle Egypt; *shabiti* figures, intended to perform menial tasks in the afterlife; and a mummified crocodile, cat and falcon from the Late Period, when animal cults reached their apogee. In the second room, look out for the sculpted heads of a nameless pharaoh and a bewigged youth from the New Kingdom, the painted coffin of a priestess of Amun bearing an uncanny resemblance to Julia Roberts, and a tautly poised bronze of the cat goddess Bastet.

On the other side of the foyer, the **Twentieth-Century Art Collection** features relatively few artists that you're likely to have heard of, but is nonetheless stimulating. In the Majakovskij Hall, named after the Soviet poet, a scumbled Expressionist portrait by **Oskar Kokoschka** faces Peter Steer's *Seaside Resort*, its languid figures posed against the white cliffs of Dover. There's a wonderfully simple Fauvist landscape by János Máttis, and two realist portraits in violet and green impasto by Gino Severini. **Marc Chagall**'s *Village in Blue* is a typically lyrical composition of floating figures, while Roberto Guttuso's *Seizure of the Land in Sicily* speaks of the urgency of the land reform cause in terms of Cubism and Social Realism. In the other room are abstracts such as István Beóthy's *Nuclear Form Nr.2* – a Möbius Strip with an extra twist, carved from teak – and a two-tone canvas based on the pyramids of Giza by the Op Artist **Victor Vasarely**.

In the corridor beyond the shop are Miróesque collages in sand, rope and chipboard by **Zoltán Kemény**, and the dangling wooden figures of Andras Böröcz's sculpture *The Hanged*. The **Ionic Pyramid** room is notable for its abstract cut-glass sculptures by German artists such as Adolf Luther and Uli Pohl, with an undertone of post-Communist angst provided by the slumped, hollowed-out figure in Magdalena Abakanowicz's *Cage No. 2*, and the Dutch artist Armando's scarlet, skull-like *Head*. **Temporary exhibitions** are held in the Doric Pyramid room.

Ground floor: antiquities and nineteenth-century art

To the right of the lobby are several rooms devoted to **ancient Mediterranean cultures** from Etruria to Athens, mainly represented by jugs and vases. Highlights include a pair of bronze greaves (shin-guards) decorated with rams' heads; terracotta tiles portraying bestial deities; a man's torso and head from the pediment of a Campanian temple; life-like busts of Roman worthies; and an Attic marble sarcophagus carved with hunting scenes.

Across the hall, the **Nineteenth-Century Art Collection** opens with a fanfare of Barbizons and Impressionists. However, the drama of **Courbet**'s wild landscapes and lifesized *Wrestlers* and the delight of **Monet**'s

Plum Trees in Blossom and **Corot**'s *Remembrance of Coubrou* aren't sustained by weaker pictures like Cézanne's *The Cupboard*, Toulouse-Lautrec's *Three Ladies in the Refectory* or Manet's *Lady with a Fan*, though *Eternal Springtime* and *The Kiss* by **Rodin** both deserve an honourable mention.

The long hall at the end displays **historical** paintings like the massive *Crowning of Emperor Francis as King of Hungary* by Johann Peter Krafft, and Karl Theodor von Piloty's *Grand Guignol Nero on the Ruins of Rome*. Sex pervades the **Symbolist and Decadent** works in the final room, notably Franz von Stuck's *The Kiss of the Sphinx*, John Quincey Adams's vampish *Lilli* and Hans Makart's *Nessus Raptures Deianera*.

Leaving this section you'll emerge into the second of two atria that are hardly used at present, though in one, two Tiepolos are hung so high up that they're almost invisible. To the rear, on the right, is the **Prints and Drawings Room** which, once it reopens, will exhibit rotating displays from the museum's extensive holdings, including works by Raphael, Leonardo, Rembrandt, Rubens, Dürer, Picasso and Chagall.

First floor: old masters

The museum's forte is its hoard of **Old Masters**, based on the collection of Count Miklós Esterházy, which he sold to the state in 1871. As a notice explains, this section was recently re-hung in what is allegedly the once-again fashionable style of stacking one painting above another, which, though it may facilitate comparisons, doesn't allow visitors to appreciate the pictures well above eye-level. The room numbering is also baffling, but the quality of the art transcends all these failings.

The **Spanish Collection** of seventy works is perhaps the best in the world outside Spain. Among the vivid altarpieces by unknown Catalonians in Room XIV, notice *The*

Bishop-Saint Enthroned, whose obvious bewilderment belies his magnificent attire. Room XV is dominated by seven **El Grecos**, most notably *Christ Stripped of His Garments*, *The Agony in the Garden*, *The Apostle St Andrew* and *The Penitent Magdalene*; though Eugenio Cajes's *Adoration of the Magi* is equally awe-inspiring. In Room XVI hang several **Murillos**, of which *Ecce Homo* and *The Holy Family with the Infant St John and Christ* are superlative. You'll also find the moving *Martyrdom of St Andrew* by **Ribera**, five **Goyas**, ranging from war scenes (*2nd of May*) to portraits of the rich (*Señora Ceán Bermudez*) and humble (*The Knife-Grinder*), plus **Velázquez**'s *Peasant's Repast*.

The **Italian Collection** is also impressive, especially rooms XVIII and XXIII. The former contains **Raphael**'s small but exquisite Esterházy *Madonna* – a Virgin and Child with the infant St John – and a picture of a youth with a Mona Lisa-esque mystique. The latter's psychological depth is matched by portraits by **Giorgione** (whose own self-portrait exhudes sensitivity) and **Titian** (of a Venetian Doge, stern and watchful in his cloth-of-gold). Tintoretto's self-portrait is less focused, while Bellini's pig-eyed *Queen of Cyprus* verges on caricature. **Tintoretto** steals the show next door with *Hercules Expelling the Faun from Omphade's Bed* and a *Supper at Emaus*. Unfortunately, **Veronese**'s *Allegory of Venice* is too high up to appreciate properly, though his *Crucifixion* is easier to admire. In Room XIII you'll find **Boccacio**'s *Adoration of the Infant Christ*, and in Room XX, the cheerfully gory *Judith with the Head of Holoferenes* and the cruel *Mocking of Job*.

Though less glamorous, the **German Collection** amply rewards a visit. Every emotion from awe to jealousy appears on the faces in **Holbein**'s *Dormition of the Virgin* in Room XVIII, while Room XIX has a dazzling array of works by **Altdorfer** and by **Cranach** the Elder. The suppressed violence of the latter's Crucifixions seem like presentiments of the Thirty Years War a century ahead, while in his *Salome with the Head of St John the Baptist* Salome displays a platter with St John's head on it with the nonchalance of a hostess bringing out the roast. Finally, **Kauffmann**'s depiction of *The Wife of Count Esterházy as Venus* shows a strumpet with her jewellery box, while **Dürer**'s *Young Man* has an enigmatic smile.

Acknowledging that art transcends nationality, Room XXI exhibits works by well-travelled artists such as **Canaletto**, who died in Warsaw after painting *The Palace of Kaunitz in Vienna*; Kauffmann (see above), whose career took her all over Europe; and **Tiepolo**, whose *St James the Great Conquering the Moors* once served as an icon for the Habsburgs.

Travel scenes and still lifes in Room XXII mark the start of the **Dutch Collection**, which leapfrogs over Room A into the rooms beyond. In Room B, the serenity of **Van Dyck**'s *St John the Evangelist* contrasts with the melodrama of **Rubens**' *Mucius Scaevola before Porsenna*, and Jordeans' *The Satyr and the Peasant*, while Room C is largely given over to **Brueghels**, from Pieter the Elder's *Sermon of St John the Baptist* to Pieter the Younger's *Blind Hurdy Gurdy Player* and Jan's *The Garden of Eden with the Fall of Man*. Also look out for *The Way to Calvary*, showing Christ being beaten through a fairy-tale medieval landscape, by the mysteriously named "Master of the Ausburg *Ecce Homo*".

The single room devoted to **English art** (A) can only muster a dullish portrait apiece by Hogarth, Reynolds and Gainsborough, and a melodramatic theatre scene by Zoffany.

Palace of Arts

Map 4, I2. Tues–Sun 10am–6pm; 200Ft, free on Tues.

Across the square from the museum is the **Palace of Arts** (*Műcsarnok*), a Grecian pile with gilded columns and a mosaic of St Stephen as patron of the arts. Its magnificent facade and foyer are in contrast to the four austere rooms used for **temporary exhibitions** (two or three at a time) or thematic avant-garde shows, which are often first-rate. Since the palace was inaugurated in 1896, its steps have been a stage for the state funeral of the painter Munkácsy, the reburial of Nagy, and other public ceremonies.

THE VÁROSLIGET

Map 4, I1. Hősök tere or Széchenyi Fürdő (Metro M1).

The **Városliget** starts just behind Hősök tere, where the fairy-tale towers of **Vajdahunyad Castle** rear above an island girdled by an artificial lake that's used for boating in the summer and, during winter, is transformed into the most splendid outdoor ice-rink in Europe. Like the park, the castle was created for the Millenary Anniversary celebrations of 1896, and proved so popular that the temporary structures were replaced by permanent ones. The castle is a catalogue in stone of architectural styles from the kingdom of Hungary, incorporating parts of two Transylvanian castles (one of the originals, the Hunyadi Castle in Romania, gives its name to the building), and a replica of the chapel at Ják in western Hungary. Though chiefly notable for its magnificent Romanesque portal, the chapel's interior is worth a look too (April–Oct Mon–Fri 9am–noon, Sun & public holidays 9am–5pm; 50Ft).

In the main wing of the castle, the **Agriculture Museum** (*Mezőgazdasági Múzeum*; Tues–Sat 10am–5pm, Sun 10am–6pm; 150Ft) traces the history of hunting and farming in Hungary. Its most interesting sections relate to the early Magyars and such typically Hungarian breeds of livestock as longhorned grey cattle (favoured for their draught power rather than their milk) and woolly pigs. Upstairs, the hunting section is notable for a prehistoric dug-out boat carved from a single piece of oak, which was found at Lake Balaton, and antique crossbows and rifles exquisitely inlaid with leaping hares and other prey.

Even if you decide to skip the museum, don't miss the hooded **statue of Anonymous** outside. This nameless chronicler to King Béla is the prime source of information about early medieval Hungary, though the existence of several monarchs of that name during the twelfth and thirteenth centuries makes it hard to date him (or his chronicles) with any exactitude.

The Petőfi Csarnok and Transport Museum

Leaving Vadjahunyad island by the causeway at the rear, you'll be on course for the **Petőfi Csarnok**, a "Metropolitan Youth Centre" about ten minutes away that regularly hosts concerts (outdoors in summer), films and parties, and a good **flea market** at weekends (©343-4327 for information in English). At the back of the building is a stairway leading to the **Aviation and Space Flight Exhibition** (*Repüléstörténeti és Űrhajózási kiállítás*; April–Nov Tues–Fri 10am–5pm, Sat & Sun 10am–6pm; 150Ft), which, among other items, contains the space capsule used by Hungary's first astronaut, Bertalan Farkas, and his Soviet colleague on the Soyuz-35 mission of 1980; and an L-2 monoplane sporting an Italian Fascist symbol, which broke world speed records in the Budapest–Rome races of 1927 and 1930. Alas, there seems to be nothing about Count László Almásy, Hungary's foremost aviator of that time, who is now better known abroad as the hero of book and film *The English Patient*. Information is in Hungarian only.

Not far away you'll come to the **Transport Museum** (*Közlekedési Múzeum*; Tues–Sun 10am–6pm; 150Ft) on the edge of the park, of which the aviation exhibition above is an outgrowth. Try to time your visit for the running of the model train set on the floor above the foyer – switched on for fifteen minutes every hour, on the hour. Captions in English explain that the Hungarian transport network of the 1890s was among the most sophisticated in Europe; starting from a low technological base, railways, canals, trams and a metro had all been created within fifty years. You can also see vintage locomotives and scale models of steamboats, and a wonderful collection of Hungarian Railways posters from 1900 to 1980. Collectors can buy Hungarian model trains in the museum shop. Outside the building are remnants of two of the Danube bridges that were wrecked in 1945: the cast-iron Erzsébet híd (replaced by a new bridge) and a few links of the original chains from the Lánchíd, which is now supported by cables.

The Széchenyi Baths

Outdoor pool: daily: summer 6am–7pm; winter 6am–4pm; 350Ft.
Turkish baths: Mon–Sat 6am–7pm, Sun 6am–1pm; 350Ft.

From the transport museum, head in the opposite direction from the castle, beyond the park's central promenade, Kós Károly sétány, where you'll see a grandiose pile that resembles a palace but is in fact the **Széchenyi Baths** (*Széchenyi Gyógyfürdő*). At the front is a statue of the geologist Zsigmondy Vilmos, who discovered the thermal spring that feeds its outdoor pool and Turkish baths. Here you can enjoy the surreal spectacle of people playing chess while immersed up to their chests in steaming water – bring your own set if you wish to participate.

Vidám Park, the circus and zoo

Map 4, H1. Széchenyi Fürdő metro (M1) or tram #72 from Arany János metro. May–Sept daily 9am–8pm; Oct–April Mon–Fri 10am–6.45pm, Sat & Sun 10am–7.15pm; 100Ft, under-14s free.

About 200m beyond the baths, on the far side of Állatkerti körút, three establishments vie for custom from families in search of entertainment. Off to the the right lies **Vidám Park**, an old-fashioned, rather shabby amusement park that has all the usual rides, though only a few operate over winter. Known as the "English Park" before the war, it was the setting for Ferenc Molnár's play *Liliom*, on which the musical *Carousel* was based. Molnár (1878–1952), one of the great Hungarian dramatists, depicted the fairground as a popular destination for country people coming to the city – which it still is. The gilded merry-go-round to the left of the entrance and the wooden switchback at the back of the fairground are both original, predating World War II. For children under the age of two there's a separate Kis Vidám Park next door (same hours; 70Ft).

The **Municipal Circus** (*Fővárosi Nagycirkusz*) is directly across the road from the baths, between the funfair and the zoo. Although the building itself dates from 1971, a permanent circus was founded here seventy years earlier, and the Hetz Theatre played to spectators around what is now Deák tér as long ago as 1783. Animal acts still play a major role in performances (mid-April to Aug Wed, Fri & Sun 3pm & 7pm, Thurs 3pm, Sat 10am, 3pm & 7pm; ©342-8300 for bookings; 350–750Ft).

To the left of the circus, Budapest's **Zoo** (*Állatkert*; daily: May–Aug 9am–7pm; April & Sept 9am–6pm; Oct & March 9am–5pm; Nov–Feb 9am–4pm; 400Ft, family ticket 1200Ft) has an Art Nouveau gateway crawling with figures of elephants, fakirs and polar bears, that sets the tone for the whimsical pavilions by Károly Kós, which seemed the last word in zoological architecture when they were opened in 1896, but are plainly awful by today's standards. The Elephant House (resembling a Central Asian mosque), Aquarium and Palmhouse are all closed for renovation, but the new garden of bonsai trees (donated by the Japanese ambassador) and children's playground (sponsored by the Lauders) hopefully augur well for improvements for the animals, given enough money and time.

The Erzsébetváros

The mainly residential **Erzsébetváros** is composed of nineteenth-century buildings whose bullet-scarred facades, adorned with fancy wrought-ironwork, conceal a warren of dwellings and leafy courtyards. It is also traditionally the **Jewish quarter** of the city, which was transformed into a ghetto during the Nazi occupation and almost wiped out in 1944–45, but has miraculously retained its cultural identity. Its current resurgence owes much to increased contacts with international Jewry, and a revival of interest in their religion and roots among the 80,000-strong Jewish community of Budapest, which had previously tended towards assimilation, reluctant to proclaim itself in a country where anti-Semitic prejudices linger. There is no better part of Pest to wander around, soaking up the atmosphere.

KIRÁLY UTCA

The official boundary between the Terézváros and Erzsébetváros runs down the middle of **Király utca**, which used to be a main thoroughfare before Andrássy út was built. In the 1870s the street contained 14 of the 58 licensed brothels in Budapest, and as late as 1934 Patrick Leigh Fermor was told that "any man could be a cavalier for five pengöes" here. After decades of shabby respectability under Communism, the street has recently become quite fashionable, with new furniture shops, patisseries and restaurants. Though not the most logical place to start exploring the Jewish quarter, it makes a wonderful approach from the direction of Andrássy út, as you can walk through the Gozsdu udvar (see p.112), entering the passage at Király utca 11 and emerging on Dob utca in the Jewish quarter.

However, approaching the area from the **Kiskörút**, as most people do, the Dohány utca (Tobacco Street) Synagogue is the obvious first objective, located only five minutes' walk from Deák tér, just off Károly körút.

THE DOHÁNY UTCA SYNAGOGUE

Map 4, D9. Astoria or Deák tér metro (M2). Mon–Fri 10am–3pm, Sun 10am–1pm; 400Ft, under-14s free, guide tape 800Ft, personal guide 1000Ft.

The splendid **Dohány utca Synagogue** (*Dohány utcai Zsinagóga*), which also contains the **Jewish Museum**, is one of the landmarks of Pest. Europe's largest synagogue and the second biggest in the world after the Temple Emmanuel in New York, it can hold 3000 worshippers, members of the **Neolog** community, a Hungarian denomination combining elements of Reform and Orthodox Judaism. Designed by a Viennese Gentile, Lajos Förster, the building epitomizes the so-called Byzantine-Moorish style that was popular in the 1850s, and attests to the patriotism of Hungarian Jewry – the colours of its brickwork (yellow, red and blue) being those of Budapest's coat of arms. During the past decade the synagogue has been restored at a cost of over $40 million, funded by the Hungarian government and the Hungarian-Jewish diaspora – notably the Emmanuel Foundation, fronted by the Hollywood actor Tony Curtis, born of 1920s emigrants.

Having admired its gilded onion-domed towers and passed through a security check, you can marvel at the **interior** by Frigyes Feszl, the architect of the Vigadó concert hall. The layout reflects the synagogue's Neolog identity, with the *bemah*, or Ark of the Torah, at one end, in the Reform fashion, but with men and women seated apart, according to Orthodox tradition. The ceiling is decorated with arabesques and Stars of David, the balconies for female worshippers are surmounted by gilded arches, and the floor is inset with eight-pointed stars. On Jewish festivals, it is filled to the rafters with Jews from all over Hungary, whose chattering disturbs their more devout co-religionists. At other times, the hall is used for concerts of classical or klezmer music, as advertised outside.

Next, visitors cross a courtyard full of simple headstones, marking the mass grave of 2281 Jews who died here during the icy winter of 1944. You can also see part of the brick wall that surrounded the ghetto, with a plaque commemorating its liberation by the Red Army on January 18, 1945. Behind the courtyard looms the cuboid, domed Heroes' Temple, erected in 1929-31 in honour of the 10,000 Jewish soldiers who died fighting for Hungary during World War I. These days it serves as a synagogue for everyday use and is not open to tourists.

The Jewish Museum

Heading upstairs to the **Jewish Museum** (*Zsidó Múzeum*), on the left-hand side of the main synagogue, notice a relief of Tivadar (Theodor) Herzl, the founder of modern Zionism, who was born and taught here. In the foyer is a gravestone inscribed with a *menora* (seven-branched candlestick) from the third century AD – proof that there were Jews living in Hungary six hundred years before the Magyars arrived. The first three rooms are devoted to

Jewish festivals, with beautifully crafted objects such as Sabbath lamps and Seder bowls, some from medieval times. In 1993, 178 items were stolen while the guards slept, but most were recovered in Romania the following year. The final room covers the Holocaust in Hungary, with chilling photos and examples of anti-Semitic propaganda. Oddly, the museum says nothing about the huge contribution that Jews have made to Hungarian society, in every field from medicine to poetry.

Upon leaving, turn the corner onto Wesselényi utca and enter the **Raoul Wallenberg Memorial Garden**, named after the Swedish consul who saved 20,000 Jews by lodging them in safe houses or, failing that, by plucking them from trains bound for Auschwitz. He was last seen alive the day before the Red Army liberated the ghetto, and it's thought that he was then arrested by the Soviets on suspicion of espionage and died in the Gulag. The park's centrepiece is a **Holocaust Memorial** by Imre Varga, shaped like a weeping willow, each leaf engraved with the names of a family killed by the Nazis. On the plinth are testimonials from their relatives living in Israel, America and Russia. Also within the grounds is the Goldmark Hall, named after Károly Goldmark, the composer of the opera *The Queen of Sheba*.

AROUND THE BACKSTREETS

Fanning out behind the synagogue is what was once the Jewish **ghetto**, created by the Nazis in April 1944. Initially, the Hungarian government feared that concentrating all the Jews within one area would expose the rest of Budapest to Allied bombing raids, but by November 1944 such considerations were forgotten, and all Jews living outside the ghetto were compelled to move there. As their menfolk had already been conscripted into labour battalions intended to kill them from overwork, the 70,000 inhabitants of the ghetto were largely women, children and old folk, crammed into 162 blocks of flats, with over 50,000 of them (in buildings meant for 15,000) around Klauzál tér alone.

Directly across the road from the Wallenberg Memorial Garden, **Rumbach Sebestyén utca** leads northwards to the **synagogue** of the so-called "Status Quo" or middling-conservative Jews (not open to the public). Though outwardly akin to the Dohány utca synagogue – with a Moorish-style facade in yellow and red brick, inset with blue crosses – its interior conforms to conservative prescriptions, with a detached gallery for women, and the *bemah* in the centre of the hall. As a plaque outside notes, the building served as a detention barracks in August 1941, from where up to 1800 Slovak and Polish refugees were deported to the Nazi death camps.

Backtracking as far as Dob utca, you'll see a **monument to Carl Lutz**, the Swiss Consul who began issuing *Schutzpasses* to Jews, attesting that they were Swiss or Swedish citizens – a ruse subsequently used by Wallenberg. Lutz was a more ambiguous figure, who ceased issuing passes and tried to prevent others from doing so after being threatened by the Gestapo. After the war he was criticized for abusing Swiss law and, feeling slighted, proposed himself for the Nobel Peace Prize. His monument – a gilded angel swooping down to help a prostrate victim – is locally known as "the figure jumping out of a window".

Just beyond Lutz's memorial, a grey stone portal at no. 16 leads into the **Gozsdu udvar**, an eerie 200-metre-long passageway connecting seven courtyards that runs through to Király utca 11. At the turn of the century this was the heart of Jewish Budapest, filled with immigrants from all over the Carpathians, plying every trade from ragpicking to hairdressing. Having fallen into disrepair, it is now scheduled for redevelopment, which the remaining residents of the flats above the udvar fear will result in it becoming an adjunct to the Madách Trade Centre, a postmodernist business complex opening onto Károly körút.

The kosher *Frölich* patisserie at Dob utca 22 presages a slew of Jewish businesses on **Kazinczy utca**, the centre of the 3000-strong Orthodox community, where one can still hear Yiddish spoken. There's a butcher's in the yard of no. 41, up to the left of Dob utca, while down to the right is a wig-makers (no. 36) that isn't Jewish but has lots of female Orthodox clients, a kosher baker (no. 28), and the non-kosher Jewish *Carmel* restaurant across the way at no. 31. Almost next door to the last stands the **Orthodox Synagogue**, an Art Nouveau edifice that melds into the curve of the street, its pediment bearing a Hebrew inscription asserting: "This place is none other than the house of God and the gate to heaven." Though its interior is off limits to the public, the gate to the right leads into an L-shaped courtyard containing a Jewish school and the *Hanna* Orthodox kosher restaurant – also accessible via an arcade on Dob utca.

The Józsefváros and Ferencváros

Separated from the Erzsébetváros by Rákóczi út, which runs out to Keleti Station, the **Józsefváros** is a weird amalgam of high and low life. Although it boasts several prestigious institutions around the Kiskörút, including the Hungarian National Museum, Eötvös Loránd University and the Erkel Theatre, the hinterland beyond the Nagykörút was nicknamed "Chicago" during the 1920s and 1930s, and is still associated with prostitution and criminal activities – though locals swear it has a real community spirit. Its tenements are the most ethnically diverse in Budapest, with gypsies, Romanians, Chinese, Turks and Arabs living cheek by jowl. While the area between the Kiskörút and Nagykörút is nothing to worry about, caution is warranted elsewehere, especially after dark.

Bordering the Józsefváros to the south is the **Ferencváros**, the most solidly working-class of the inner-city districts, and chiefly of interest for the wonderful market hall on Vámház körút and the Applied Arts Museum on Üllői út.

MÚZEUM KÖRÚT

Map 4, D10. Astoria (M2) or Kálvin tér (M3) metro; tram #47 or #49 along the Kiskörút.

Part of the Kiskörút, **Múzeum körút**, separates the Belváros and Józsefváros. Aside from being curved rather than straight, it resembles Andrássy út in miniature, lined with trees, shops and grandiose buildings. Immediately beyond the Astoria junction stands the old faculty of the **Eötvös Loránd Science University** (known by its Hungarian initials as ELTE). It is named after the physicist Loránd Eötvös, whose pupils included many of the scientists who later developed the US atomic bombs at Los Alamos, including Edward Teller, "Father of the Hydrogen Bomb".

At no. 7, on the other side of the körút, is an incredibly dilapidated apartment block built in 1852, whose courtyard resembles a ruinous Venetian palazzo. Further along, remnants of the **medieval walls** of Pest can be seen in the courtyards of nos. 17 and 21. Originally 2km long and 8m high, the walls gradually disappeared as the city was built up on either side, but fragments remain here and there.

Staying on the outer edge of Múzeum körút, you'll find the **Múzeum Kávéház** at no. 12, one of the earliest coffee houses in Pest, whose original frescoes and Zsolnay ceramic reliefs dating from 1885 still grace what has long since become a restaurant. Dining here is a must, but it's essential to reserve; see p.173, for details. At the next corner, just before the National Museum, you can wander off down Bródy Sándor utca to see the nondescript **Radio Building** (nos. 5–7), where ÁVO guards fired upon students demanding access to the airwaves, an act which turned the hitherto peaceful protests of October 23, 1956 into an uprising against the secret police and other manifestations of Stalinism.

Hungarian National Museum

Map 4, E11. Kálvin tér metro (M3). May–Sept Tues–Sun 10am–6pm, Oct–April Wed–Sun 10am–4pm; 250Ft.

Like the National Library on Várhegy, the **Hungarian National Museum** (*Magyar Nemzeti Múzeum*) was the brainchild of Count Ferenc Széchényi (father of István), who donated thousands of prints and manuscripts to form the basis of its collection. Housed in a Grecian-style edifice by Mihály Pollack, it was only the fourth such museum in the world when it opened in 1847, and soon afterwards became the stage for a famous event in the 1848 Revolution, when Sándor Petőfi first declaimed the *National Song* from its steps, with its rousing refrain – "Choose! Now is the time! Shall we be slaves or shall we be free?" ("Some noisy mob had their hurly-burly outside so I left for home," complained the director.) Ever since, March 15 has been commemorated here with flags and patriotic speeches.

The museum is fairly well adapted for foreign visitors, with some captions and explanatory texts in English, as well as info-touch machines giving extra information on exhibits. Its highlights include the Hungarian Crown Jewels and Coronation Regalia; medieval, Turkish and Renaissance artefacts; and relics from the Communist era.

The Crown Jewels and Coronation Regalia

The museum's most precious exhibits are housed in a constantly guarded chamber on the ground floor, off to the left of the foyer (no cameras allowed). **St Stephen's Crown** symbolizes over a thousand years of statehood, and the national coat of arms faithfully reproduces the distinctive bent cross that surmounts the crown. It actually consists of two crowns joined together: the cruciform crown that was sent as a gift by Pope Sylvester II to Stephen for his coronation in 1000; and a circlet given by the Byzantine monarch to King Géza I seven decades later, made on the eastern coast of the Black Sea. They are thought to have been joined during the reign of Béla III. Since then the crown has been smuggled to safety in a haycart during the Mongol invasion; stolen by a lady-in-waiting and hidden in the cradle of László V's baby (whose weight bent the cross); buried in Transylvania to hide it from the Habsburgs; and abducted to Germany by Hungarian Fascists in 1945, whence it was taken to the US. Here it reposed in Fort Knox until the Carter administration returned it to Hungary in 1978, outraging emigrés who felt that this conferred legitimacy on the Communist state.

You can also see Géza's Byzantine silk coronation robe and crystal-headed sceptre, a fourteenth-century gold-plated orb and a sixteenth-century sword made in Vienna, used for the coronation of Hungarian kings. Under the Dual Monarchy, the Habsburg emperors ruled Hungary in the name of St Stephen, and travelled to Budapest for a special coronation ceremony, traditionally held in the Mátyás Church on Várhegy.

Hungarian history exhibition

The museum's main **exhibition** traces Hungarian history from the Árpád dynasty to the end of Communism. St Stephen's marble sarcophagus and a copy of the Lehel Horn that was supposedly blown at the battle of Ausburg in 955 are the highlights of Room 1, while in Room 2 you'll find the Anjou Fountain from the royal palace at Visegrád (see p.140). Don't miss the beautiful saddles inlaid with hunting scenes in Room 3, the Gothic pew used by Mátyás and Beatrice in Room 4, or the Renaissance Báthory pew from Nyírbátor in Room 5. A Turkish leather kaftan from the battle of Mohács and the gold-embroidered tunic of Prince Gábor Bethlen of Transylvania in Room 7 speak of the 150 years when Hungary was divided and its destiny decided by intriguers and warlords.

The oldest **portraits** in Hungary are owned by the museum, with the portrait of Ferenc Nádasdy, the "Black Knight", hanging in Room 8, though the portrait of his wife, the infamous "Blood Countess" Báthory, is kept in storage. The Reform era and the *belle époque* are covered in Rooms 11–18, followed by World War II and the **Communist era** in Room 20. The last features newsreel footage and such items as a radio set dedicated to Stalin's seventieth birthday, a fragment of the Stalin statue and the crest of Party headquarters torn down by crowds in 1956, and kitsch tributes to János Kádár, who reimposed Communist rule with a vengeance, but later liberalized it to the point that his successors felt able to abandon it entirely.

KÁLVIN TÉR

Map 4, D12. Kálvin tér metro (M3).

Múzeum körút ends at **Kálvin tér**, a busy intersection above a metro underpass, whose chief landmarks are the *Korona Hotel* (see p.73) and a hoarding advertising the *Blue Angel* strip club. The latter is incongruously located near the **Szabó Ervin Library** (Mon, Tues & Thurs 9am–9pm, Sat & Sun 9am–1pm), whose ornate reading room miraculously survived the heavy streetfighting around Kálvin tér in 1944 and 1956, as did the Fountain of Justice, installed outside in 1929 as a reminder of the injustice inflicted on Hungary by the Treaty of Trianon, which originally featured a relief of Lord Rothermere (see p.84).

The continuation of the Kiskörút and the Applied Arts Museum on Üllői út are covered on p.124.

TO THE NAGYKÖRÚT AND BEYOND

Blaha Lujza tér metro (M2); tram #4 or #6.

The segment of the Józsefváros between the Kiskörút and the Nagykörut is a good place to ramble, especially around **Mikszáth Kálmán tér**, beyond the library, a neighbourhood of crumbling churches and parochial schools, raucous wine cellars and workshops. The József körút section of the Nagykörút marks the beginning of the **red-light district** around **Rákóczi tér**, a shabby square whose market hall and Chinese food stores impart an air of normality by day, though by night the streetwalkers on the Nagykörút are less discreet. The district has been a centre of downmarket prostitution since the 1860s, but, unlike on Király utca, the trade resumed in the 1960s and has flourished unhindered since the end of Communism, together with the porn industry. After some vicious turf wars, street prostitution and the strip clubs are now largely controlled by the Ukrainian mafia.

Further north, **Köztársaság tér** marks a return to bourgeois respectability, with the **Erkel Theatre** (named after the composer of the national anthem, Ferenc Erkel) drawing smartly dressed crowds most evenings. This is the second home of Hungarian opera after the Opera House on Andrássy út. Across the square, no. 26–27 once housed the Budapest Party headquarters, which was attacked by insurgents during the Uprising. Many of the occupants were summarily executed on suspicion of being members of the ÁVO, including the Budapest Party Secretary, Imre Mező, a friend of Kádár's. His death was undoubtedly a factor in Kádár's defection to the Soviets, which led to him being installed as the country's ruler after the Uprising had been crushed. Today, the building is the headquarters of the Socialist Party – the former Communists (see "History" p.255).

At the end of Rákóczi út, **Baross tér** and **Keleti Station** are a hub of activity from dawn until the small hours, but no place to hang around. The square is named after Gábor Baross, the Minister of Transport responsible for the phenomenal expansion of Hungary's railways in the late nineteenth century, who determined that the lines of communication between Vienna and the Balkans should run through Budapest, not Zagreb.

KEREPESI CEMETERY

Map 2, F6. Tram #23 or #24 from Keleti Station (M2). Daily: July & Aug 8am–8pm; Sept–June 8am–sunset; free.

Kerepesi Cemetery (*Kerepesi temető*) is the Père Lachaise of Budapest, where the famous, great and not-so-good are buried. As the entrance on Fiumei út is only ten minutes' walk from Baross tér, it's hardly worth taking a tram. With the plan opposite you can track down the florid **nineteenth-century mausoleums** of Kossuth, Batthyány, Deák and Petőfi (whose family tomb is here though his own body was never found). Don't miss the Art Nouveau funerary arcades between Batthyány's and the novelist Jókai's mausoleums, nor the nearby tomb of the diva Lujza Blaha, the "Nation's Nightingale", whose effigy is surrounded by statues of serenading figures. Other notables include the composer Erkel, the confectioner Gerbeaud, and three chess grandmasters whose tombs are engraved with the chess moves that won them their titles. The most recent VIP to be interred in Kerepesi was József Antall, Hungary's first post-Communist Prime Minister, who died in 1993.

In Communist times, Party members killed in the Uprising were buried in a prominent position near the entrance, and government ministers in honourable proximity to Kossuth. Unlike the tombs of the martyrs of 1848, or

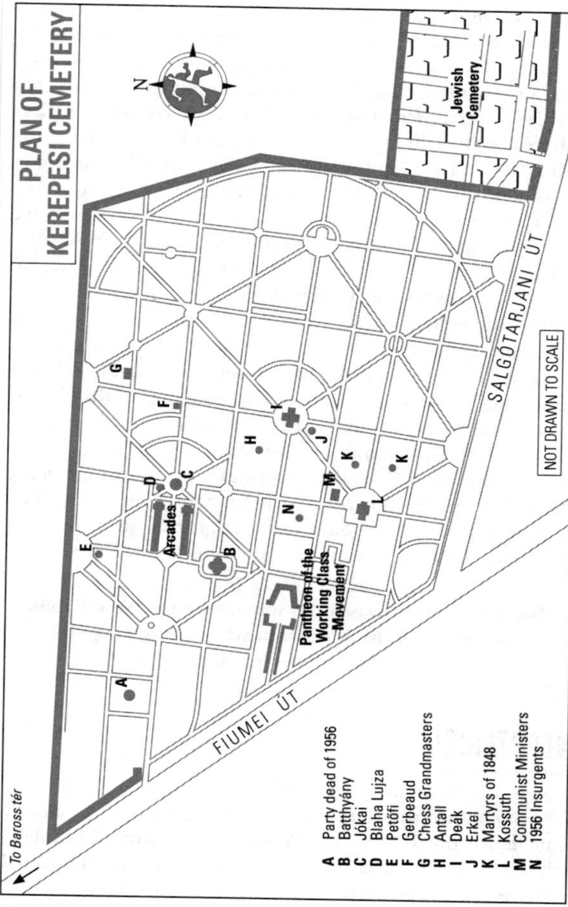
PLAN OF KEREPESI CEMETERY
N
Jewish Cemetery
SALGÓTARJÁNI ÚT
NOT DRAWN TO SCALE
FIUMEI ÚT
To Baross tér
Arcades
Pantheon of the Working Class Movement
A Party dead of 1956
B Batthyány
C Jókai
D Blaha Lujza
E Petőfi
F Gerbeaud
G Chess Grandmasters
H Antall
I Deák
J Erkel
K Martyrs of 1848
L Kossuth
M Communist Ministers
N 1956 Insurgents

the insurgents slain in 1956 (only recently buried here), which express their faith in God, Hungary and liberty, the apparatchiks' tombs are devoid of any sentiment, implying a lack of confidence in their own ideology. This is even palpable in the **Pantheon of the Working Class Movement**, a hideously ugly necropolis for personages who "Lived for Communism and the People", which was so shoddily built that it is now falling apart. Most of the dead are stacked in concrete filing cases and a few have been withdrawn by their relatives to be reburied elsewhere.

Beyond the wall at the far end of the cemetery lies an overgrown **Jewish cemetery** (Mon–Fri & Sun 8am–2pm), with some beautiful Art Nouveau tombs of artists, politicians and industrialists, including many interesting tombs designed by the brilliant early twentieth-century architect Béla Lajta. That of Manfred Weiss, founder of the Csepel ironworks, is still maintained by Csepel's council, in gratitude and by way of apology for the fact that Weiss had to sign his factory over to the government in return for being allowed to leave Hungary with his family in 1944. The cemetery gates are on Salgótarján utca, two stops by tram #37 from the Kerepesi entrance on Fiumei út.

Tram #37 continues all the way out to the New Public Cemetery in the X district, where Imre Nagy is buried (see p.130).

NÉPSTADION

Map 2, G5. Népstadion metro (M2).

The **Népstadion** district, north of Kerepesi út, is chiefly notable for the 76,000-seat **People's Stadium** (*Népstadion*) where league championship and international **football** matches, concerts by foreign pop stars and events such as the national dog show are held. Its **Sport and Training Museum** (*Testnevelési és Sportmúzeum*; daily except Fri 10am–4.30pm; 100Ft) features temporary exhibitions on sports themes, in Hungarian only. The stadium itself was built in the early 1950s by 50,000 Budapesters who "volunteered" their labour, unpaid, on Soviet-style "free Saturdays". Stalinist statues of healthy proletarian youth line the court that separates it from the smaller **Kisstadion** and the indoor **Sportcsarnok**, which also hosts occasional concerts. The Népstadion **bus station** completes this concrete ensemble.

Otherwise, the only reason to come is to catch trolleybus #75 along Stefánia út, behind the Sportcsarnok, to admire the **Geological Institute** (no. 14). The last of the three edifices in Budapest designed by Ödön Lechner, its exterior is as striking as the Postal Savings Bank (see p.85) and the Applied Arts Museum (see overleaf), with a gingerbread facade, scrolled gables and steeply pitched Transylvanian roofs patterned in bright blue tiles, crowned by figures holding globes on their backs. Sadly, you can't see what the interior is like.

From the Geological Institute, you can continue along Stefánia út by trolleybus #75 to reach the Városliget (see p.103).

FERENCVÁROS

Kálvin tér or Ferenc körút metro (M3).

Ferencváros (Franz Town), the IX district, was developed to house workers in the latter half of the nineteenth century, and remains the most working-class of Budapest's inner suburbs. During the 1930s and 1940s, its population confounded Marxist orthodoxy by voting for the extreme right, who returned the favour by supporting the local football team FTC (known as Fradi). This association made FTC the popular underdogs in the 1950s when the Party favoured such teams as MTK and Vasas, but has visibly revived in the nineties. However, the inner section of the Ferencváros is comparatively bourgeois, with the only call to venture further being the Applied Arts Museum on Üllői út. See p.212 for more on Fradi and the football scene in general.

Ferencváros begins at **Vámház körút**, the section of the Kiskörút running from Kálvin tér to the Szabadság híd, where the largest section of the **medieval walls** of Pest can be found in the courtyard of no. 16. Nearer the bridge stands the recently restored **Nagycsarnok**, Budapest's main **market hall** (Mon 6am–4pm, Tues–Fri 6am–6pm, Sat 6am–2pm), which is noted for its ambience as much as for its produce. Tanks of live fish can be found downstairs and stalls festooned with strings of paprika at the back. Mrs Thatcher endeared herself to locals here by haggling during a visit in 1984, an event that is still recalled, setting a trend for all visiting statespeople. Between the market hall and river stands the Budapest **Economics University** (*Budapesti Közgazdaság-tudományos Egyetem*), formerly the Main Customs Building, which was recently given a face-lift and is now a delightful sight at night when it's reflected in the river. Until 1989 the university was named for Karl Marx and his statue still stands in the main hall.

Applied Arts Museum

Map 4, F13. Ferenc körút metro (M3). Tues–Sun 10am–6pm; 200Ft, photo permit 200Ft, video permit 1500Ft.

The **Applied Arts Museum** (*Iparművészeti Múzeum*) is worth a visit purely to see the building, which is one of the finest works of Ödön Lechner. Lechner strove to create a uniquely Hungarian form of architecture, emphasizing the Magyars' Central Asian and Turkic roots, but was also influenced by the then fashionable style of Art Nouveau. Inaugurated by Emperor Franz Josef during the Millennial celebrations of 1896, the museum is topped by an enormous dome covered in green and yellow tiles, and its portico is adorned with Turkic motifs on a yolk-coloured background, both from the Zsolnay porcelain factory in Pécs. By contrast, the all-white interior is reminiscent of Moghul and Moorish architecture: at one time it was thought that the Magyars came from India.

Though much of the museum is given over to temporary exhibitions, there is a permanent display of **arts and crafts** ranging from glassware and pottery to textiles, leather working and wrought iron. The section entitled Style 1900 is devoted to the movement variously known as Jugendstil, Secessionist or Art Nouveau, and features everything from William Morris wallpaper to Tiffany vases and stained-glass panels by such Hungarian masters as József Rippl-Rónai and Miksa Róth. Owing to an enlightened purchasing policy, the museum owns one of the finest collections of this kind in the world.

The Kilián Barracks and Corvin Cinema

Map 4, F13. Ferenc körút metro (M3).

One block beyond the Applied Arts Museum, the underpass at the junction of the Nagykörút will bring you out on either side of Üllői út beside two buildings associated with the 1956 Uprising. On the right side stands the former **Kilián Barracks**, a nineteenth-century edifice whose Hungarian garrison was the first to join the insurgents. As the Uprising spread this became the headquarters of Colonel Pál Maleter, who was appointed Minister of Defence in the revolutionary government of Imre Nagy.

Though professional soldiers formed the core of the resistance, its shock troops were civilians – many of them teenagers, some as young as 12 years' old. Their base was the **Corvin Cinema** across the road, set back within a circular lane opening out on Üllői út and the Nagykörút, which proved impenetrable to Soviet tanks. While the barracks are now given over to businesses ranging from a photocopying bureau to a massage parlour, the cinema is still just that, but since the fall of Communism its heroic past has been honoured by memorial plaques and a statue of a young insurgent carrying a rifle.

Further out

While the centre of Budapest is hardly short of attractions, it would be a shame to overlook some of the ones **further out** towards the city limits. **The Statue Park**, with its outmoded Communist memorials, is the prime destination on the outskirts, for Hungarians and foreigners alike. After that, it really depends on your inclinatons whether you want to visit the **Budakeszi Game Park** on the outskirts of Buda or the **Farkasrét and New District cemeteries** that complete the roll-call of illustrious Hungarian dead begun at Kerepesi.

STATUE PARK

Map 2, C9. Suburban bus from stand #6 on Kosztolányi Dezső tér. May–Oct daily 10am–6pm; Nov–April Sat, Sun & public holidays 10am to dusk. May be closed in bad weather (☎227-7446). 200Ft.

Easily the most popular site on the outskirts, the **Statue Park** (*Szoborpark*) brings together 42 of the monuments that once glorified Communism in Budapest. The idea was suggested by a historian during the period of transition to democracy and put into practice following the municipal assembly's ruling that each district should decide the fate of its own statues, with the museum finally opening in autumn

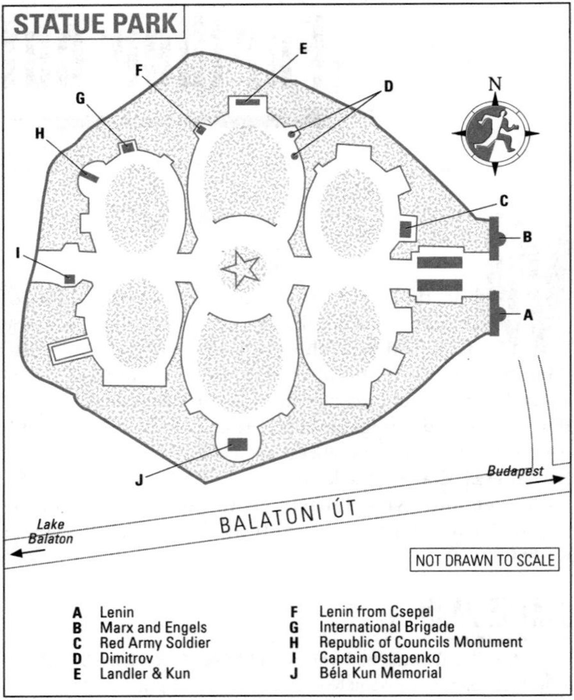

1993. The site is beside Balatoni út in the XXII district, 15km from the city centre: a twenty-minute bus ride from Kosztolányi Dezső tér in Buda (which can be reached by tram #49 from the Kiskörút or Szent Gellért tér). City passes aren't valid on this service.

The Statue Park's outsized gate is clearly visible from the highway, its bogus Classical facade framing giant statues of

Lenin, Marx and Engels. Lenin's once stood beside the Városliget, while Marx's and Engels' are carved from granite quarried at Mauthausen, the Nazi concentration camp later used by the Soviets. Inside the grounds you'll encounter the Red Army soldier that guarded the foot of the Liberation Monument on Gellért-hegy, and dozens of other statues and memorials, large and small. Here are prewar Hungarian Communists like Béla Kun (secretly shot in Moscow on Stalin's orders) and Jenő Landler (afforded a place in the Kremlin Wall); Dimitrov, hero of the Comintern; and the Lenin statue from outside the Csepel ironworks.

Artistically, the best statues are the Republic of Councils Monument – a giant charging sailor based on a 1919 revolutionary poster, that makes a fantastic slide for kids – and Imre Varga's Béla Kun Memorial, with Kun on a tribune surrounded by a surging crowd of workers and soldiers (plus a bystander with an umbrella). Budapesters fondly remember the statue of Captain Ostapenko that stood on the highway to the Balaton and Vienna, where hitch-hikers would arrange to meet their friends (a locality still known as "Ostapenko"), while the removal of the monument to the Hungarian contingent of the International Brigade in the Spanish Civil War (three robotic figures with fists clenched to their heads) provoked a heartfelt debate that few of the others engendered.

Among the **souvenirs** on sale are small busts of Lenin, cans of air from "the last breath of socialism", and a selection of revolutionary songs that was a retro hit in 1997 (which can be heard playing from a 1950s' radio set). There's also a fairly informative English-language brochure (400Ft).

BUDAKESZI GAME PARK

Map 2, A5. Bus #22 from Moszkva tér (M2) to the Korányi Körház stop, or a yellow striped #22 to the MÁV Sanatorium. Daily 9am to dusk; 140Ft.

Better known to natives than it is to tourists, the **Budakeszi Game Park** (*Vadászkert*), right on the city limits, offers a chance to view fauna that is otherwise elusive in the Buda Hills, to breathe fresh air and to escape from the city – with the caveat that you should avoid coming at weekends or national holidays, and, in order to really get back to nature, get away from the zoological enclosures. Since bus #22 stops fairly near to the Szépjuhászné halt on the Children's Railway, you can also visit the park as an extension of the "railway circuit" in the Buda Hills (p.61).

Oddly, the *Hotel Tanne* is better signposted than the *Vadászkert* itself, whose entrance is fifteen minutes' walk past the hotel. Turn off Budakeszi út, and head on past a **quarry** with steep sandy slopes which children can slide down, and the *Vadászkert* **restaurant** (daily 11am–11pm), where shameless carnivores can consume the species in the park.

Away from the enclosures near the entrance (boars and deer to the left, fowl to the right) and the wooden **lookout tower** that affords a lovely view of the wooded hills and the village of Budakeszi with Budapest nowhere in sight, the woodland **paths** are pretty much deserted, and if it wasn't for the lack of signposting one could easily follow the *A túra* (5km) or *B túra* (3km) circuits posted at the entrance. As things are, however, you'd do better to simply follow the swathe cut for telephone pylons, where all kinds of wildflowers and butterflies flourish, and nobody ever goes.

FARKASRÉT CEMETERY

Map 2, C6. Tram #59 from Moszkva tér to the entrance on Nemetvölgyi út. Daily 8am–7pm; free.

Another notable necropolis is the Wolf's Meadow or **Farkasrét Cemetery** (*Farkasréti temető*), in the hilly XI district. One of the largest cemeteries in Buda, it contains the graves of many poets, writers and musicians, of whom the best known is **Béla Bartók**. His remains were ceremonially interred here in July 1988 following their return from America, where the composer died in exile in 1945. His will forbade reburial in Hungary so long as there were streets named after Hitler or Mussolini, but the return of his body was delayed for decades to prevent the Communists from capitalizing on the event. The Hungarian-born conductor **Sir Georg Solti** was buried alongside Bartók in 1998. Ironically, Farkasrét also contains the grave of **Mátyás Rákosi**, Hungary's Stalinist dictator, who died in exile in the USSR and was evidently deemed unworthy of inclusion in the Pantheon of the Working Class Movement at Kerepesi. Also look out for gravestones inscribed in the ancient runic Székely alphabet.

The real attraction, however, is the amazing **mortuary chapel by Imre Makovecz**, whose wood-ribbed vault resembles the throat and belly of a beast. This awesome structure is one of Makovecz's finest designs, and can't help but make anyone who sees it curious to know more about his work, which can also be seen at Viségrad (see p.141), but, as it is in almost constant use by mourners, visitors should be as discreet as possible.

NEW PUBLIC CEMETERY

Map 2, I6. Tram #28 or #37 from Népszínház utca near Blaha Lujza tér (M2), or Fiumei út. Daily 8am–7pm; free.

The **New Public Cemetery** (*Új köztemető*) in the industrial X district is the largest in Budapest, reflecting the city's growth in the latter half of the nineteenth century. Located beyond the breweries of Kőbánya, near the end of one of the longest tram rides in Budapest, its significance lies in the fact that it was here that Imre Nagy, Pál Maleter and other leaders of the 1956 Uprising were secretly buried in unmarked graves in 1958, after their death sentences were carried out at the Military Court of Justice (p.52). The police removed any flowers left at **Plot 301** until 1989, when the deceased were accorded a ceremonial funeral in Hősök tere before being returned to their graves, which were dignified by the erection of 301 crosses and a Transylvanian-style gateway. The plot lies in the furthest corner of the cemetery, a thirty-minute walk from the main entrance on Kozma utca (accessible by minibus in summertime). Alongside lies Hungary's largest **Jewish cemetery** (Sun–Fri 8am–2pm), where Ernő Szép (author of *The Smell of Humans*) and illustrious rabbis are buried.

Excursions from Budapest

Although many provincial towns in Hungary are within three hours' journey of Budapest, the attractions covered in this chapter are all within an hour

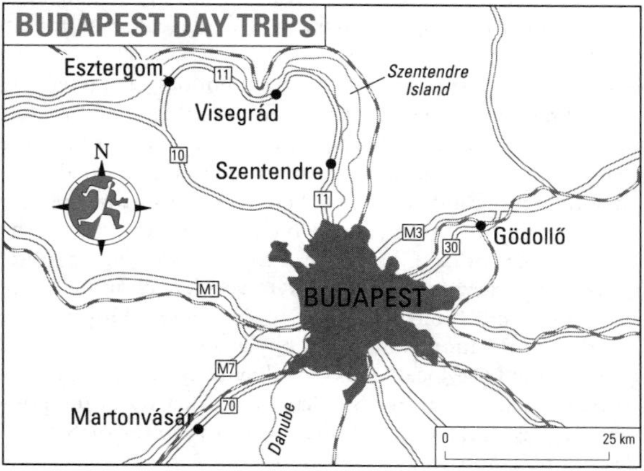

or so's travel. Foremost among them are the sites on the Danube Bend – the artists' colony and former Serbian settlement of **Szentendre** and the cathedral town of **Esztergom**, where the Danube forms the border between Hungary and Slovakia; if you've got time, the medieval ruins and Makovecz buildings at **Visegrád** are also worthwhile.

SZENTENDRE

Map 8. 45min by HÉV train from Batthyány tér (M2).

Szentendre (St Andrew), 20km north of Budapest, is the most popular tourist destination in the vicinity of the capital and the easiest to reach. Despite its rash of souvenir shops, the centre remains a delightful maze of houses in autumnal colours, with secretive gardens and lanes winding up to hilltop churches. Szentendre's location on the lower slopes of the Pilis range is not only beautiful, but ensures that it enjoys more hours of sunlight than anywhere else in Hungary, making it a perfect spot for an artists' colony.

Before the artists moved in, Szentendre's character had been forged by waves of refugees from Serbia. The first followed the catastrophic Serb defeat at Kosovo in 1389, and the second, the Turkish recapture of Belgrade in 1690, precipitating the flight of 30,000 Serbs and Bosnians, 6000 of whom settled in Szentendre, which became the seat of the Serbian Orthodox Church in exile. Prospering through trade, the Serbians replaced their wooden churches with stone ones and built handsome town houses. However, as Habsburg toleration waned and phylloxera (vine-blight) and floods ruined the local economy, they trickled back to their own country, so that by 1890 less than a quarter of the population was Serb. Only about seventy families of Serbian descent remain today.

The Town

Szentendre's bus and train (HÉV) stations are next to each other, fifteen minutes' walk south of the centre. The jetty for ferries and hydrofoils between Budapest and Esztergom lies 500m to the north. For a free map of town and any **information**, drop into Tourinform at Dumsta Jenő utca 22, a few minutes up the road leading into the centre, on the far side of the pedestrian underpass outside the HÉV station (March–Oct Mon–Fri 9.30am–4.30pm, Sat & Sun 10am–2pm; Nov–Feb Mon–Fri 10am–4pm; ©26/317-965). Bear in mind that Szentendre's **museums** open at weekends only between November and March.

When you feel hungry, make a beeline for the tiny *Aranysárkány* ("Golden Dragon") **restaurant** at Alkotmány utca 1A, just uphill from Fő tér, which serves delicious Hungarian dishes such as honeyed goose with red cabbage, at very reasonable prices (daily noon–11pm).

Churches, museums and crafts

The **Požarevačka Church**, 100m before Tourinform (Fri–Sun 11am–5pm), is the first evidence of a Serbian presence. Typical of the churches in Szentendre, it was built in the late eighteenth century to replace an older wooden structure. Beyond the Bükkös stream, Dumtsa Jenő utca continues past the **Marzipan Museum and Pastry Shop** at no. 12, where the marzipan creations include a model of the Hungarian Parliament, while a left turn at Péter-Pál utca brings you to the **Peter-Paul Church**, built in 1708, whose original furnishings were taken back to Serbia after World War I. For details of organ recitals there, ask at Tourinform.

Just beyond the church, **Fő tér** swarms with tourists and horse-drawn carriages, with diverging streets and alleys leading to various galleries and museums. Don't miss the

Margit Kovács Museum on Vastagh György utca (Tues–Sun 10am–6pm; 100Ft), whose wonderful collection of ceramic hats never fails to delight. Her themes of legends, dreams, love and motherhood give her graceful sculptures and reliefs universal appeal; although her work isn't particularly well known abroad, in Hungary, Kovács, who died in 1977, is duly honoured as the nation's greatest ceramicist.

The museum is down a sidestreet from the **Blagoveštenska Church** on Fő tér, whose icons evoke all the richness and tragedy of Serbian history. Look out for the tomb of a Greek merchant of Macedonian origin to the left of the entrance, and the Rococo windows and gate facing Görög utca. Next door, a portal carved with emblems of science and learning provides the entrance to a former Serbian school, now the **Ferenczy Museum** (mid-March to Oct Tues–Sun 10am–4pm; Nov to mid-March Fri–Sun same hours; 100Ft) exhibiting paintings by the Impressionist Károly Ferenczy, and of his eldest son Valér and younger twins Nóemi and Béni, who branched out into Expressionism, textiles and bronzeware.

From Fő tér you can ascend an alley of steps to gain a lovely view of Szentendre's rooftops and gardens from **Templom tér**, where **craft fairs** are frequently held to help finance the restoration of the Catholic **parish church**. Of medieval origin, with Romanesque and Gothic features, it was rebuilt in the Baroque style after falling derelict in Turkish times. The frescoes in its sanctuary were collectively painted by the artists' colony. North of Templom tér, the burgundy spire of the Orthodox episcopal cathedral or **Belgrade Church** rises above a walled garden; it is rarely open except for services (Sat 5pm, 6pm in summer; Sun 10am & 4pm), though you can view a **Serbian Ecclesiastical History Collection** (mid-March to Oct Wed–Sun 10am–4pm; Nov to mid-March Fri–Sun same hours; 100Ft) in the episcopal palace, whose icons, vestments and crosses come from churches in Hungary that fell empty after the Serbs returned to the Balkans and the last remaining parishioners died out. The palace is entered from Patriarka utca, around the corner from the church.

From the church you can follow a lane down to Bogdányi utca, where the **Wine Museum** (daily 10am–10pm; 100Ft) does a fair job of describing Hungary's wine-making regions using maps, wine-bottle labels and other artefacts. The sting in the tail is the invitation to sample half a dozen wines for an extra 600Ft – more than you'd pay to drink twice as much in a regular *borozó*. Five minutes to the north you'll reach a square flanked by the **Lázár Cross** honouring King Lázár of Serbia, whom the Turks beheaded after Kosovo. His body was brought here by the Serbs and buried in a wooden church; when the relic was taken back to Serbia the place was marked by a cross in his memory. The Kovács **Blue Dye Shop** at no. 36 showcases a traditional style of folk dyeing that was once popular with ethnic Germans and is now fashionable amongst Hungarians. You'll find more examples of local crafts up the hill at Angyal utca 5, where **paper-maker** László Vincze operates his mill and gives demonstrations by appointment (Mon–Fri 7am–5pm, Sat 7am–2pm; ©26/314-328; 100Ft).

The Village Museum

The **Szentendre Village Museum** on Sztaravodai út, 4km west of town (April–Oct Tues–Sun 9am–5pm; 200Ft), is one of Szentendre's principal attractions. Hungary's largest open-air museum of rural architecture (termed a *Skanzen*, after the first such museum, founded in a Stockholm suburb in 1891), it will eventually include "samples" from ten different regions of Hungary – though only four exist so far. The museum is accessible by buses from stand 8 of the bus terminal near the HÉV station in

Szentendre, though services are pretty infrequent after noon.

Downhill from the entrance is a composite village from **zabolcs-Szatmár** in northeastern Hungary, a region oted for its backwardness. The brochure points out the ner distinctions between the various humble dwellings scattered among the barns and woven pigsties. The homes of the poorest squires were barely superior to those of their tenants, yet rural carpenters produced highly skilled work, such as the circular "dry mill", the wooden belltower from Nemesborzova, and the carving inside the church from Mándok (on a hilltop).

The second village "unit" is from the Great Plain, with a house from Süsköd with a beautiful facade on the street, and a visitors' room or "clean room" laid out for Christmas celebrations with a nativity crib and a church-shaped box. Beyond it lies a far more regimented unit originating from the ethnic **German** communities of the Kisalföld (Little Plain) in Transdanubia. Neatly aligned and whitewashed, the houses are filled with knick-knacks and embroidered samplers bearing homilies like "When the Hausfrau is capable, the clocks keep good time." Beyond lies the Western Transdanubia unit.

Demonstrations of traditional crafts such as weaving, pottery and basket-making usually take place on the first and third Sunday of each month as well as on public holidays – but check at the museum (✆26/312-304) or Tourinform for precise dates. Local festivals are also celebrated here, such as the grape harvest in October, when folkloric programmes and grape-pressing take place.

VISEGRÁD

Bus (30min) or ferry (1hr 40min) from Szentendre; bus from the Árpád híd terminal (1hr 15min) or hydrofoil (50min) or ferry (3hr) from the Vigadó tér pier in Budapest.

Approaching **Visegrád** from the south, the hillsides start to plunge and the river twists shortly before you first catch sight of the citadel and ramparts of the ancient fortified site whose Slavic name means "High Castle". It hasn't changed much since 1488 when János Thuroczy described its "upper walls stretching to the clouds floating in the sky, and the lower bastions reaching down as far as the river". At that time, courtly life in Visegrád was nearing its apogee and the palace of King Mátyás and Queen Beatrice was famed throughout Europe as a "paradiso terrestri". Today, Visegrád is a mere village that manages to conceal the remains of the palace off its main street, Fő utca, until the last moment, though the ramparts snaking down the hillside from the citadel and Solomon's Tower near the riverside are plainly visible from a distance.

The ruins

The **layout** of the ruins dates back to the thirteenth century, when Béla IV began fortifying the north against a recurrence of the Mongol invasion, while the construction of a royal palace below the hilltop citadel was a sign of greater security during the reign of the Angevins. However, its magnificence was effaced by the Turkish conquest, and later mud washing down from the hillside gradually buried the palace entirely. Later generations doubted its very existence until the archeologist János Schulek unearthed one of the vaults in 1934.

Now partially excavated and reconstructed, the **Royal Palace** (Tues–Sun: April–Oct 9am–5pm; Nov–March 8am–4pm; 100Ft) spreads over four levels or terraces. Founded in 1323 by the Angevin king Charles Robert, it was the setting for the Visegrád Congress of 1335, attended by the monarchs of Central Europe and the Grandmaster of the Teutonic Knights. Although nothing remains of this palace, the **Court of Honour** constructed for his successor Louis, which provided the basis for additions by kings Sigismund and

Mátyás, is still to be seen on the second terrace. Its chief features are the pillastered **Renaissance loggia** and two panels from the red marble **Hercules Fountain**. The upper storey of heavily carved and gilded wood disappeared long ago, as did most of the royal suites and the chapel on the third terrace, used by Mátyás and Beatrice, but you can still see a perfect copy of the **Lion Fountain**, bearing Mátyás' raven crest and surrounded by dozens of sleepy-looking lions.

By walking north along Fő utca and turning right onto Solamon torony utca, you'll reach **Solomon's Tower**, a mighty hexagonal keep buttressed by concrete slabs. The **Mátyás Museum** inside the tower (May to early Nov Tues–Sun 9am–5pm; 100Ft) exhibits finds from the palace, including a copy of the white Anjou Fountain of the Angevins and the red marble *Visegrád Madonna* carved by Tomaso Fiamberti – the probable sculptor of the Lion and Hercules fountains. In July the ruins provide a stage for **pageants** and **films** intended to recreate the splendour of Visegrád's Renaissance heyday.

You can also visit the triangular **citadel** on the hilltop (May–Sept daily 10am–6pm; Oct–April Sat & Sun 10am–4pm; 100Ft), which can be reached in forty minutes by the "calvary" footpath (signposted *Fellegvár)* starting on Kálvaria utca, off Mátyás király utca, or by catching a bus (June–Aug only) from the Mátyás statue, which follows the scenic Panorama autóút into the hills. Though only partly restored, the citadel is still mightily impressive, commanding a superb view of Nagymaros and the Börzsöny Mountains on the east bank of the Danube. A **museum** within the citadel focuses on the lives of local hunters and fishermen during the Middle Ages.

The Visegrád Hills

Thickly wooded and crisscrossed with paths, the **Visegrád Hills** are a popular rambling spot. From the car park near the citadel, you can follow the autóút and then a signposted path to the **Nagy-Villám observation tower**, or *Kilátó* (March–Oct daily 9am–7pm; Nov–Feb Sat & Sun 9am–6pm unless there's snow). Sited at the highest point on the Danube Bend, it offers a view that stretches as far as Slovakia. Alongside is a **summer bobsleigh course** (*Nyári Bob*), where for 150Ft you can race down a one-kilometre run (April–Oct, except on rainy days when the brakes are rendered ineffective).

One kilometre north of the observation tower lies Mogyoró-hegy (Hazelnut Hill) and a collection of wooden **buildings by Imre Makovecz**. As a promising architect in the Kádár years, Makovecz was branded a troublemaker for his outspoken nationalism, banned from teaching and "exiled" to the Visegrád forestry department in 1977. Here he refined his ideas over the next decade, acquiring a following of students for whom he held summer schools. Employing cheap, low-technology methods in a specifically Magyar way, he taught them how to construct temporary buildings using raw materials such as branches and twigs. The Cultural House near *Jurta Camping* is an excellent example, with a turfed roof and a light, homely interior. The oesophagus-like crypt of the Farkasrét Cemetery in Budapest (see p.132) is another notable example of his organic style of architecture.

ESZTERGOM

Map 9. By bus from the Árpád híd terminal (1hr 30min), train from Nyugati Station (1hr 30min), or hydrofoil (1hr 10min) from the Vigadó tér pier in Budapest.

Beautifully situated in a crook of the Danube facing Slovakia, **Esztergom** is dominated by its basilica, whose dome is visible for miles around – a richly symbolic sight, as it was here that Prince Géza and his son Vajk (the future king and saint Stephen) brought Hungary into the fold of

Roman Catholic (not Orthodox) Christendom. Even after the court moved to Buda following the Mongol invasion, Esztergom remained the centre of Catholicism until the Turkish conquest, and resumed this role in the 1820s. Though the Church was persecuted during the Rákosi era, from the 1960s onwards the Communists settled for a modus vivendi; during the 1990s it regained much of its former influence. Esztergom itself makes an ideal day-trip, combining historic monuments and small-town charm in just the right doses. The only drawback is the infrequency of direct buses between Visegrád and Esztergom, which makes it difficult to see both towns in one day. Coming by bus from Visegrád usually entails changing at Dömös (2hr).

The Town

If you do arrive by bus from Visegrád, get off near the Basilica Hill rather than travelling on to the bus station where services from Budapest terminate. Arriving at the train station, 1km further south, buses #1 and #5 run into the centre, while hydrofoils from Budapest tie up on the Danube embankment of Prímás-Sziget (Primate's Island), fifteen minutes' walk away. For **information**, drop into Gran Tours on the corner of Rákóczi tér and Kossuth utca, in the lower town between Prímás-Sziget and Bazilika-hegy (Oct–April Mon–Fri 8am–6pm; May–Sept Mon–Fri 8am–6pm, Sat 9am–noon; ©33/417-052).

As in Szentendre, **restaurants** near the tourist sites are geared to coach parties and a fast turnover, but none of them is so bad or expensive that you feel compelled to look elsewhere. Indeed, it's hard to resist a meal in the cavernous cellars of the *Prímás Pince* (daily 10am–9.30pm), beneath Bazilika-hegy. On Prímás-Sziget, the *Hotel Esztergom*'s restaurant is excellent, or there's the terraced rustic-style *Szálma Csárda* near the Budapest ferry-dock, serving fish and poultry.

The Basilica

Built upon the site of the first cathedral in Hungary, where Vajk was crowned as King Stephen by a papal envoy on Christmas Day 1000 AD, Esztergom's **Basilica** is the largest in the country, measuring 118m in length and 40m in width, capped by a dome 100m high. Liszt's *Gran Mass* (*Gran* being the German name for Esztergom) was composed for its completion in 1869. Admission (March–Sept

Cardinal Mindszenty

When the much-travelled body of **Cardinal József Mindszenty** was finally laid to rest with state honours in May 1991, it was a vindication of his uncompromising heroism – and the Vatican realpolitik that Mindszenty despised.

As a conservative and monarchist, he had stubbornly opposed the postwar Communist takeover, warning that "cruel hands are reaching out to seize hold of our children, claws belonging to people who have nothing but evil to teach them". Arrested in 1948, tortured for 39 days and nights, and sentenced to life imprisonment for treason, Mindszenty was freed during the Uprising and took refuge in the US Embassy, where he remained for the next fifteen years – an exile in the heart of Budapest.

When the Vatican struck a deal with the Kádár regime in 1971, Mindszenty had to be pushed into resigning his position and going to Austria, where he died in 1975. Although his will stated that his body should not return home until "the red star of Moscow had fallen from Hungarian skies", his reburial occurred some weeks before the last Soviet soldier left, in preparation for the pope's visit in August of that year. Nowadays the Vatican proclaims his greatness, without any hint of apology for its past actions.

daily 7am–6pm; Oct–Feb Tues–Sun 7am–5pm) is free, but tickets are required for the spooky **crypt** (9am–4.45pm; 50Ft) where Cardinal Mindszenty (see box on p.143) is buried; the **cupola** (May–Oct 9am–5pm; 80Ft), reached by 300 steps and offering a superb view of Esztergom; and the collection of bejewelled croziers and kitsch papal souvenirs in the **treasury** (daily: May–Oct 9am–4.30pm; Feb–April, Nov & Dec 10am–4pm; 160Ft). The last is at the back of the nave, whose main altarpiece was painted by the Venetian Michelangelo Grigoletti, based on Titian's *Assumption* in the Frari Church in Venice. Don't miss the lavish red and white marble **Bakócz Chapel**, whose Florentine altar was salvaged from the original basilica that was destroyed by the Mongols.

The Castle Museum

Near the basilica are the reconstructed remains of the palace founded by Prince Géza, now presented as the **Castle Museum** (Tues–Sun: April–Oct 9am–5pm; Nov–March 10am–4pm; 160Ft). A royal seat for almost three hundred years, it was here that Béla III entertained Philip of France and Frederick Barbarossa on their way to the Third Crusade. The Renaissance prelate János Vitéz made it a centre of humanist culture, where Queen Beatrice spent her widowhood. Although it was sacked by the Turks and twice besieged before they were evicted in 1683, enough survived to be excavated in the 1930s. Traces of the frescoes that once covered every wall can be seen in the vaulted living hall from Béla III's reign, from which stairs ascend to the study of Archbishop Vitéz – known as the **Hall of Virtues** after its allegorical murals. Beyond lies the **royal chapel**, whose Gothic rose window and Romanesque arches were executed by craftsmen brought over by Béla's French wives, while the rooftop offers a panoramic view of Esztergom and the river.

During June and July, **plays** and **dances** are staged in the **Rondella** bastion on the hillside. Descending the hillside after your visit, notice the monumental **Dark Gate** – a tunnel built in the 1820s as a short cut between church buildings on either side of the hill – and the former primate's wine cellars, now the *Prímás Pince* restaurant.

The Víziváros and Prímás-Sziget

Below the castle ramparts lies the picturesque **Víziváros** district of Baroque churches and seminaries, where practising choirs can often be heard. Beyond the Italianate Baroque **Víziváros Parish Church**, the old Primate's Palace at Berényi utca 2 houses the **Christian Museum** (Tues–Sun 10am–6pm; 150Ft), Hungary's richest hoard of religious art, which includes the largest collection of Italian prints outside Italy; Renaissance paintings and wood carvings by German and Austrian masters; and the unique "Lord's Coffin of Garamszentbenedek", a wheeled, gilded structure used in Easter Week processions. From the parish church you can cross a bridge onto **Prímás-Sziget**, a popular recreation spot. A little way south of the landing stage for ferries to the Slovak town of Štúrovo, you'll see the elegant stump of the Mária Valeria **bridge** that connected the two towns before it was blown up in 1945.

LISTINGS

Accommodation

The range of **accommodation** in Budapest is increasing, but so are the prices, which are now far closer to Western European levels than ever before. Predictably, demand is heaviest and charges at their peak over summer, when the city can feel like it's bursting at the seams. Most hotels also raise their rates during the busy periods at Christmas and New Year, and for the Hungarian Grand Prix and the Autumn Music Weeks. Even so, it should always be possible to find somewhere that's reasonably priced, if not well situated.

Budget travellers will find that the majority of **hotels** are out of their range, even during low season (Nov–March, excluding New Year). **Pensions**, however, are cheaper: little different from smaller hotels, they often have en-suite bathrooms and other mod cons. For both hotels and pensions, it's essential to phone ahead and book.

If you're on a tight budget, your safest bet is a **private room**, arranged through a tourist agency. Though its location might not be perfect, the price should be reasonable and you can be sure of finding one at any time of year, day or night. Finally, the very cheapest options are generally **hostels**, which fill rapidly but can be unbeatable bargains, and **campsites**, where tent space can usually be found, even if all the bungalows are taken.

Of the city's four main **booking agencies**, listed below, both Cooptourist and Budapest Tourist specialize in private rooms and apartments, and the latter will also book bungalows. IBUSZ will make reservations in hotels, private rooms and apartments, while Express deals with the cheaper hostel and student-type accommodation. Note that Tourinform (see p.9) will not book accommodation, but can give information about where to look.

ACCOMMODATION PRICE CODES

All accommodation in this guide is graded according to the price bands given below. Note that prices refer to the **cheapest available double room in high season** or the price of **two people sharing a tent** in a campsite. 100Ft is roughly equivalent to $0.45 or DM1.

① Under 2000Ft
② 2000–4000Ft
③ 4000–6000Ft
④ 6000–8500Ft
⑤ 8500–13,000Ft
⑥ 13,000–20,000Ft
⑦ 20,000–27,000Ft
⑧ 27,000-40,000Ft
⑨ over 40,000Ft

ACCOMMODATION BOOKING AGENCIES

Budapest Tourist

Nyugati Station, downstairs in the underpass in front of the station ©332-6565. Mon–Fri 9am–5.30pm, Sat 9am–noon.
VIII, Baross tér 3, across the square from Keleti Station ©333-6587. Mon–Fri 9am–4.30pm.
Déli Station, in the mall by the metro entrance ©355-7167. Mon–Thurs 9am–5pm, Fri 9am–4pm.
VII, Erzsébet körút 41 ©342-6521. Mon–Thurs 10am–6pm, Fri 10am–5pm, Sat 9am–1pm.

V, Roosevelt tér 5 ©317-3555. Mon–Thurs 9am–4.30pm, Fri 9am–4pm.

Cooptourist

Skála Metro department store, opposite Nyugati Station ©312-3621. Mon–Fri 9am–4.30pm.
V, Bajcsy-Zsilinszky út 17 ©311-7034. Mon–Fri 9am–5pm.
V, Kossuth tér 13 ©332-6387. Mon, Tues, Thurs & Fri 8am–4pm, Wed 8am–5pm.

Express

V, Semmelweis utca 4 ©317-8845 or 317-8600. Mon–Thurs 8.30am–noon & 12.45–4.30pm, Fri 8.30am–noon & 12.45–3pm.

IBUSZ

Ferenciek tere 10, in the Párisi udvar on the corner of Petőfi Sándor utca ©318-1120. Mon–Fri 8.15am–5pm.
VII, Dob utca 1 ©322-7214. Mon–Fri 8am–6pm, Sat & Sun 8am–4pm.

HOTELS AND PENSIONS

Both hotels and pensions are in high demand, so it's sensible to **book** before leaving home or, failing that, through an agency (see above) or any airport tourist office on arrival. Star ratings give you a fair idea of standards, though facilities at some of the older three-star places don't compare with their Western equivalents, even if room prices are similar; you may get a better deal out of season, when almost all hotels reduce their rates.

The greatest choice of hotels can be found in **Pest**, where there's more in the way of restaurants and nightlife – and more traffic noise, too. The prime spots are along the river bank, with views across to Várhegy; having said that, all the really grand hotels were destroyed during the war, and their replacements don't quite have the same elegance. Staying out of the centre is a viable option, since most places are within reach of a metro station.

VÁRHEGY, VÍZIVÁROS, TABÁN AND GELLÉRT-HEGY

Alba Hotel

Map 5, E6. I, Apor Péter utca 3 ©375-9244. Bus #86 from Batthyány tér (M2).

Four-star hotel well situated by the Lánchíd, below Várhegy. Modern, comfy interior, but slightly lacking in atmosphere. Rooms have minibar and TV and there's an underground car park. ⑥.

Astra Hotel

Map 5, F3. I, Vám utca 6 ©214-1906. Batthyány tér metro (M2).

Brand-new small hotel in a converted 300-year-old building, at the foot of steps leading up to Várhegy. Nine well-furnished, a/c rooms with minibar. ⑥.

Budapest Hilton

Map 5, D3. I, Hess András tér 1–3 ©488-6600. Várbusz from Moszkva tér (M2).

By the Mátyás Church on Várhegy, with superb views across the river, this five-star hotel incorporates the remains of a medieval monastery and hosts summertime concerts in the former church. Luxurious to a fault. ⑧.

Dunapart Hotel

Map 5, G4. I, Szilágyi Dezső tér 33 ©355-9244. Batthyány tér metro (M2).

A floating four-star hotel moored upriver from the Lánchíd, open year-round unless ice endangers the boat. Rooms on the river side are quiet, and all are cramped enough to remind you that you're on a boat (only the suites have double beds). All rooms have a/c and TV; breakfast included. ⑥.

Gellért Hotel

Map 3, H14. XI, Szent Gellért tér 1 ©385-2200. Tram #47 or #49 from Deák tér.

One of Budapest's most famous old hotels, whose character will hopefully survive the hotel's gradual refurbishment. The facade, floodlit at night, is magnificent, as is the thermal pool (free for guests). The hotel's beer hall (*söröző*) serves good food and there's also an excellent coffee shop. ⑧.

Kulturinnov Hotel

Map 5, D3. I, Szentháromság tér 6 ©355-0122, fax 375-1886. Várbusz from Moszkva tér (M2).

First-floor hotel well positioned for sightseeing, in an extraordinary neo-Gothic building right by Mátyás Church. Spacious, quiet rooms; breakfast included. The hotel hosts cultural events, concerts and exhibitions. ⑤.

Victoria Hotel

Map 5, F5. I, Bem rakpart 11 ©457-8080. Bus #86 from Batthyány tér (M2).

Pleasant, small hotel on the embankment directly below the Mátyás Church, with excellent views of the Lánchíd and the river. A/c rooms have minibar and TV. Sauna and parking facilities. ⑥.

ÓBUDA, BUDA HILLS AND BEYOND

Beatrix Panzió

Map 2, B4. II, Szehér út 3 ©275-0550, fax 394-3730. Bus #56 from Moszkva tér (M2).

Friendly eighteen-room pension in the villa district northwest of Moszkva tér. There's a bar on the ground floor, plus a sauna. ⑤.

Budapest Hotel

Map 2, B5. II, Szilágyi Erzsébet fasor 47 ©202-0044. Bus #56 or tram #56 from Moszkva tér (M2).

Cylindrical tower facing the Buda Hills, opposite the lower terminal of the Cogwheel Railway, 500m from Moszkva tér. A recent refurbishment has slightly improved on the Seventies-look interior. Good views over city, especially from the café at the top. ⑥.

Buda Villa Panzió

Map 2, C5. XII, Kiss Áron utca 6 ©275-0091, fax 275-1687, *budapans@hungary.net*. Bus #156 from Moszkva tér (M2).

Comfortable small pension in the hills just above Moszkva tér. There's a bar in the lounge on the first floor; breakfast is included; and the small garden is perfect for relaxing in after a day's sightseeing. ⑤.

Csillaghegy Strand Hotel

Map 2, C5. III, Pusztakúti utca 3 ©368-4012. HÉV train to Csillaghegy from Batthyány tér (M2).

Situated in the northern suburbs, but only ten minutes by HÉV from Batthyány tér. Free entry to the hotel's outdoor thermal pool; breakfast included. ③.

Pál Vendégház Panzió

Map 7, A4. III, Pálvölgyi köz 15 ©388-7099. Bus #65 from Kolosy tér.

Small, welcoming pension with eight double rooms, situated in the hills near the Pálvölgy Stalactite Cave. ④.

Panda Hotel

Map 2, C4. II, Pasaréti út 133 ©394-1932, fax 394-1002, *panda@magnet.hu.* Bus #5 from Moszkva tér (M2).

Pleasant, modern hotel only a ten-minute bus ride from Moszkva tér. All rooms have TV and minibar, most have showers, and three have baths. Sauna available. ⑤.

San Marcó Panzió

Map 7, E4. III, San Marcó utca 6 ©388-9997. Bus #60 from Batthyány tér (M2).
Friendly Óbuda pension that's always highly recommended. Shared bathrooms. ④.

Touring Hotel

Map 2, E1. III, Pünkösdfürdő utca 38 ©250-3184. HÉV train to Békásmegyer from Batthyány tér (M2).
On the northern edge of the city, about 11km from centre, but only 15min by HÉV. Basic one-star hotel with tennis court, pool tables and restaurant. All rooms have TV and minibar and there's a swimming pool at the *strand* situated down the road. Ten percent discount for HI cardholders. ④.

Tusculanum Hotel

Map 2, E3. III, Záhony utca 10 ©388-7673. HÉV train to Aquincum from Batthyány tér (M2).
Comfortable, if characterless, new establishment, near the ruins of Aquincum. Rooms all come with bathroom and TV, and breakfast is included. Guests can use the tennis court next door. ⑤.

MARGIT SZIGET

Danubius Grand Hotel

Map 2, E4. XIII, Margit sziget ©329-2300. Bus #26 from Nyugati pu. (M3).
The island's original *fin-de-siècle* hotel, now totally refurbished for wealthy tourists here to enjoy the seclusion and fresh air. Its uglier modern sister hotel next door, the *Thermal*, is now home to the sauna, gym, and the thermal springs that made this a fashionable spa resort around the turn of the century. ⑧.

BELVÁROS

Art Hotel

Map 6, D8. V, Királyi Pál utca 12 ©266-2166, fax 266-2170. Kálvin tér metro (M3).

Small hotel in a quiet street near Kálvin tér. Rooms are cramped, but all have a/c, phone and TV (Hungarian and German channels). Facilities include a sauna, fitness room and laundry service. ⑥.

Astoria Hotel

Map 6, F6. V, Kossuth utca 19 ©317-3411, fax 318-6798, *astoria@hungary.net*. Astoria metro (M2).

Refurbished, vintage hotel on the major junction in central Pest to which it gave its name. Good-sized rooms all have a sofa, safe, minibar, phone and TV. As well as the wonderful coffee house, there's a restaurant complete with Hungarian gypsy band. ⑦.

Atrium Hyatt

Map 6, B1. V, Roosevelt tér 2 ©266-1234, fax 266-9101, *atriumhyatt@pannoniahotels.hu*. Vörösmarty tér metro (M1) or tram #2 to the Lánchíd.

Overlooking the Lánchíd and the Danube, this five-star hotel has just undergone a major refurbishment, with the atrium now dominated by a replica of one of the first Hungarian planes. Rooms are a/c, and feature all the facilities you'd expect; apartments are available too. The hotel has its own business centre, pool, gym and sauna. ⑨.

Carmen Mini Hotel

Map 6, F5. V, Károly körút 5/b ©352-0798. Deák tér (M1/2/3) or Astoria metro (M2).

Small hotel in a couple of converted flats in the centre of town, a minute's walk from the main synagogue. Rooms have TV, bath and shower. Breakfast included. ⑤.

City Panzió Mátyás

Map 6, B6. V, Március 15 tér 8 ©338-4700, fax 317-9086, *matyas@taverna.hu*. Ferenciek tere metro (M3).

Centrally located place offering simple rooms with TV, minibar, and a buffet breakfast in the *Mátyás Pince* restaurant downstairs, which is painted inside rather like the Mátyás Church. Overlooks the main road leading onto the Erzsébet híd, so ask for a courtyard room if you want some quiet, though corner rooms compensate with a great view of the river. Secure parking. ⑥.

ELTE Peregrinus Vendégház

Map 6, C8. V, Szerb utca 3 ©266-4911, fax 266-4913. Kálvin tér metro (M3).

Elegant but friendly place in a quiet street in central Pest. Double rooms are spacious with high ceilings but cramped bathrooms. It belongs to the university, and so all rooms have writing tables to meet the needs of academic visitors. Buffet breakfast included. ⑤.

Inter-Continental Hotel

Map 6, B1. V, Apáczai Csere János utca 12–14 ©327-6333, fax 327-6357, *budapest@interconti.com*. Vörösmarty tér metro (M1) or tram #2 to the Lánchíd.

Five-star hotel overlooking the Danube. Its recent purchase by the Inter-Continental chain is bringing a much needed refurbishment. Rooms have all the usual mod cons, but best of all is the first-floor *Bécsi Kávéház*, serving some of the finest cakes in the city. ⑧.

Kempinski Hotel Corvinus

Map 6, D3. V, Erzsébet tér 7–8 ©266-1000, fax 266-2000, *hotel@kempinski.hungary.net*. Deák tér metro (M1/2/3).

A flashy five-star establishment on the edge of the Belváros, which counts Madonna and Michael Jackson amongst past guests. Tastefully furnished rooms offer every luxury, right down to a phone extension in the bathroom. Swimming pool, sauna, solarium, fitness room and underground garage. ⑨.

K&K Opera

Map 4, C7. VI, Révay utca 24 ©269-0222, fax 269-0230, *kk.hotel.opera@kkhotel.hu*. Opera metro (M1).

Bright, modern and fully a/c four-star hotel by the Opera House, with its own parking space. Rooms – all with minibar, TV, safe and phone – are pleasantly furnished. Buffet breakfast included. ⑦–⑧.

Marriott Budapest

Map 6, B3. V, Apáczai Csere János utca 4 ©266-7000, fax 266-5000. Vörösmarty tér (M1) or Ferenciek tere metro (M3).

There's a view of the Danube from every room in this older, five-star hotel. Excellent buffet grill and an afternoon string quartet in the lounge area. Facilities include a sauna, squash court, parking and baby-sitting service. ⑨.

Medosz Hotel

Map 4, D5. VI, Jókai tér 9 ©374-3000. Oktogon metro (M1).

Ugly but comfortable hotel in a former trade union hostel overlooking a square near Oktogon. Small, bright rooms with bath and TV make this good value for the location. ④.

Nemzeti Hotel

Map 4, G9. VIII, József körút 4 ©269-9310, fax 314-0019, *nemzeti@pannoniahotels.hu*. Blaha Lujza tér metro (M2).

Small but elegant rooms in an Art Nouveau-style place overlooking Blaha Lujza tér. The bar and glass-roofed restaurant are both magnificent, albeit with a touch of the Seventies about them. Breakfast included. ⑥.

BEYOND THE NAGYKÖRÚT

Benczúr Hotel

Map 4, H3. VI, Benczúr utca 35 ©342-7970, fax 342-1558. Hősök tere metro (M1).

Modern, soulless hotel on a leafy street off Andrássy út, with a nice garden at the back and parking in the yard (850Ft extra). Pleasant rooms all have bath, TV and phone. In the other wing of the building is the *Hotel Pedagógus*, a sister establishment offering a few less frills and a slightly cheaper rate. ⑤–⑥.

Central Hotel

Map 4, H3. VI, Munkácsy Mihály utca 5–7 ©321-2000. Bajza utca metro (M1).

Spacious rooms with balconies in this former Communist Party hotel on the corner of Andrássy út. Pleasant wooden furniture and old wallpaper give the rooms a nice old-fashioned feel; all have TV and minibar. Even the bathrooms are spacious. Be warned that the rooms overlooking the main road are noisy. ⑥.

Radio Inn

Map 4, H3. VI, Benczúr utca 19 ©322-8437, fax 322-8284. Bajza utca metro (M1).

Spacious, if slightly gloomy rooms complete with kitchen, extra living room and TV. Situated in a leafy street, by the Chinese and Vietnamese embassies. Pleasant garden. ⑤.

Thermal Hotel Helia

Map 2, E4. XIII, Kárpát utca 62–64 ©270-3277. Trolleybus #79 from Margit híd or Dózsa György út (M3).

Finnish-owned modern four-star hotel with thermal baths, well situated near the river in northern Pest. ⑧.

HOSTELS

For those on a tight budget, **hostels** are definitely worth considering. By far the cheapest option is to stay in one of the numerous hostels converted from private flats, where beds and mattresses are crammed into every room. At the other end of the price scale are the privately run summer-only student dormitories, many located in the university area south of Gellért-hegy.

Finding a bed in a hostel is not difficult: arriving by international train, you'll get information whether you need it or not, and the larger hostel organizations – *Universum* and *More Than Ways* – even provide transport from the station to their hostels. Otherwise, the Tourist Information Centre office in Keleti Station (see p.7) has information on hostels and can make bookings (daily: June–Aug 7.30am–9pm; Sept–May 7.30am–7pm; ©343-0748). A Hostelling International card can be obtained from Express (see p.151) if needed, though in practice there don't seem to be any age or membership requirements.

Caterina Youth Hostel

Map 4, E6. V, Andrássy Út 47 ©291-9538 or 342-0804. Oktogon metro (M1). Open all year.

Thirty-two beds crammed into every corner of an apartment on the third floor of a grand block in Pest. Laundry facilities. ①.

Citadella

Map 3, G13. I, Citadella sétány ©466-5794. Bus #27 from Móricz Zsigmond körtér, then a ten-minute walk to the top of the hill. Open all year.

Romantically located right in the old citadel atop Gellért-hegy, with breathtaking views. Reservations can be made direct or through Budapest Tourist. Ten- and fourteen-bed dorms ① per person, doubles ④.

Diáksport Hotel

Map 2, F5. XIII, Dózsa György út 152 ©340-8585. Dózsa György út metro (M3). Open all year.

Singles, doubles and triples, plus dorms with four, six, nine and twelve beds. This is the centre of the *More Than Ways* student organization and, with a 24-hour bar, it's a lively place. Dorms ①, doubles ③.

KÉK Somogyi Kollégium

Map 2, E6. XI, Szüret utca 2–18 ©371-0066. Tram #61 from Moszkva tér or Móricz Zsigmond körtér. Open July & Aug.

Around the back of Gellért-hegy, double rooms in the hostel of the Gardeners' and Foresters' University. ③.

Hostel Landler

Map 2, E6. XI, Bartók Béla út 17 ©463-3621. Tram #47 or #49 from Deák tér (M1/2/3). Open July & Aug.

One of the older hostels, housed in the Baross Gábor Kollégium, near the Gellért Baths. Doubles ③.

Martos

Map 2, E6. XI, Sztoczek utca 5–7 ©463-3777. Tram #47 or #49 from Deák tér (M1/2/3). Open July & Aug.

Basic student accommodation near the Gellért Baths in the university district of the city. En-suite rooms are more expensive. Doubles ②–③.

Strawberry Youth Hostel

Map 4, E14. IX, Ráday utca 43–45 ©218-4766, or reservations 06-20/528-724. Kálvin tér metro (M3). Open July & Aug.

The older of two *Strawberry* hostels near Kálvin tér, with basic student hostel furniture in dorms or two- to six-bed rooms. Internet access. Discount for HI cardholders. ②.

Teréz Guest House

Map 4, G9. VIII, Bezerédj utca 6 ©333-2452. Blaha Lujza tér metro (M2). Open all year.

Cheapest of the cheap, with home cooking too. Two rooms in a private flat, jam-packed with beds and mattresses, ranging from 300 to 900Ft in price. Parking in courtyard. ①.

CAMPING

Budapest's **campsites** are generally well equipped and pleasant, with trees, grass and sometimes even a pool. They can be crowded between June and September, though, when smaller places might run out of space. It is, however, illegal to camp anywhere else, and the parks are patrolled to enforce this. The campsites listed here are all in Buda, since the Pest ones are far out and not very inviting. Tourinform (see p.9) can point you in their direction if you need them.

Csillebérci Camping

Map 2, B6. XII, Konkoly Thege M. út 21 ©395-6537. Bus #21 from Moszkva tér (M2), then a short walk. Open all year.

Large, well-equipped site with space for 1000 campers. A range of bungalows also available. 500Ft per person plus 600Ft tent fee, 1000Ft for a car.

Római-Fürdő Camping

Map 2, E2. III, Szentendrei út 189 ©368-6260. HÉV from Batthyány tér (M2). Open all year.

Huge site with space for 2500 campers beside the road to Szentendre in Római-Fürdő (25min by HÉV). Higher than average rates include use of the nearby swimming pool. 800Ft per person plus 700Ft tent fee, 1000Ft for a car.

Zugligeti Niche Camping

Map 2, B5. XII, Zugligeti út 101 ©200-8346. Bus #158 from Moszkva tér (M2). Open April–Oct.

Small, terraced ravine site in the woods with space for 260 campers and good facilities including a pleasant little restaurant occupying the former tram station at the far end. At the end of the #158 bus route, opposite the chairlift up to János-hegy. 600Ft per person plus 400Ft tent fee.

Restaurants

It's remarkably easy to spend your time in Budapest going from restaurant to coffee house, with a bit of sightseeing and shopping in between. The culinary scene has improved enormously in recent years, with the Hungarian love of food finally being translated into good food and service in its restaurants, giving the prospective diner a lot more choice – and satisfaction.

Though you can no longer dine like a king in the city's top restaurants for a penny, you can still eat very well without breaking the bank. Some of the places listed here are rough-and-ready, others glittering citadels of *haute cuisine* – it's worth checking out both ends of the spectrum. As forint **prices** rise continuously, we have classified restaurants in comparative terms. You should expect to pay no more than $11/£7 per head for a full meal with drinks in a **cheap** place; around $16/£10 in an **inexpensive** one; $23/£15 in a **moderate** restaurant; $40/£26 in an **expensive** one; and upwards of $55/£36 in a **very expensive** establishment. For places that we haven't included below, you can generally reckon that the further from the Belváros or Várhegy they are, the cheaper they are likely to be. Most restaurants with Hungarian gypsy bands will be touristy and expensive.

A food glossary

What follows is by no means a comprehensive list of Hungarian dishes, though by combining names and terms it should be possible to decipher most things that you're likely to see on a menu, or to ask for basic items.

Soups (*levesek*)

erőleves	meat consommé with noodles (*tésztával* or *metélttel*), liver dumplings (*májgombóccal*), or a raw egg placed into it (*tojással*)
gombaleves	mushroom soup
gulyásleves	goulash in its original Hungarian form as a soup
halászlé	a rich paprika fish soup
jókai bableves	bean soup flavoured with smoked meat
tarkonyos borjúraguleves	lamb soup flavoured with tarragon

Appetizers (*előételek*)

hortobágyi palacsinta	pancake stuffed with minced meat and served with creamy paprika sauce
körözött	a paprika-flavoured spread made with sheep's cheese and served with toast
rántott gomba	mushrooms fried in breadcrumbs, sometimes stuffed with sheep's cheese (*juhtúróval töltött*)

Fish dishes (*halételek*)

fogas	a local fish of the pike-perch family
harcsa	catfish

pisztráng	trout
ponty	carp

Meat dishes (*húsételek*)

bélszin	sirloin
csirke	chicken
kacsa	duck
kolbász	spicy sausage
liba	goose
máj	liver
marha	beef
őz	venison
sertés	pork
vaddisznó	wild boar
bécsi szelet	Wiener schnitzel
cigányrostélyos	"gypsy-style" steak with brown sauce
hagymás rostélyos	braised steak piled high with fried onions
paprikás csirke	chicken in paprika sauce

Accompaniments (*köretek*)

galuska	noodles
hasábburgonya	chips
krokett	potato croquettes
rizs	rice

Vegetables (*zöldségek*)

bab	beans
burgonya/krumpli	potatoes
gomba	mushrooms
hagyma	onions
lecsó	tomato and green pepper stew
káposzta	cabbage
paprika – édes or *erős*	peppers – sweet or hot

Snacks are covered at the end of this chapter, though you should also look at the chapters on bars and coffee houses as these sometimes serve food.

It's wise to **reserve** a table if you're determined to eat in a particular restaurant; if you haven't, and it's full, you can usually find an alternative within a couple of blocks. Booking is a must on August 20, St Stephen's Day, when restaurants fill up as the crowds who have been watching the firework displays by the Danube turn their thoughts to food.

The standard policy for **tipping** is to give an extra ten to fifteen percent of the total when you pay your bill. Some restaurants include this in their menu prices, but they will not always draw your attention to the fact. Don't be shy about querying the bill since even established restaurants can have a tendency to err when it comes to asking for money, and as a tourist you are an easy target for being ripped off. Favoured tactics include issuing menus without prices, hiking up the bill or charging exorbitant amounts for the wine. Be sure to check the price beforehand, especially if you are ordering any fancy extras, like expensive *Tokaji* dessert wines or foreign spirits.

RESTAURANTS

CENTRAL BUDA

Belga Söröző

Map 5, F5. I, Bem rakpart 12 ©201-5082. Batthyány tér (M2), then tram #19 or walk.

Daily noon–midnight. Moderate.

Basement restaurant with a small terrace overlooking the tramlines and the river. Good menu and a very large selection of Belgian beers.

Gusto's

Map 3, E2. II, Frankel Leo utca 12 ©316-3970. Tram #4 or #6 from Moszkva tér or the Nagykörút.

Mon–Sat 10am–10pm. Inexpensive.

A cosy little bar near the Buda side of Margit híd, with a small summertime terrace. Its small menu includes good salads and wines, as well as the best *tiramisu* in town. Booking essential.

Horgásztanya

Map 5, F4. I, Fő utca 27 ©201-3780. Batthyány tér (M2).

Daily noon–11pm. Inexpensive.

Fish restaurant near the river, whose specialities include several varieties of *halászlé* or fish soup, cooked with hot paprikas for extra bite and brought to your table in miniature kettle pans. Rather relaxed service.

Horváth

Map 5, A5. I, Krisztina tér 3. Tram #18 from Déli pu. (M2).

Daily noon–11pm. Inexpensive.

Small popular restaurant just down from Déli Station, near the tunnel beneath Várhegy. Despite its name, which means "Croat" in Hungarian, it serves traditional Hungarian dishes; the speciality of bone marrow served with toast and garlic is recommended.

Márkus Vendéglő

Map 3, B3. II, Lövőház utca 17 ©212-3153. Moszkva tér metro (M2).

Daily 9am–1am. Cheap.

Friendly Hungarian restaurant near Moszkva tér, with a small terrace facing the revamped market building. Serves reliable Hungarian food, such as Jókai bean soup and Wiener schnitzel with chips and pickled cucumbers.

Marxim

Map 3, C3. II, Kis Rókus utca 23. Tram #4 or #6 or a five-minute walk from Moszkva tér (M2).
Mon–Fri noon–1am, Sat noon–2am, Sun 6pm–1am. Cheap.
Popular pizza restaurant located just off Margit körút, whose decor makes humorous digs at Stalin and Communism in general.

Söröző a Szent Jupáthoz

Map 3, B4. II, Retek utca 16. Moszkva tér (M2).
Daily 24 hours. Cheap.
Steamy cellar just off Moszkva tér that's well known for its hearty servings of Hungarian stews and other meat dishes. Good for the starving.

ÓBUDA AND THE BUDA HILLS

Búfelejtő

Map 2, C6. XI, Németvölgyi út 136. Tram #59 from Moszkva tér (M2).
Daily 11am–midnight. Inexpensive.
The "Comforter" offers the consolation of fine Hungarian food and a pleasant terrace opposite the Farkasrét cemetery.

Fenyőgyöngye

Map 2, C4. II, Szépvölgyi út 155 ©325-9783. Bus #65 from Kolosy tér.
Daily noon–midnight. Inexpensive.
A pleasant restaurant out in the woods on the northwest edge of the city, serving standard Hungarian fare. Recommended are the Transylvanian stuffed cabbage, and the *Füredi Fimom Falatok* – spicy sausage wrapped in pork and served in a paprika sauce.

Gigler

Map 7, E2. III, Föld utca 50/c. Bus #60 from Batthyány tér (M2).
Tues–Sat noon–10pm, Sun noon–4pm. Inexpensive.
One of the few remaining old-style restaurants in Óbuda, located just downhill from the Kiscelli Museum (see p.64).

Family-run and frequented by locals, it offers good wine from the barrel and outside seating in a courtyard.

Kikelet Vendéglő

Map 2, D5. II, Fillér utca 85 ©212-5444. Bus #49 from Moszkva tér (M2).

Daily noon–midnight. Moderate.

On the Rózsadomb above Moszkva tér, with a view over the city and outside seating under the shade of chestnut trees. The tempting aroma from the barbecue wafts across the garden, but the menu is limited; ask what else they have on offer – usually garlic chicken. The beer's superior to the wine on offer.

Kisbuda Gyöngye

Map 7, E3. III, Kenyeres utca 34 ©368-6402. Bus #60 from Batthyány tér (M2).

Daily noon–midnight. Expensive.

Good food in finely decorated turn-of-the-century-style surroundings out in Óbuda. Pleasant courtyard and violin music. Booking essential.

Náncsi Néni

Map 2, B4. II, Ördögárok út 80 ©397-2742. Bus #56 from Moszkva tér (M2).

Daily noon–11pm. Moderate.

Popular garden restaurant in the leafy Hűvösvölgy, ten minutes' walk from the bus stop. Excellent food and a jolly atmosphere, with chequered tablecloths and live accordion music. The witty lines chalked up on boards around the garden include one saying "free glass of champagne for lovers". Booking essential.

CENTRAL PEST

Al-Amir

Map 4, D8. VII, Király utca 17 ©352-1422. Deák tér (M1/2/3).

Daily 11am–11pm. Inexpensive.
Syrian restaurant serving excellent salads and hummus, making it a haven for vegetarians in this city of carnivores. If that isn't enough, the array of Arabic sweets is also very enticing. No alcohol served.

Berlini Sörkatakomba ("Beer Catacombs")

Map 4, D12. IX, Ráday utca 9 ©217-6757. Kálvin tér (M3).
Daily 11am–3am. Inexpensive.
Smoky cellar restaurant near Kálvin tér with a genial atmosphere; popular with the younger generation. Serves up lots of that old Hungarian staple – different meats deep-fried in breadcrumbs.

Biarritz

Map 4, A4. V, Balassi Bálint uca 2 ©302-3943. Kossuth tér (M2).
Daily 11am–midnight. Moderate.
Close to Parliament, with a small summer terrace. Good salads and light dishes, and a cheery environment.

Café Kör

Map 6, E1. V, Sas utca 17 ©311-0053. Arany János utca metro (M3).
Mon–Sat 10am–10pm. Moderate.
Popular and airy café-cum-restaurant near the Basilica. The menu of flavoursome grilled meats and salads is supplemented by specials written up on the wall. The pike-perch in garlic sauce, and the grilled Gomolya cheese with salad are both recommended. Booking essential.

Cyrano

Map 6, C3. V, Kristóf tér 7-8 ©266-3096. Vörösmarty tér metro (M1).
Daily 11am–5pm & 6.30pm–midnight. Expensive.
Standards are high in this popular joint close to Vörösmarty tér, which has a designer interior and designer-clad waiters. The movie *Cyrano* was filmed partly in Hungary, and the restaurant's chandelier was used on the set, hence its name.

Fatál

Map 6, B8. V, Váci utca 67 ©266-2607. Ferenciek tere (M3).
Daily 11.30pm–2am. Inexpensive.

Don't be deterred by the name of this place, which means "Wooden Dish" in Hungarian. Servings are gargantuan, but avoid the "vegetable feast", which is mostly batter. Guests have to endure an embarrassing wait on arrival behind the velvet rope at the bottom of the steep stairs, and solo diners are relegated to the long table at the end. Check the bill, as mistakes are not unknown. The entrance is on Pintér utca, a narrow alley off Váci utca, down towards the Nagycsarnok.

Fausto's

Map 6, G6. VII, Dohány utca 3 ©269-6806. Astoria metro (M2).
Daily noon–3pm & 7pm–midnight. Expensive.

Fresh daily specials and homemade pasta in perhaps the best Italian restaurant in town, located near the main synagogue. Specializes in food from northern Italy, and has a good selection of Italian wines and spirits.

Fészek Klub

Map 4, E7. VII, Kertész utca 36 ©322-6043. Tram #4 or #6 from Nyugati tér (M3) or Blaha Lujza tér (M2).
Daily noon–2am. Inexpensive.

A long-established artists' club that draws many of its diners from that world. Delightful leafy courtyard for summer dining, with cool arcades and a grand dining room in winter, though the food and service can be a letdown. Entry 50Ft unless you book in advance.

Gandhi

Map 4, A7. V, Vigyázó Ferenc utca 4 ©269-4944. Tram #2 to Roosevelt tér.
Daily noon–11pm. Cheap.

Despite its name, this vegetarian cellar restaurant near Roosevelt tér is not limited to Indian cuisine, offering two set menus, a wide selection of salads, and forty types of tea. It's all very meditative and calming, with prayer wheels for the Hindu, Buddhist, Muslim, Jewish and Christian faiths – Gandhi apparently named all five when asked which religion he belonged to.

Govinda

Map 6, A7. V, Belgrád rakpart 18. Ferenciek tere (M3).

Tues–Sun noon–9pm. Cheap.

Hare Krishna vegetarian restaurant overlooking the river. Serves good set meals, accompanied by the whiff of soporific incense. No alcohol served. No credit cards.

King's Hotel

Map 4, E8. VII, Nagydiófa utca 25–27 ©352-7675. Tram #4 or #6 from Nyugati tér (M3) or Blaha Lujza tér (M2).

Daily noon–9.30pm. Moderate.

Mehadrin kosher food – in a town where it's hard to find much that's kosher – in the old Jewish ghetto five minutes' walk from the Dohány utca synagogue.

Kiskacsa

Map 4, D8. VII, Dob utca 26, Deák tér metro (M1/2/3).

Mon–Sat noon–11pm. Cheap.

Small friendly joint ten minutes up from the big synagogue, serving traditional Hungarian fare. You get three dice with your bill and if you roll three sixes your meal is on the house.

Krónikás

Map 4, B2. XIII, Tátra utca 2 ©269-5048. Tram #4 or #6 from Nyugati tér (M3) or tram #2 from Kossuth tér (M2).

Daily noon–midnight. Moderate.

Excellent cellar restaurant just off the Szent István körút near the Margit híd, with a good range of vegetarian dishes on the menu. Of the desserts, the *turógombóc* is a Hungarian favourite that deserves a mention – a delicious breadcrumbed large ball of curd cheese and sour cream sprinkled with sugar.

Lou Lou

Map 4, A7. V, Vigyázó Ferenc utca 4 ©312-4505. Tram #2 to Roosevelt tér.

Mon–Fri noon–3pm & 7pm–midnight, Sat 7pm–midnight.

Atmospheric small French restaurant near the Lánchíd, serving excellent French and Hungarian food, supported by a good wine list. Booking strongly advised.

Marquis de Salade

Map 4, C5. VI, Hajós utca 43 ©302-4086. Arany János utca metro (M3).

Daily 11am–midnight. Moderate.

Trendy place that has just expanded into a vast downstairs section, offering Japanese, Greek, Azerbaijani and other cuisines. Zesty salads make this a favourite destination for vegetarians. Special business lunch offer from 11am to 6pm. No credit cards.

Mérleg

Map 6, C1. V, Mérleg utca 6 ©317-5910. Deák tér metro (M1/2/3) or Tram #2 to the Lánchíd.

Mon–Sat 8am–11pm. Inexpensive.

Small, popular place near the Lánchíd, serving simple Hungarian food.

Múzeum Kávéház

Map 6, E8. VIII, Múzeum körút 12 ©267-0375. Astoria metro (M2).

Mon–Sat 10am–1am. Expensive.

Excellent food in a grand setting next to the Hungarian National Museum. The interior decoration dates from 1885, and includes Zsolnay porcelain tiles from Pécs in southern Hungary and frescoes by Károly Lotz. Attentive service, quiet piano music, and a massive tome of a menu. Specialities of the house are the turkey or beef "Museum-style" – wrapped up in bacon and served with a dill sauce with mushrooms and delicious garlic noodles. Booking essential.

Okay Italia

Map 4, C3. XIII, Szent István körút 20. Nyugati pu. metro (M3).
Daily noon–midnight. Inexpensive.
One of the most popular Italian restaurants in Budapest, and not just because of the mini-skirted waitresses. Bright interior, speedy service, and delicious pasta and pizza.

Shalimar

Map 4, E7. VII, Dob utca 50 ©352-0297. Tram #4 or #6 from Nyugati tér (M3) or Blaha Lujza tér (M2).
Daily noon–1am. Inexpensive.
Indian cellar restaurant on the edge of the Jewish quarter. The standard of food is helped by the presence of an Indian chef, though it's let down by a shortage of authentic ingredients.

Via Luna

Map 4, C6. V, Nagysándor József utca 1 ©312-8058. Arany János utca metro (M3).
Daily noon–11.30pm. Inexpensive.
Popular Italian restaurant a few minutes' walk from Szabadság tér. Widely spaced tables, with bunches of dried herbs decorating the interior, giving a rustic trattoria feel. Good fresh salads, soups, and Parma ham, but the canned vegetables and olives would cause a scandal if the restaurant was in Italy.

OUTER PEST

Bagolyvár

Map 4, H1. XIV, Állatkerti körút 20 ©321-3550. Hősök tere (M1).
Daily noon–11pm. Moderate.

Sister to the illustrious *Gundel* restaurant next door (see below), so standards are high, but prices much lower. Prides itself on creating the atmosphere of a prewar middle-class home and serves up home-style cooking to match. Pleasant terrace backing onto the zoo.

Chez Daniel

Map 4, E4. VI, Szív utca 32 ©302-4039. Kodály körönd metro (M1).

Daily noon–10.30pm. Expensive.

An excellent French restaurant in a cellar, run by idiosyncratic master chef, Daniel, that's arguably the best in town. The new courtyard dining area has just the right atmosphere. Booking recommended.

Gundel

Map 4, H1. Állatkerti körút 2 ©321-3550. Hősök tere (M1).

Daily noon–4pm & 7pm–midnight. Very expensive.

Budapest's most famous restaurant since 1894, it's now run by the Hungarian-American restaurateur, George Lang. Zsolnay porcelain and silver service, a ballroom, garden and terrace and a gypsy band maintain the atmosphere of elegance from before the war, when *Gundel* was the haunt of Budapest's social elite. Its menu is fantastically expensive, though the all-you-can-eat Sunday brunch (11am–3pm; 3400Ft) offers a cheaper way to sample its delights. Booking and smart dress required.

Kispesti Halásztanya

Map 2, H8. XIX, Városház tér ©282-9873. Kőbánya-Kispest metro (M3), then bus #93.

Daily 11am–midnight. Moderate.

Established fish restaurant with a huge terrrace, out in the suburb of Kispest. Excellent catfish and carp dishes in a traditional style, served to the strains of a Hungarian gypsy band, make the long trip worthwhile. No credit cards.

Paprika Csárda

Map 4, I4. XIV, Dózsa György út 72 ©352-1380. Hősök tere metro (M1).
Daily 10am–11pm. Cheap.
No-frills eatery with a terrace on the edge of the Városliget, ten minutes' walk from the Museum of Fine Arts. Traditional Hungarian dishes featuring lots of paprika, including some fine fish recipes – with fresh fish if they come from the gruesome tanks in the window.

FAST FOOD AND SNACKS

Budapest has taken to **fast food** in a big way, and new fast-food outlets and snack bars are opening all the time. A Hungarian institution is the *Étkezde* – a small, lunchtime diner where customers share tables and eat hearty homecooked food. None of the places listed below takes credit cards.

Duran Sandwich Bar

Map 4, B7. V, Október 6 utca 15. Arany János utca metro (M3).
Mon–Fri 8am–6pm, Sat 9am–1pm.
A sandwich and coffee bar – still a rare combination in Budapest, oddly enough.

Falafel

Map 4, D6. VI, Paulay Ede utca 53. Opera metro (M1).
Mon–Fri 10am–8pm, Sat 10am–6pm.
Small self-service falafel joint five minutes' walk from the Opera House. You can eat as much as you can cram into the pitta bread. Some seating in the upstairs gallery.

Gresham Borozó

Map 6, C1. V, Mérleg utca 2. Deák tér metro (M1/2/3) or tram #2 along the Pest riverbank to the Lánchíd.
Mon–Fri 7am–10pm, Sun 8am–4pm.
Good Hungarian food, fast service, and the staff can help you

with the menu, which is written in Hungarian. Packed out with diners at lunchtime, when it's non-smoking, but more of a bar in the evenings.

Kádár Étkezde

Map 4, E8. VII, Klauzál tér 10. Tram #4 or #6 from Nyugati tér (M3) or Blaha Lujza tér (M2).

Mon–Sat 11.30am–3.30pm; closed mid-July to mid-Aug.

Cheap lunch place in the heart of the Jewish quarter. The food, such as *sólet*, the bean stew speciality served on Fridays and Saturdays, is that of the non-kosher assimilated Budapest Jewry. Friendly atmosphere, with diners sharing tables equipped with soda siphons, and photos and caricatures of Hungarian and visiting celebrities on the walls.

Marie Kristensen Sandwich Bar

Map 4, E12. IX, Ráday utca 7. Kálvin tér metro (M3).

Mon–Fri 10am–8pm.

In theory this place behind Kálvin tér has a Danish flavour, but in practice it is basically a decent regular sandwich bar.

Mini Étkezde

Map 4, E7. VII, Dob utca 45. Tram #4 or #6 from Nyugati tér (M3) or Blaha Lujza tér (M2).

Mon–Fri 11.30am–3pm; closed mid-July to mid-Aug.

Another cheap lunchtime diner just off Klauzál tér.

New York Bagels

Map 4, E6. VI, Bajcsy-Zsilinszky út 21. Arany János utca metro (M3). **Map 6, F6.** Top of the East-West Centre. Astoria metro (M2).

Mon–Fri 7am–10pm, Sat & Sun 9am–10pm.

A chain restaurant with outlets around the city, serving New York-style bagels and fillings – and they have English-language papers to read. The *Astoria* branch has great views.

Self-service Canteen

Map 6, B2. V, Szende Pál utca 3. Vörösmarty tér metro (M1).

Mon–Fri noon–3pm.

Standard Hungarian food at this super-cheap lunch spot just round the corner from Vörösmarty tér.

Zöldfaló Salad Bar

Map 3, B5. XII, Csaba utca 8 (entrance in Hajnóczy utca). Moszkva tér metro (M2).

Mon–Fri 10am–6pm.

Five minutes' walk from Moszkva tér, this place serves good falafels and as much salad as you can eat.

Coffee houses and patisseries

Coffee houses (kávéház) are one of the city's big treats. At the end of the nineteenth century Budapest had hundreds of them, providing meeting places for the city's bohemian intelligentsia – artists, writers, journalists and lawyers. Living conditions in the rapidly growing city were often poor, and the coffee houses offered warmth and a place to work, with sympathy drinks or credit for those down on their luck. Stories abound of the quirks of some of the regulars, such as the writer who would always come to his table at three o'clock in the morning and work all night by candlelight.

Today's coffee houses and **patisseries** (*cukrászda*) are less romantic but still full of character, whether fabulously opulent, with silver service, or homely and idiosyncratic. They are still very much in use, with daily life in Budapest punctuated by the consumption of black coffee drunk from little glasses or cups (*eszpresszó*), though cappuccinos are now standard fare too.

BUDA

Angelika

Map 3, F5. I, Batthyány tér 7. Batthyány tér metro (M2).

Daily 10am–8pm.

Quiet, old-fashioned place with large, comfortable furniture in beautiful vaulted rooms next to St Anne's Church in the Víziváros.

Daubner

Map 7, E7. II, Szépvölgyi út 20. Bus #60 from Batthyány tér.

Daily 10am–7pm.

Ten minutes' walk up from Kolosy tér, towards the Pálvölgyi Caves. Excellent cakes and pastries: recommended are the *szilvás papucs* (plum slippers) – plums folded in a Danish pastry. The long queues at weekends testify to the place's popularity.

Miró

Map 5, C3. I, Úri utca 30. Várbusz from Moszkva tér metro (M2).

Daily 9am–midnight.

Groovy place with a young, relaxed atmosphere, down the road from the Mátyás Church on Várhegy. Furnished in a Miróesque style, with curious, not very comfortable, chairs. Snacks and sandwiches.

Ruszwurm

Map 5, D3. I, Szentháromság tér 7. Várbusz from Moszkva tér metro (M2).

Daily 10am–8pm.

Diminutive Baroque coffee house near the Mátyás Church that is the oldest in Budapest, operating since 1827. Almost impossible to get a seat in summer. Delicious cakes and ices.

PEST

Astoria Kávéház

Map 6, F6. V, Kossuth utca 19. Astoria metro (M2).

Daily 7am–11pm.

A grand, turn-of-the-century coffee house-cum-bar on the ground floor of the *Astoria Hotel*, whose central location makes it a convenient meeting place. You can sit around in small leather armchairs and watch the locals discuss their business.

Bécsi Kávéház

Map 6, B1. V, Apáczai Csere János utca 12. Vörösmarty tér metro (M1) or tram #2 to the Lánchíd.

Daily 9am–9pm.

On the first floor of the *Inter-Continental Hotel*, this place is said by many to have the best cakes in the city. Smooth service and, if you are lucky, a table by the window overlooking the river.

Eckermann

Map 4, D6. VI, Andrássy út 24. Opera metro (M1).

Mon–Fri 8am–10pm, Sat 9am–10pm.

Café near the Opera House, set up by the Goethe Institute next door. Excellent large coffees, tasty Balkan *burek* pastry and other snacks, and free Internet access.

Frölich

Map 4, D8. VII, Dob utca 22. Deák tér metro (M1/2/3) or Astoria metro (M2).

Tues–Thurs 8am–5pm, Fri 8am–2pm; closed Jewish holidays.

A kosher patisserie five minutes' walk from the Dohány utca synagogue, presided over by the cheery Mrs Frölich and her daughter. Mr Frölich appears from time to time covered in flour in his cake-stained overalls bearing specialities like *flodni*, an apple, walnut and poppy-seed cake.

Gerbeaud

Map 6, C2. V, Vörösmarty tér 7. Vörösmarty tér metro (M1).

Daily 9am–10pm.

A Budapest institution with a gilded salon and terrace. Popular with tourists, the cakes are great and the creamy and chocolatey Mexican coffee superb – though it's quite pricey. The *Kis Gerbeaud* round the corner is a cheaper, stand-up version.

Ibolya

Map 6, C6. V, Ferenciek tere 5. Ferenciek tere metro (M3).

Daily 6am–10pm.

Iced coffee outside in the summer, or sticky cakes, *Szalon sör* (a beer from the southern Hungarian town of Pécs), and a smoky atmosphere indoors all year round.

István Cukrászda

Map 4, B7. V, Október 6 utca 17. Arany János utca metro (M3).

Daily 10am–6pm.

Small cake shop near the Basilica. You pay for your cakes and coffee on the ground floor, then head upstairs to find a table. Your order arrives on the mini-lift.

Kaffee Károlyi

Map 6, D7. V, Károlyi Mihály utca. Ferenciek tere metro (M3).

Daily 9am–9pm.

A minute's walk from Ferenciek tere. Good Italian coffee, served to the sounds of the 1970s and 1980s.

Király

Map 4, D8. V, Király utca 19. Deák tér metro (M1/2/3).

Daily 10am–midnight.

Cosy café above a patisserie serving delicious cakes and ice cream, all made on the premises.

Lukács

Map 4, F4. VI, Andrássy út 70. Kodály körönd metro (M1).

Mon–Fri 8am–8pm, Sat & Sun 10am–8pm.

One of the older coffee houses, recently restored to its full grandeur. In the 1950s this was apparently the local café for the

Communist secret police, who had their headquarters down the road at no. 60.

Múzeum Cukrászda

Map 6, F7. VIII, Múzeum körút 10. Astoria metro (M2).
Daily 24 hours.
Friendly hangout next to the National Museum, with *pogácsa* (cheese scones) on the table. Fresh pastries arrive early in the morning.

Művész

Map 4, D6. VI, Andrássy út 29. Opera metro (M1).
Daily 8am–midnight.
Stunning old coffee house that's now getting a bit shabby. Valued for its location, just across from the Opera House, its decor and its clientele – mainly writers and fur-hatted old ladies. The cakes and service are average.

New York

Map 4, F8. VII, Erzsébet körút 9–11. Blaha Lujza tér metro (M2).
Daily 9am–10pm.
The cappuccinos and cocktails are mediocre, but the opportunity to admire the wonderful Art Nouveau decor is more than worth the cost. Cavorting satyrs, nymphs and cherubs, lashings of gold leaf, and caricatures of journalists who frequented the place in the 1950s and 1960s all decorate the walls. The exterior was rammed by a Soviet tank during the Uprising and still looks a mess. There's a restaurant downstairs, but it's overpriced and nothing special.

Szalay

Map 4, A5. V, Balassi Bálint utca 5. Kossuth tér metro (M2).
Wed–Sun 8am–4pm.
Just near the Parliament, this is one of the few remaining old-style cake shops in Budapest, run by a dynasty of bakers. Excellent cakes and ice creams.

Zsolnay

Map 4, D4. VI, Teréz körút 43. Nyugati pu. metro (M3).

Daily 10am–10pm.

In spite of its unlikely location on the first floor of the *Béke Radisson Hotel* and its modern interior, the *Zsolnay* is a popular meeting place. Its cakes, served on Zsolnay porcelain, are close contenders for the best in town.

Bars and clubs

Budapest's nightlife scene is small – spend a few evenings drinking and clubbing and you'll be spotting familiar faces – but it's constantly changing, with venues opening and closing, becoming the place to be seen or losing their credibility.

Insofar as you can generalize, most places that style themselves "**drinkbars**" mainly serve cocktails. The majority of *borozó* or **wine bars** are nothing like their counterparts in the West, being mainly working men's watering holes. Conversely, **beer halls** (*söröző*) are often quite upmarket, striving to resemble an English pub or a German bierkeller, and serving full meals. The addition of *pince* to the name of an outlet for wine (*bor*) or beer (*sör*) signifies that it is in a cellar. Most places open around lunchtime and stay open until after midnight, though bars with outdoor seating usually close at 10pm.

Some **clubs** and **discos** in the city are still run under the aegis of universities, though there are an increasing number of private ventures, some of which have a fairly strict entrance policy. It's hard to draw a firm line between drinking and dancing places, as many bars play live music or have a disco. Various mafias operate in town – Russian, Ukrainian, and others – and there is a big demand for bouncers, whose presence is felt at many of the bars and clubs in town. The best advice is not to mess with them.

BARS

BUDA

Bambi

Map 3, F2. I, Frankl Leó utca 2–4.

Mon–Fri 7am–9pm, Sat & Sun 9am–8pm.

One of the few surviving Socialist-Realist bars, with red plastic-covered seats and stern waitresses serving drinks, plus breakfast, lunch, snacks and cakes all day long.

Kecskeméti Borozó

Map 3, C4. II, Széna tér.

Mon–Sat 9am–11pm.

Smoky, sweaty and crowded stand-up wine bar by Moszkva tér, on the corner of Retek utca. A notice on the wall says: "We do not serve drunks", but this warning doesn't seem to be put into practice. However, they do serve up that staple Hungarian bar fare, *zsirós kenyér,* bread with lard, paprika and onions.

Kisposta

Map 3, B5. XII, Krisztina körút 6.

Mon–Sat 8am–midnight, Sun 9am–11pm.

The "Little Post Office" has managed to preserve its 1960s interior and unique atmosphere. A collection of drunks and assorted others dance to the sounds of Tibor and his drum machine playing Hungarian classics and foreign golden oldies, though you might struggle to recognize them. An experience.

Libella

Map 3, I14. XI, Budafoki út 7.

Mon–Sat 8am–11pm, Sun 10am–11pm.

Friendly unmarked bar near the *Gellért Hotel.* A young, alternative crowd comes here for bar snacks, chess and draughts.

Miniatűr Eszpresszó

Map 3, D2. II, Rózsahegy utca 1.

Mon–Sat 7pm–3am.

Small bohemian bar with red velvet furnishings and piano music after 9pm. If you win approval from the owner, you get to sit in the inner room by the pianist.

Móri Borozó

Map 3, C4. I, Fiáth János utca 16.

June–Aug daily 4–11pm; Sept–May Mon–Sat 2–11pm, Sun 2–9pm.

This cheap and cheerful neighbourhood wine bar just up from Moszkva tér, opposite the extraordinary Swan House shopping complex, attracts a young crowd. Darts and bar billiards in the room at the far end.

Park Café

Map 2, E6. XI, Kosztolányi Dezső tér 2.

Daily noon–5pm.

Trendy music bar in the middle of a park by the Feneketlen-tó (Bottomless Lake) where the city's bright young things go to see and be seen. An ideal location in summer, when customers spill out into the park. Occasional live acts.

Rácz kert Söröző

Map 3, F11. I, Hadnagy utca 12, by the Rác Baths.

March–Oct daily 5pm until late.

This place on the edge of the Tabán is one of the few places where you can drink outside after 10pm, as there are no neighbours to disturb. Excellent atmosphere and good bar snacks and food.

Teázó

Map 3, F10. I, Attila út 27.

Daily 11am–1am.

Quiet place near Dózsa György tér, west of Várhegy, that specializes in tea, but sells alcohol too.

Vinceller Borozó

Map 3, E4. I, Fő utca 71.

Daily 8am–10pm.

Agreeable wine cellar down the road from the Király Baths.

PEST

Café Mediterrán

Map 4, E6. VI, Liszt Ferenc tér 11.

Daily 10am–2pm.

There's a relaxed atmosphere in this place, which has red walls, cane furniture and an outdoor terrace and offers English bitter on tap.

Café Pardon

Map 4, D4. VI, Szondi utca 11.

Daily 10am–1am.

If they have the ingredients, they'll mix you the cocktail of your choice – otherwise it's Czech beer, with the accompaniment of live piano music. This is a fun place for a post-dinner drink.

Café Vian

Map 4, E6. VI, Liszt Ferenc tér 9.

Daily 10am–midnight.

Relaxed place with a light interior, offering drinks, various cocktails and a big selection of "French bistro food" (sandwiches, salads, desserts and homemade pastries). Cabaret/music shows three times a week.

Crazy Café

Map 4, D4. VI, Jókai utca 30.

Open noon–1am.

Lively and very long cellar bar with a huge variety of beer and a karaoke machine.

Darshan Udvar

Map 4, F12. VIII, Krúdy Gyula utca 7.

Mon–Wed 11am–midnight, Thurs & Fri 11am–2am, Sat & Sun 6pm–midnight.

This is the largest bar in a growing complex of bars, cafés and shops. Set at the back of a courtyard, with oriental/hippy decorations, good food and world music. The service is leisurely.

Paris-Texas

Map 4, E13. IX, Ráday utca 22.

Daily 9am–dawn.

Stylish bar near Kálvin tér with a very French atmosphere. Good bar snacks.

Portside

Map 6, G6. VII, Dohány utca 7.

Sun–Thurs noon–2am, Fri & Sat noon–4am.

Large cellar bar offering beer and delicious food – the grilled cheese with vegetables is a vegetarian's delight. Pool tables to the left of the entrance.

Sixtusi Kápolna

Map 4, E8. VII, Nagydiófa utca 24.

Mon–Sat 6pm–1am. Usually closed during the Sziget Festival in mid-Aug.

The "Sistine Chapel" is rather like the brown bars of Amsterdam, attracting a friendly crowd of non-business expats. There is no street sign announcing the place, just two steamed-up windows.

Talk-Talk Café

Map 6, E7. V, Magyar utca 12–14.

Daily 9pm–1am.

There's a good atmosphere in this bar just behind the *Astoria Hotel*, though it's marred by slow service.

DANCE SPOTS

With posters all around town advertising raves and discos, it won't take long to find your way around Budapest's small clubbing scene. In addition to the places listed below, you'll also find raves advertised in the **Almássy tér Centre** (Map 4, G7), at two tram sheds (*remiz*) at XI, Bartók Béla út 137 (Map 2, D7) and II, Budakeszi út 3 (Map 2, C5). For a different experience, look out for the regular cinetrip raves held at the Rudas Baths (*www.c3.hu/cinetrip/*), with films and weird lighting alongside the music. All the places listed below, with the exception of *Vox*, are in Pest.

E-Klub

Map 2, G6. X, Népliget (at the Planetarium).

Fri & Sat 8pm–5am.

Formerly in block E of the Technical University across the

Turntable wizards

Budapest may not rate as the rave capital of the world, but it has thrown up a few local stars. Names to look out for include DJ Palotai, probably the best underground name on the circuit, and close behind, DJ Cadik, DJ Titus and DJ Mango, who are all **drum'n'bass DJs**. You can find them at raves organized around town by the pirate radio station, Tilos Rádió. If you're into **goa**, the slightly gentler version of your run-of-the-mill techno, look out for DJ Virág and Oleg. Of the **mainstream** DJs, the best names are DJ Pedro, a regular at the *Underground* bar, and DJ Tommy Boy, both playing mainly acid jazz. One other master of the turntables is London-based DJ Norman Austin, an expert in house music.

river, this once-wild cattle market for engineering students has been exiled to outer Pest. Today a more mixed crowd packs the two discos on different floors, and there's beer galore. Live rock music on Fridays.

E-Play

Map 4, C–D3. VI, Teréz körút 55.

Thurs–Sat 8pm–dawn.

Housed in the top of the magnificent Nyugati Station, this is a newly decked-out techno haunt for the fast and flashy.

Garage Café

Map 4, B7. V, Arany János utca 9

Daily 11am–2am.

Cool, spacious and hip bar with a brick interior and a restaurant serving excellent food. Wednesday is the best night for dancing, with house DJ Tommy Boy.

Közgáz DC

Map 4, D13. IX, Fővám tér 8.

Fri 8.30pm–3am.

Massive, sweaty party scene at the southern end of the Economics University, with a live rock band and non-stop disco, two films and a karaoke show, plus a "tea house", ice-cream bar and lots of beer.

Made Inn

Map 4, G3. VI, Andrássy út 112.

Restaurant: daily noon–3am. Dancing: Wed–Sun 10pm–4am.

You can't miss the gleaming sports cars parked outside this ultra-trendy disco and hangout for jetsetters, dressed (or barely dressed) in the flashiest MTV fashions. The outdoor patio is packed in summer, and there's good food in the restaurant on the ground floor. Live bands play most Fridays, with a Greek band most Sundays. Cover 500Ft.

Nincs Pardon

Map 4, G7. VIII, Almássy tér 11.

Daily noon–4am.

Bar/nightclub with a small dance floor, variable music, and open sandwiches at the bar. Packed on Saturdays.

Old Man's Music Pub

Map 4, F8. VII. Akácfa utca 13.

Daily 3pm–dawn.

Very popular place in the centre of town, though expensive by Hungarian standards. Good for dancing and Hungarian food.

Petőfi Csarnok

Map 2, F5. XIV, Zichy Mihály út 14.

The raves organized by Tilós Rádió and other DJs are the best dance events at this large youth centre near the back of the Városliget. Otherwise it offers everything from Greek folk dancing (Sun in summer) down to the Kelly Family club. Turn up on the wrong night and you'll stumble into the Star Trek club.

Piaf

Map 4, D6. VI, Nagymező utca 20.

Daily 10pm to well after dawn.

This fashionable bar on "Broadway" charges 300Ft to enter unless you know a regular and can say their name at the door (you have to ring). Basically it's a room and a cellar graced by the odd film star and lots of wannabes, with occasional jazz or rock sets.

Süss fel nap

Map 4, B3. V, corner of Honvéd utca and Szent István körút.

Daily 8pm–4am.

Big club with endless small rooms all filled to bursting by a young crowd. Mixed music and occasional live acts.

The Club

Map 6, B2. V, Apáczai Csere János utca 13.

Daily 10.30pm–2am.

Cavernous place with two bars and a spacious dance floor. Models of angels hang from the ceiling, but the crowd is far from angelic. Regular house and techno.

Trocadero (Franklin Trocadero)

Map 4, B3. V, Szent István körút 15.

Tues–Sat 9pm–4am.

The best place in town for Latin music, and the best dancers too. Hot and steamy once it gets going.

Undergrass

Map 4, E6. VI, Liszt Ferenc tér 10.

Daily 7pm–4am.

Funky music in this air-conditioned dance bar under the *Café Mediterrán*.

Underground

Map 4, D5. VI, Teréz körút 30.

Wed–Sat 8pm–5am, Mon, Tues & Sun 8pm–1am.

Live music, if there is any, begins at 8pm. There's a small dance space, but to be honest it's better here for just hanging out, drinking and eating – the food is surprisingly good. DJ Pedro is one of the star DJs you'll find here.

Vox

Map 3, B2. II, Márcibányi tér 5/a.

Daily 8pm–3am.

Live acts and funky music in this popular dive near Moszkva tér.

Gay Budapest

Budapest's gay scene has taken wing in recent years, with new, openly gay clubs replacing the old, covert meeting places, and the appearance of a trilingual monthly listings magazine, *Mások* ("Outsiders"). However, gays must still tread warily as attitudes can be hostile, and lesbians remain several steps behind. The Magyar euphemism for gay is *meleg* – warm.

Aside from the places listed below, the Király Baths and, to a lesser extent, the Rudas Baths and the sun terrace of Palatinus pool on Margit sziget are all hangouts for gay men, while the mud bath (*iszapfürdő*) at the nearby Lukács Baths is a popular place to meet; see p.217 for addresses and opening times. The most popular **cruising spots** on the Buda side are the Vérmező park by Déli Station (though you should take care, as the park is not particularly safe after dark) and the park at the Buda end of the Margit híd, while in Pest there is the Danube promenade from Erzsébet híd to Vigadó tér. The Népliget behind the Planetarium is another meeting place, though it's notoriously dangerous.

All the restaurants listed below, which are frequented by gay people, are relatively cheap. The bars we've listed are mainly frequented by men; for women the best bars are the *Angyál* and *Capella*.

Háttér (Background) is a gay help and information line on health and any other issues, operating 6–11pm every evening (©329-3380; English generally spoken).

RESTAURANTS

Club 93

Map 4, E9. V, Vas utca 2. Astoria metro (M2).

Daily 11am–midnight.

A cheap pizzeria, popular after 8pm. Its gallery and window seating make it a good place to peoplewatch.

Fenyőgyöngye

Map 2, C4. II, Szépvölgyi út 155 ©325-9783. Bus #65 from Kolosy tér.

Daily noon–midnight.

A pleasant restaurant out in the woods on the northwest edge of the city, serving the usual Hungarian fare. Recommended are the Transylvanian stuffed cabbage and the *Füredi Fimom Falatok* – spicy sausage wrapped in pork and served in a paprika sauce.

Kis Sün

Map 4, D4. VI, Podmaniczky utca 29 &269-4072. Nyugati pu. (M3).

Daily 11am–11pm.

Friendly place near Nyugati Station. Divided up with partitions, making for a more intimate atmosphere.

BARS

Action Bár

Map 6, E8. V, Magyar utca 42. Kálvin tér metro (M3).

Daily 9pm–4am.

Chiefly for gay men looking for one-night stands, this bar has sex videos and a dark room for close encounters.

Amstel River Café

Map 6, C5. V, Párisi utca 6. Ferenciek tere metro (M3).

Mon–Fri 9am–11pm.

Not on the river, but between Váci and Petőfi utcas, this Dutch-style pub attracts a large foreign clientele and is welcoming to gays.

Angyál Bár

Map 4, G7. VII, Szövetség utca 33. Tram #4 or #6 from Blaha Lujza tér metro (M2).

Thurs–Sun 10am–dawn.

Budapest's premier gay club, which looks a bit like an airport lounge, but has an interesting crowd. Saturdays are men-only, but Fridays and Sundays are popular with women. Has a dark room.

Capella

Map 6, A7. V, Belgrád rakpart 23. Ferenciek tere metro (M3).

Mon & Tues 9pm–2am, Wed–Sun 9pm–5am.

Drag queens, jungle music and lots of kitsch. The best transvestite show in town takes place every night from Wednesday to Sunday. A very mixed joint, with men, women and a lot of straights too. Bizarrely, the xenophobic Smallholders Party has its headquarters on the same strip of the river bank, sharing the block with the *Capella* and an Arab butchers.

Darling

Map 6, D6. V, Szép utca 1. Astoria metro (M2).

Daily 7pm–3am.

A small beer-house and video gallery that gets "warmer" after 9pm and stays open till late. Has a dark room.

Mystery Bar-klub

Map 4, C6. V, Nagysándor József utca 3. Arany János utca metro (M3).

Mon–Sat 9pm–4am.

Very small bar near the Arany József metro stop. Quiet place for talking rather than dancing – there's no disco. If the door's locked you might have to wait to be let in.

No Limit

Map 6, E5. V, Semmelweis utca 10. Astoria metro (M2).

Daily 10am–5am.

Small bar with a mirror on the ceiling to make it appear bigger. Downstairs there's dancing and videos. Fairly expensive drinks with names like "Boy Cocktail". A hangout for male prostitutes.

Live music

Live music is one of the city's strengths, and most evenings you can choose from classical, folk and jazz performances. Now that Budapest is on the world circuit, a large number of foreign performers include it on their tour schedule, with some artists returning regularly.

See Directory on p.252 for details of ticket agencies.

If you can't get tickets for a performance, it is always worth persevering with the staff at the ticket office or door, as there is often some way in, even if it costs a bit extra – for instance, the Music Academy puts aside tickets each performance for a fire and a police officer, which are often not used, and it also has space on its top balcony.

OPERA, BALLET AND CLASSICAL MUSIC

You can enjoy **opera** in Budapest at a very reasonable price; the surroundings are magnificent, and you can even afford to treat yourself to several glasses of (Hungarian) champagne in the bar during the interval. Of the two venues, the grandest is the State Opera House, a nineteenth-century pile on Andrássy út, while the Erkel Theatre is much more modern. Most productions are in

Hungarian, a custom introduced by Mahler when he was director of the State Opera House in Budapest. Fans prefer their opera "old style", with lavish sets and costumes (so it's not surprising that they are very keen on **operetta**), and they interrupt with ovations after particularly bravura passages. However, productions are severely handicapped by the lack of money and by the ridiculously big repertoire that the two opera houses maintain.

The city excels in its variety of **classical music** performances, with only pre-Baroque being poorly represented. There are several concerts every night of the year, especially during the Spring and Autumn festivals (see p.223 & 226). The top **orchestras** in the city are the Hungarian Radio and Television Symphony Orchestra under the baton of Tamás Vásáry, the pianist/conductor who has transformed the ensemble since he took over in 1992; the Budapest Festival Orchestra under Iván Fischer; and the excellent Liszt Ferenc Chamber Orchestra led by János Rolla.

Four places of worship that host concerts throughout the year are the **Mátyás Church** on Várhegy (see p.19); the **Lutheran Church** on Deák tér (see p.77), including free performances of Bach before Easter – information for these is posted by the church entrance; **St Stephen's Basilica** in central Pest (see p.81); and the **Dohány utca synagogue** (see p.109).

The opera, theatre and concert halls all close at the end of May for the summer, reopening in mid-September, though there is a summer season of outdoor concerts at the open-air venues in town.

Weekly and monthly listings magazines cover the events, and **information** can also be obtained from Tourinform and the main ticket offices. Regular concerts are held at the following venues.

Bartók Memorial House (*Bartók Emlékház*)

Map 2, C4. II, Csalán utca 29 ©394-2100.

Concerts, not just of Bartók's music, are held in the villa where he used to live, most Fridays at 11am.

Budapest Convention Centre (*Budapest Kongresszusi Központ*)

Map 3, B12. XII, Jagelló út 1–3 ©209-1990.

Modern and uninspiring concert hall behind the *Novotel*, hosting big concerts.

Erkel Theatre

Map 4, H9. VIII, Köztársaság tér 30 ©333-0540.

A modern venue for operas, ballet and musicals, near Blaha Lujza tér (M2).

Hungarian State Opera (*Magyar Állami Operaház*)

Map 4, D6. VI, Andrássy út 22 ©302-4290.

Budapest's grandest venue, with gilded frescoes and three-tonne chandeliers – a place to dress up for. The box office is on Dalszínház utca, by the side entrance to the building (Tues–Sat 11am–7pm, Sun 10am–1pm & 4–7pm); returns are also sold at Andrássy út 18. Prices are higher for performances on Friday and Saturday.

Music Academy (*Zeneakadémia*)

Map 4, E6. VI, Liszt Ferenc tér 8 ©342-0179.

Nightly concerts and recitals in the magnificent *Nagyterem* (Great Hall) or the smaller *Kisterem*.

Old Music Academy (*Régi Zeneakadémia*)

Map 4, F5. VI, Vörösmarty utca 35 ©322-9804.

Concerts every Saturday morning by young musicians in the concert hall in the Liszt Memorial Museum.

Pesti Vigadó

Map 6, B3. V, Vigadó tér 1 ©327-4322.

Another fabulously decorated hall, though the acoustics are inferior. Box office opens at 1pm.

FOLK MUSIC AND TÁNCHÁZ

Hungarian **folk music and dancing** underwent a revival in the 1970s, drawing inspiration from communities in Transylvania, which were regarded as pure wellsprings of Magyar culture. Enthusiasts formed "dance houses" or **táncház** to revive traditional instruments and dances. Visitors are welcome to attend the weekly gatherings (100Ft admission) and learn the steps. Muzsikás, Téka and Kalamajka groups play sounds from Transylvania, and another popular new sound on the *táncház* scene is that of the Gyimes (Ghimes in Romanian) region in eastern Transylvania.

Details of events are available from the free magazines *Where Budapest*, *Budapest Sun*, *Budapest Week*, or on the Internet at *www.datanet.hu/tanchaz/thclub.htm*. Many of these places close for summer, so check before you go.

Almássy téri Szabadidő Központ

Map 4, G7. VII, Almássy tér 6 ©267-8709.

This cultural centre sometimes hosts concerts by foreign acts, as well as large-scale Hungarian folk and Roma gatherings.

City Cultural Centre (*Fővárosi Művelődési Ház*)

Map 2, E7. XI, Fehérvári út 47 ©203-3868.

Muzsikás dance house for children on Tuesday from 5.30 to 6.30pm, and Téka dance house every Friday at 5.30–6.30pm for children and then until midnight for adults.

Downtown Cultural Centre (*Belvárosi Művelődési Ház*)

Map 4, C11. V, Molnár utca 9 ©317-5928.

The Kalamajka ensemble plays to a packed dance floor on Saturday nights at this downtown Pest cultural centre. Instruction for children from 5pm and for adults from 7pm. A jamming session often develops in the bar upstairs as the evening rolls on.

Fonó Budai Zeneház

Map 2, E7. XI, Sztregova utca 3 ©206-5300. Tram #18 or #47; get off at stop at Fehérvári út 108.

This large, lively concert venue out in Kelenföld is a twenty-minute tram ride from Deák tér, but one of the best folk venues in town, with old Transylvanian groups appearing every Wednesday. Concerts start 8pm. Every first Thursday of the month is Gyimes night.

Gyökér Club

Map 4, D4. VI, Eötvös utca 46, near Nyugati Station (entrance round the corner in Szob utca).

In the "Root" club there is a Gyimes dance house on Tuesday from 8pm, and straight Hungarian on Friday from 9pm. Pleasant atmosphere and good restaurant, but watch out for the watered-down wine.

Marcibányi téri Szabadidő Központ

Map 3, B2. II, Marcibányi tér 5/A ©212-5504.

Muzsikás plays every Thursday night from 8pm. Not a dance house as such – the group just plays and people sit round in a very informal atmosphere. On Wednesdays there is Gyimesi from 8pm.

JAZZ

Although **jazz** is currently fashionable in Budapest, regular venues are few in number. Some bands appear at local cultural centres, others in some of the venues listed.

Art Café

Map 6, C3. V, Vörösmarty tér 1 ©327-4340.

Daily 7pm–2am; live music from 9pm.

On the ground floor of the large modern block on this central Pest square, often featuring live blues bands. Popular with foreign visitors.

Hades Jazztaurant

Map 4, F5. VI, Vörösmarty utca 31 ©352-1503.

Mon–Fri noon–2am, Sat 5pm–2am.

Pleasant bar/restaurant with live music.

Jazz Café

Map 4, A2. V, Balassi Bálint utca 25 ©132-4377.

Mon–Fri 3pm–3am, Sat & Sun 6pm–3am.

Small underground club with blue neon lighting. One of the few places in town with live jazz every night, starting at 8pm.

Jazz Fél Tíz

Map 4, F12. VIII, Baross utca 30.

Daily 6pm–2am.

Slightly lugubrious interior and wideboys hanging around at the door, but the music, which starts at 9.30pm, is often good – including blues and bluegrass.

Kosztolányi Művelődési Ház

Map 4, D12. IX, Török Pál utca 3.

Daily 5–10pm.

The world-famous Benkó Dixieland Band plays here every Wednesday evening when not touring abroad.

Közgáz Jazz Klub

Map 4, E14. IX, Kinizsi utca 2–4 ©217-5110.

Fri 8pm–midnight.

Belongs to the Budapest Economics University and favours

progressive jazz. The self-indulgently brilliant local ethno-jazz wizard Mihály Dresch and his quartet play here to a crowd of loyal fans (usually Feb–May & Sept–Dec Fri, but call to check).

Long Jazz Club

Map 4, E9. VII, Dohány utca 22–24 ©322-0006.
Daily 6pm–2am.
Good jazz venue on the corner of Sip utca near the *Astoria*, attracting top names like the double bassist Aladár Pege and pianist Ifj Szakcsi Lakatos.

POP AND CONTEMPORARY DANCE MUSIC

Merlin Klub

Map 6, E4. V, Gerloczy utca 4 ©317-9338.
Good food, a relaxed atmosphere and a variety of performances. The Roma gypsy group Ando Drom plays regularly and there's theatre too, sometimes in English. The entrance is through a courtyard and up the stairs to the first floor.

Petőfi Csarnok

Map 2, F5. XIV, Zichy Mihály út 14 ©342-4327.
Huge purpose-built youth centre near the back of the Városliget, hosting concerts by local and big-name foreign bands and contemporary dance performances.

Sportcsarnok

Map 2, G5. XIV, Stefánia út 1–3 ©251-6855.
Indoor stadium next to Népstadion metro station (M2), which hosts big jazz, rock and dance events. Entrance on the upper level by the walkway from the metro station.

Trafó

Map 4, G14. IX, Liliom utca 41 ©456-2054.

Probably the best contemporary arts centre in town, housed in an old transformer station. Exhibitions, music, dance, and theatre performances. A very happening place, with both Hungarian and foreign acts.

Theatre and cinema

There are some beautiful theatres in Budapest, and if you're undeterred by the language barrier it can be a very rewarding experience. For a cheaper night out, the cinema is a good option, with foreign films usually screened in their original language.

To find out **what's on**, look out for flyers and check out the listings magazines *Budapest Week* and *Budapest Sun*. Full cinema listings are given in the Hungarian publications *Pesti Est* (free) and *Pesti Műsor (PM)* under the heading *Budapesti mozik műsora*. The free theatre listings publication, *Súgó*, available from theatre foyers, is published in English in July and August.

See Directory on p.252 for details of ticket agencies.

THEATRE

Hungarians show great taste when it comes to building theatres: take the splendid mass of the newly restored Comedy Theatre (*Vígszínház*) at XIII, Szent István körút 14 (Map 4, B2). Theatre tickets range from 200Ft to 1000Ft, but there are two obstacles to enjoying the performances: the language barrier and the melodramatic stage manners and stiff productions that remain the fashion in Hungary. Recently, however, the number of **alternative theatre** venues around town has been growing. The most acclaimed new company is the **Moving House** (*Mozgó ház*) group, whose inventive combinations of music and movement under the direction of László Hudi have won international acclaim. Their *Cherry Orchard* (*Cseresznyéskert*), which carried off the Best Show award at the International Theatre Festival in Sarajevo in 1998, uses the original Chekhov play as a starting point for its playful ideas. When not touring in Europe, you can catch them at the Trafó (see overleaf).

Puppet theatres are covered under "Children's Budapest" on p.232.

The National Theatre

The continuing lack of a **National Theatre** in Hungary has become something of a scandal. The nation's prime dramatic institution used to stand on Blaha Lujza tér, but in 1964 the Communist regime used the building of the metro as an excuse for knocking the building down. Since then the theatre company has been housed temporarily in an ugly cramped theatre on Hevesi Sándor tér, up towards the Városliget, while arguments have raged on about where the new theatre should be. After years of wrangling it all seemed decided in 1998, as the city authorities started work on a theatre on Deák tér, next to the bus station. However, after a soundproof underground car park had been built at great expense, the new government decided to put a stop to the work, saying they wanted to move the site to the Városliget. The debate continues, with little sign of a conclusion.

Katona József Theatre

Map 6, C5. V, Petőfi Sándor utca 6.

The company here remains the most impressive mainstream group in town, winning plaudits at the Old Vic in London and the Odéon in Paris, with performances of Hungarian and non-Hungarian theatre. The box office opens at 2pm, and tickets for any unoccupied seats are sold just before the show starts at 7pm.

Merlin Theatre

Map 6, E4. V, Gerlóczy utca 4 ©317-9338.

The Merlin is near Deák tér, its entrance through a courtyard and up the stairs to the first floor. It sometimes hosts visiting British companies.

Operetta Theatre

Map 4, D6. VI, Nagymező utca 17 ©332-0535.

Hungary excels at operetta, and here you can see works by Lehár, Kálmán and other local stars who achieved international fame with their work, as well as more modern musicals. The building, located on "Broadway", a few blocks from the Opera House, is also splendid.

Szkéné Színház

Map 2, E6. XI, Műegyetem rakpart 3.

A small theatre housed in the main building of the Technical University near the *Gellért Hotel*, this has been an alternative venue for many years, dating back to the bad old days of Communism.

Trafó

Map 4, G14. IX, Liliom utca 41 ©456-2054.

A new contemporary arts centre in a former transformer station under the dedicated direction of cultural impresario György Szabó. It pulls full houses with Hungarian and foreign theatre and dance performances.

FILMS AND CINEMA

There are over 35 **cinemas** in Budapest, many of them multi-screen, with tickets at less than £2. Hollywood blockbusters naturally dominate the **mainstream cinemas**, though serious film buffs should look to the **art cinemas** (*art mozi*), which specialize in more alternative and obscure films. Their provenance is indicated thus: *Angol* (British), *Lengyel* (Polish), *Német* (German), *Olasz* (Italian), and *Orosz* (Russian); films are usually screened in their original language, subtitled in Hungarian. In the summer there are also **outdoor** and **drive-in cinemas** on the edge of town.

In listings magazines, you'll find the *art mozi* list at the end of the mainstream cinemas. Here, the times of shows are cryptically abbreviated to *n8* or *1/4 8* for 7.15pm; *f8* or

HUNGARIAN FILM

Hungarians have an impressive record in film, and many of the Hollywood greats were **Hungarian emigrés**, such as Michael Curtiz, George Cukor, and actors Béla Lugosi, Tony Curtis and Leslie Howard. In the Communist years **Hungarian films** continued to make waves, with Károly Makk, István Szabó, Márta Mészáros and many others making films that managed to say much about the oppressive regime in spite of its restrictions. In recent years the film industry has been languishing, robbed by the collapse of Communism of both its subject matter and its financing. Occasional flickerings like Ildikó Enyedi's *My Twentieth Century* and Makk's *The Gambler* have not marked a lasting recovery. There has been an increase in the number of co-productions with foreign studios, placing a wholly different set of pressures on the nation's film-makers, but, given the great tradition the industry enjoys here, Hungarian directors should be capable of producing more surprises.

1/2 8 for 7.30pm; and *h8* or *3/4 8* for 7.45pm. "*Mb.*" indicates the film is dubbed, and "*fel.*" or "*feliratos*" means that it has Hungarian subtitles.

Budapest has some beautiful movie houses – check out the Moorish interior of the Uránia at VIII, Rákóczi út 21 (Map 4, E9) and the coffered ceiling of the turn-of-the-century Puskin at V, Kossuth Lajos 18 (Map 6, E6).

Cirko-gejzir

Map 4, A3. V, Balassi Bálint utca 15–17.

One of the best alternative cinemas, with a regular selection of films from around the globe. In one week you could come across films by Almodovar, Tarkovsky, Jarmusch, Wenders and Rohmer, and even the latest Iranian classic.

Corvin Budapest Filmpalota

Map 4, F13. VIII, Corvin köz 1 ©459-5050.

The glitzy Film Palace, near the Ferenc körút metro station (M3), is a modern jungle of cinemas, popcorn and drinks. You can catch the latest foreign releases here, and in February it hosts the Hungarian Film Festival. Reduced ticket prices on Wednesdays.

Művész

Map 4, D5. VI, Teréz körút 30 ©332-6726.

Alternative cinema near the Oktogon with one larger and several smaller rooms named after big film personalities.

Toldi

Map 4, C6. V, Bajcsy-Zsilinszky út 36–38 ©311-2809.

Next door to Arany János utca metro station (M3), the Toldi is one of the more dynamic, alternative cinemas in town, with a bar and a bookshop where people congregate. Every year it hosts the Titanic Film Festival, showcasing Hungarian and foreign independent films.

Sports

The Hungarian passion for sport has not been dimmed by the years of under-financing. Spectator sports such as horse-racing, football and the Hungarian Grand Prix are very popular, with facilities at football stadia gradually being transformed alongside their European counterparts. Supporters are pretty friendly everywhere, apart from the rowdy skinhead supporters of FTC football team (see below). Participatory sports have suffered similarly from a lack of funding, but you can find tennis, squash and riding facilities dotted around the capital.

SOCCER

While **international matches** are held at the 76,000-seater Népstadion stadium, national football revolves around the turf of four **premier league teams**. Ferencvárosi Torna Club (aka FTC or Fradi), whose colours are green and white, are based at IX, Üllői út 129, near the Népliget metro stop. Their fans are keen to fight with supporters of Újpesti Torna Egylet, the 1998 champions whose ground is at IV, Megyeri út 13 (three stops on bus #30 from Újpest Központ metro station). The rivals of these two teams are MTK, the 1997 winners of both the cup and the league, based at VIII, Salgótarján utca 12–14 (tram #37 from Blaha Lujza tér), and Honvéd-Kispest, based at XIX, Új temető út 1–3 (tram #42 from Határ út metro stop to the end of the line). Matches are played on Saturday afternoons and Monday evenings; see *Programme* magazine or any Hungarian newspaper for details. For more details on the leading clubs see the *Rough Guide to European Football.*

HORSE-RACING

Horse-racing, like so many things, was introduced from England by the great Count Széchenyi in 1827. Both **flat-racing** (*galopp*) and **trotting** (*ügető*) tracks lie on the eastern side of Pest, where you can have a great afternoon's entertainment. Today, racing is in crisis, however, as investment has dwindled due to the the falling attendance at the tracks.

The atmosphere at both tracks is informal, but photographing the race-goers is frowned upon, since many attend without telling their spouses or employers. Races are advertised in *Fortuna* magazine, and you can get details of the horses running in a leaflet sold at the betting windows at the courses. **Betting** operates on a tote system, where your returns are affected by how the odds stand at the close of betting. The odds at any time are shown on the screens near the windows. The different types of bet you can make are *tét* (placing money on the winner); *hely* (on a horse coming in the first three); and the popular *befutó* (a bet on two horses to come in either first and second or first and third). You state what type of bet you want to make, and then give the numbers of the horses you are backing. Winnings are paid out about fifteen minutes after the end of the race.

Flat racing takes place at Kincsem Park (*Lóversenytér*), X, Albertirsai út 2, north of the International Fair grounds

(Map 2, H5; Pillangó utca metro stop and a ten-minute walk; ©334-2956). Punters gather here every Sunday afternoon during the racing season (March–Nov). The big races are in May (*Nemzeti* and *Milleniumi díj*), July (the **Hungarian Derby** is early in the month), and October, with the Hungarian St Leger on the first Sunday.

Trotting takes place at the Ügetőpálya, VIII, Kerepesi út 11 (Map 2, F6; bus #95 or trolleybus #80 from Keleti Station). Even though the crowd is small and elderly, trotting is a legendary sport in Hungary, as captured in the cult film *We Never Die* (*Sose halunk meg*) made in the early 1990s. There's a 2pm start on Saturday, and a 4pm one on Wednesday.

GRAND PRIX RACING

First held in 1986, the **Hungarian Grand Prix** takes place every summer at the purpose-built **Formula 1 racing track** at Mogyoród, 20km northeast of Budapest (Map2, L2). It is usually scheduled for early August, though every year financial uncertainties spark off rumours that this is the last year it will be held. Details are available from Tourinform or any listings magazine.

You can reach the track by special buses from the Árpád Bridge bus station; trains from Keleti Station to Fót, and then a bus from there; or by HÉV train from Örs vezér tere to the Szilasliget stop, which is 1800m northeast of Gate C. **Tickets** (available from Ostermann Formula 1 office, V, Apáczai Csere János utca 11 and from tourist offices) cost £8/$12 for a standing ticket on the first practice day, £50/$75 for a standing ticket and £200/$300 for a seat in the gold tribune on the Sunday, with a three-day pass costing £60/$90 to £260/$390. The price is partly determined by the location, and whether you book in advance or not.

PARTICIPATORY SPORTS

TENNIS AND SQUASH

Tennis courts can be booked at the *Thermal Hotel Helia* in north Pest, XIII, Kárpát utca 62 (©270-3277), at the Euro-Gym on Margit Island (©269-3228), and at Marczibányi tér 13 (©214-5433). The last of these is next to the City Squash Club (©212-3110), one of a growing number of **squash courts** in the city, where they rent out rackets, shoes and balls. The *Marriott Hotel* in central Pest also has courts, though these cost a bit more.

SKIING AND ICE-SKATING

If it's a snowy winter, you can **ski** at Normafa in the Buda Hills; equipment can be rented from Suli Sí in the Komjádi swimming complex at II, Árpád Fejedelem utca 8 (©212-0330). You can skate at the **ice rink** by Hősök tere in the Városliget (City Park) between November and March; skates can be hired.

Information about the city's extensive bath and swimming facilities is given on p.217.

HORSE-RIDING

If you want to go **horse-riding**, you can head out to the Great Plain, where there are many small riding schools; ask at Tourinform for further information (see p.9). Pegazus at Budapest V, Ferenciek tere 5, in the office facing you as you walk into the courtyard rather than the one on the street front (©317-1552), also organizes horse-riding at venues outside the city. Alternatively, you can go horse-riding year-round at the Petneházy school at II, Feketefej utca 2–4 (Tues–Fri 9am–noon & 2–4pm, Sat & Sun 9am–1pm; ©397-1208).

Baths and pools

Budapest has a long bathing tradition going back to Roman times or even earlier, and a visit to the city's baths should not be missed. There are three different types of bath: *gyógyfürdő*, a thermal bath in its original Turkish form, as at the Rudas and Király, or in the magnificent nineteenth-century settings of the Gellért and Széchenyi; *uszoda*, a proper swimming pool like the Sport; and *strand*, a summer pool in a verdant setting, like the Palatinus or Csillaghegy.

The best way to enjoy the **steam baths** (*gözfürdő*) is to move from room to room, moving on when the heat gets too much. A good circuit is to work up a sweat in the "dry steam" room; then to head to a moderate pool (around 28°C), and once you have cooled down, go into the thick and misty "wet steam"; from there into the cold plunge for as long as you can bear it, and then into the hot water (42°C), where your skin will tingle madly. Then you either start again, or go and chill out in one of the larger pools in the complex. Before getting dressed in the Rudas and Király, a good way to cool down is to go and relax in the rest rooms on your way to the changing rooms. Remember to make a note of the cabin/locker number, and, when you leave the pool, find the attendant who will then unlock it for you. It is customary to give him or her a small tip of 100–200Ft.

Gellért Gyógyfürdő

Map 4, B14. XI, Kelenhegyi út 4 ©466-6166.

May–Sept daily: 6am–7pm; Oct–April Mon–Fri 6am–7pm, Sat & Sun 6am–5pm; 1200Ft for both main and steam baths, 700Ft after 5pm. Turkish bath: May–Sept Mon–Fri 6am–7pm, Sat & Sun 6am–5pm; Oct–April Mon–Fri 6am–5pm, Sat & Sun 6am–2pm; 700Ft for the steam baths only. Evening swimming in summer Fri & Sat 8pm–midnight, depending on the weather.

The most popular of the city's baths, and also the most expensive, the Gellért has it all: a magnificent main pool for swimming, hot pools for sitting around in both inside and outside on the terrace, fabulous Art Nouveau steam baths, and a large outdoor area, including a wave machine in the main pool and shaded terraces – and, of course, a restaurant where you can get your daily dose of meat fried in breadcrumbs. In the main pool, swimming caps are compulsory; you can get free blue plastic ones by the exit from the changing rooms. The baths attract a lot of foreigners, and staff usually speak German or English.

Király Gyógyfürdő

Map 3, E3. II, Fő utca 84.

Men, Mon, Wed & Fri 6.30am–7pm; women, Tues & Thurs 6.30am–7pm, Sat 6.30am–noon; 450Ft.

Fabulous Turkish baths, though sadly it is now customary to wear swimming costumes rather than the dinky little aprons they used to give out. Of all the steam baths, this is the one most popular with the gay community.

Hajós Alfred Uszoda (aka Sport)

Map 3, G1. Margit sziget.

Daily 6am–6pm

One of the nicest places for proper swimming – a beautiful 1930s lido at the southern end of the island, with a small sauna, and two large outdoor pools against a backdrop of trees; one is normally given over to water polo. In the winter you can swim out along a channel to the larger of the pools without walking outside. The buffets on the terrace and in the entrance hall serve excellent pastries.

The Palatinus Strand

Map 7, H7. Margit sziget.

May–Sept daily 8am–6pm; 400Ft.

Halfway up the islands on the west, the Palatinus has a large outdoor set of pools, including a wave pool and children's pools, all set in a big expanse of grass. The sunroof above the changing rooms is a gay centre.

Lukács Fürdő

Map 3, E1. II, Frankl Leó út 25–29.

Mon–Fri 6am–7pm, Sat & Sun 6am–5pm; 450Ft.

Two small but delightful pools in the grounds of this bath-cum-hospital complex. Buy your tickets in the folly entrance hall (ask for the *uszoda* if you want the pool) and follow the courtyard round to the left, past the plaques put up by grateful patients. It also has steam and mud baths (*iszapfürdő*), the latter being particularly popular with gays.

Rác Gyógyfürdő

Map 3, F11. I, Hadnagy utca 8–10.

Men, Tues, Thurs & Sat 6.30am–6pm; women, Mon, Wed & Fri 6.30am–6pm; 450Ft.

Small modernized Turkish baths on the southern edge of the Tabán, in one of the few remaining buildings of the old Serb quarter. Popular with gays as a meeting place.

Rudas Gyógyfürdő

Map 3, G12. I, Döbrentei tér 9.

Mon–Fri 6am–5pm, Sat 6am–noon; 450Ft.

One the original Turkish baths in the city, with a beautiful interior, at its best when the sun shines through the hole in the dome to light up the interior. Still operates the apron system, so swimming things are not needed in the steam section; in the larger pool to the left of the entrance the usual rules apply. The steam baths are for men only – women can only get a look when *Cinetrip* raves are held in the baths (see p.190).

Széchenyi Fürdő

Map 4, I1. XIV, Állatkerti körút 11 (entrance opposite the Circus).

Mid-May to mid-Sept daily 6am–6pm; mid-Sept to mid-May Mon–Fri 6am–6pm, Sat & Sun 6am–4pm; 350ft.

Magnificent nineteenth-century complex in the Városliget with sixteen pools in all, including the various medicinal sections. You'll probably use just the three outdoor pools – the hot one with people playing chess that appears in so many photos of the city, a cool pool for swimming, and a shallower children's pool. There is also a mixed sauna with hot and cold pools across the far side of the hot pool from the changing rooms. Chess sets are not provided – bring your own if you want to play. There are separate steam baths for men on Mondays, Wednesdays and Fridays, and for women on Tuesdays, Thursdays and Saturdays.

Csillaghegyi Strand

Map 2, E2. III, Pusztakúti út 3.

May 10–Sept 15 daily 6am–7pm; Sept 16–May 9 Mon–Fri 6am–7pm, Sat 6am–3pm, Sun 6am–noon; 300Ft.

Large outdoor complex spreading up the hillside north of Óbuda. Ten minutes by train from Batthyány tér, and close to the Csillaghegy HÉV stop, with a large cold main pool and smaller warmer pools. Nude sunbathing on the upper slopes.

Festivals

Whatever time of the year you visit Budapest, there's almost certain to be something happening. Of the events listed in this chapter, the biggest are the Spring Festival in late March/early April, and the Autumn Festival from late September to late October – both of which feature music, ballet and drama, including star acts from abroad. Many theatres, concert halls and dance houses close down during the long, hot months of July and August, though open-air performances are staged in their place. The city's population returns from the countryside for the fireworks on August 20, and life returns to normal in the city as school starts the following week. The new arts season holds fire until the last week of September, when there is a rash of music festivals and political anniversaries. The opening performance at the State Opera House is traditionally *Bánk Bán*, by Ferenc Erkel.

JANUARY

Farsang

January 6 to Ash Wednesday. This is the season of carnivals and balls, and Farsang is the Hungarian way of saying farewell to winter, as well as fattening everyone up before fasting begins in Lent. Revellers usually take to the streets in fancy dress during one weekend in January; they process across the Lánchíd and down to Vörösmarty tér, where their apparel is judged. Unfortunately the inclement weather at this time of year often dampens the event's spirit.

FEBRUARY

Bears and Spring

February 2. Tradition has it that if the bears in Budapest Zoo come out of their cave on this date and catch sight of their shadows, they will return to their lairs to sleep, and the winter will be a long one. If the sun doesn't shine, it means that spring is just around the corner.

Hungarian Film Festival

Two weeks of the latest films from the Hungarian studios. Tickets can be bought at the central venue, the Corvin Filmpalota on Ferenc körút (see p.210), which usually shows films with English translations.

MARCH–APRIL

Declaration of Independence of 1848

March 15. A public holiday in honour of the 1848 Revolution, which began with Petőfi's declaration of the *National Song* from the steps of the National Museum. Budapest decks itself out with Hungarian tricolours, and there are speeches and gatherings outside the museum and by Petőfi's statue on Marcius 15 tér. The more patriotic citizens wear little cockades in the national colours (red, white and green) pinned to their lapels.

Budapest Spring Festival

Late March/early April. The city's major arts festival: classical music concerts in venues across the city, as well as some jazz and folk; exhibitions, including the World Press Photos show; dance, including the folk dance festival in the Budapest Sportcsarnok; theatre and cinema, with a series of Hungarian films with English subtitles often showing in one cinema in town.

Easter

Late March/early April. Easter is a low-profile holiday in Hungary. Easter Saturday is marked by processions in churches, while on Easter Monday *locsolkodás* (splashing) takes place, when men and boys visit their female friends to spray them with cologne. Kids get a painted egg or money in return for splashing, while the men receive *pálinka* (schnapps). This is a tamer version of an older village tradition where a bucket of water was used instead of the perfume bottle. Regular events in the weeks preceding Easter are arts and craft fairs in the Museum of Ethnography, with traditional folk skills like egg painting on display; and free performances of Bach's *St John Passion* in the big, yellow Lutheran church on Deák tér.

MAY

Labour Day

May 1. Though still a public holiday, citizens are no longer obliged to parade past the Lenin statue near the Városliget. Instead the major trade unions put on a big do in the park, with shows, games, talks, and of course food and drink in large quantities.

JUNE

Book Week

First week. Vörösmarty tér and Liszt Ferenc tér are lined with stalls, as Hungarian writers gather from neighbouring countries and further afield. Authors sign books for the punters, and there is singing and dancing on the temporary stages in the two squares.

WOMUFE

Early June. A two- to three-day event at the Budai Parkszínpad in the park by Kosztolányi Dezső tér, hosting a collection of world music stars.

World Music Day

Nearest weekend to June 21. Musical events around town mark this day, which the French introduced.

Budapesti Bucsú

Last weekend. "Bucsú" means farewell in Hungarian, and the first Budapesti Bucsú was held in 1991 to celebrate the departure of Soviet troops from the country. Now it's an annual city-wide celebration of music, with events in the Tabán, the park at the Buda side of the Erzsébet híd, and in Hősök tere, where there is a large outdoor classical music performance.

JULY

Bastille Day

July 14. Street ball outside the French Institute near the Lánchíd in Buda, with music, dancing and fireworks.

Hungarian Derby

Early July on a Sunday. Hungary's premier race meeting, held at the Lóversenytér, north of the International Fair grounds at X, Albertirsai út 2 (©334-2956; Pillangó utca metro-M2). See p.214 for further information.

AUGUST

Hungarian Grand Prix

Usually second weekend. The Hungarian Grand Prix takes place at the Hungaroring circuit at Mogyoród on the north-eastern edge of the city.

Budafest

Mid-August. Opera and ballet festival in the State Opera House.

Sziget Festival

Mid-August. The biggest rock and pop festival in Europe takes place on Óbudai-sziget, an island north of the centre. Rock, pop, world music, dance, theatre, films and children's events.

St Stephen's Day

August 20. A public holiday in honour of Hungary's national saint and founder, with day-long rites at his Basilica, a craft fair and folk dancing at different venues in the Várhegy, and a spectacular fireworks display at 9pm. Over a million people line the Danube to watch the fireworks fired off from Gellért-hegy, and the traffic jam that follows is equally mind-blowing. Restaurants are also packed that night, so book well ahead if you want to eat out.

SEPTEMBER

Budapest Wine Festival

Early September. The centrepiece of this festival is on Vörösmarty tér, where you can walk around the wine stalls tasting and buying wines. There may also be concerts and a procession.

BNV: Budapest National Fair

Early September. The largest consumer trade fair of the year takes place in the Budapest International Fair Centre at X, Albertirsai út 10 (©263-6000).

European Heritage Days

Late September. A Council of Europe initiative which takes place all over the Continent, with public buildings opened to the public for a weekend. Tours (in Hungarian) take you round the Art Nouveau Geological Institute on Stefánia út, the former Post Office Savings Bank in Hold utca, and the Interior Ministry on Roosevelt tér.

Budapest Music Weeks

Late September to early November. City-wide music events starting around the anniversary of Bartók's death on September 25.

Budapest Autumn Festival

Late September to mid-October. This is the lesser of the two big arts festivals, but stronger on contemporary music. There are also exhibitions, opera and theatre performances.

OCTOBER

Music of Our Time

Early October. Two weeks of contemporary music played by Hungarian and foreign artists.

Titanic Film Festival

Early October. An annual show of independent films shown over ten days in October, usually at the Toldi Cinema by Arany János utca metro station (M3).

Arad martyrs anniversary

October 6. Commemoration of the shooting of the thirteen Hungarian generals in 1849 in Arad in present-day Romania, when the 1848 revolution was crushed by the Austrians with Russian help. Wreaths are laid at the "Eternal Flame" at the junction of Báthory and Hold utca (Map 4, B5), erected on the spot where Count Lajos Batthyány, the Prime Minister of the short-lived independent government, was shot.

Commemoration of the Uprising

October 23. A national holiday to commemorate the 1956 Uprising and the declaration of the Republic in 1990. Ceremonies take place in Kossuth tér, by the Nagy Imre statue nearby, and at Nagy's grave in the New Cemetery (see p.130).

NOVEMBER

All Souls' Day

November 1. Cemeteries stay open late around this day and candles are lit in memory of departed souls, making for an incredible sight as darkness falls.

DECEMBER

Mikulás

December 5–6. St Nicholas's Day. On December 5, children clean their shoes and put them in the window for "Mikulás", the Santa Claus figure, to fill with sweets. Naughty children are warned that if they behave badly, all they will get is *virgács*, a gold-painted bunch of twigs from Mikulás' little helpers. Nowadays most children get sweets, twigs and presents.

Christmas

December 24–25. The main celebration is on December 24, when the city becomes eerily silent by late afternoon. Children are taken out while their parents decorate the Christmas tree (until then the trees are stored outside, and on housing estates you can often see them dangling from windows). When the children return home, they wait outside until the bell rings, which tells them that "little Jesus" (*Jézuska*) has come. Inside, they sing carols by the tree, open presents, and start the big Christmas meal, which is traditionally spicy fish soup, amongst other things. In the preceding weeks there are Christmas fairs in several locations in town, the best being in the Museum of Ethnography, where traditional crafts are demonstrated.

New Year's Eve

December 31. Revellers gather on the Nagykörút, engaging in trumpet battles at the junction with Rákóczi út. In the Opera House there is an all-night ball; tickets, which are expensive, can be bought from the usual tickets agencies on p.252.

Kids' Budapest

Budapest offers a healthy range of activities for kids from state-of-the-art playgrounds to roller-skating parks, with concessions on most entry tickets for under-14s. Don't expect anything too high-tech, however, as a lack of cash dogs the facilities and some of the city's playgrounds have become pretty run-down. There is no doubting the average Hungarian's love of children, though. They will talk to children on buses and give their seats up for parents carrying small babies; old ladies will loudly berate parents for not dressing their babies adequately (which for Hungarians means not putting a hat on in the mildest of weather); and if you are pushing a baby buggy, help is usually quickly forthcoming when you want go upstairs.

Since the city is still very much lived in and offices have not yet taken over the centre of town, there are a lot of **playgrounds** in squares and parks, such as in Klauzál tér and the Károlyi kert near Astoria – although the best of the pack is the adventure playground in the zoo. If you want to jump around and get rid of excess energy there are trampolines in big cages at the Buda end of the Margit híd and in the Városliget, south of the Széchenyi baths.

More ideas for children are listed below, or look out for *Budapest for Children* by Bob Dent (City Hall, 1992), which is still available in some English-language sections of bookshops.

Shops selling toys and games are listed under "Shopping" on p.247.

PARKS AND OUTDOOR ACTIVITIES

Caves

There are several **caves** in the Buda Hills that are open to the public, which are good fun for children as long as they aren't scared of the dark. The Castle Caves at Úri utca 9, below Várhegy (*Várbarlang*; map 5, D4; daily 9.30am–7.30pm) exhibit some entertaining remains of human activity including a pile of skulls and a giant head, while the Pálvölgy Stalactite Caves at Szépvölgyi út 162 (*Pálvölgyi cseppkőbarlang*; Tues–Sun 10am–4pm) and the Szemlő-hegy Caves at Pusztaszeri út 35 (*Szemlőhegyi barlang*; map 7, D7; April–Oct Mon & Wed–Fri 10am–3pm, Sat & Sun 10am–4pm; 160Ft) display dramatic geological formations.

Görzenál Skatepark

Map 7, H6. III, Árpád fejedelem útja ©250-4800. Szentendre HÉV to Timár utca.

Daily 10am–8pm.

Space to rollerblade, skateboard and cycle, with ramps and jumps, all to your heart's content.

Margit sziget

Map 2, E4.

A great open space where you can hire **bikes** and four-person **trikes**, or take a trip round the island on the train on wheels that leaves from by the strange sculpture at the southern end of the island. The **Palatinus open-air baths**, halfway down on the west of the island, have a wave machine and lots of small pools for kids. The low point of the island is the zoo across on the east – a smelly and sorry-looking place. Otherwise the island's scenery is varied, with a rose garden, ruins, and big open spaces for frisbee and ball games, all creating a very pleasant atmosphere. If you go back once the children are in bed you can hear the nightingales singing.

Városliget

Map 4, I1.

This is where you'll find the largest concentration of activities for children. Besides the park itself you have the **zoo** (*Állatkert*; daily: May–Aug 9am–7pm; April & Sept 9am–6pm; Oct & March 9am–5pm; Nov–Feb 9am–4pm), which also has one of the best adventure playgrounds in the city. Next door is the **circus** (mid-April to end Aug: Wed, Fri & Sun 3pm & 7pm, Thurs 3pm, Sat 10am, 3pm & 7pm; ©342-8300 for bookings), and beyond that the **Amusement Park** (May–Sept daily 9am–8pm; Oct–April Mon–Fri 10am–6.45pm, Sat & Sun 10am–7.15pm), which is enjoyable in its shabby way. Across the road from the circus is the outdoor **Széchenyi Baths** (daily: summer 6am–7pm; winter 6am–4pm; Turkish baths: Mon–Sat 6am–7pm, Sun 6am–1pm), with a large children's pool. If you want to stay above water level, there is rowing in summer and ice-skating in winter on the lake by Hősök tere (Nov–March Mon–Fri 9am–1pm & 4–8pm, Sat & Sun 10am–2pm & 4–8pm depending on the weather). For kids, the pick of the park's many museums is the **Transport Museum** (*Közlekedési Múzeum*; Tues–Sun 10am–6pm), with vehicles of all kinds, and a model train set that runs on the hour every hour until 5pm. Across the way, on the first floor of the Petőfi Csarnok, is its **Aviation and Space** display (*Repüléstörténeti és űrhajózási kiállítás*; April–Nov Tues–Fri 10am–5pm, Sat & Sun 10am–6pm).

MUSEUMS

Metro Museum

Map 6, E3. Below ground at Deák tér.

Tues–Sun 10am–6pm.

The small *Földalattivasút Múzeum* next to the metro station still preserves some of the original track the trains first ran on, as well as the original wooden carriages, decorated with old advertisements.

Szentendre Village Museum

Map 8, A1.

April–Oct Tues–Sun 9am–5pm; 200Ft.

Children's programmes every weekend, a playground, and frequent folk craft and folk dancing displays.

Telephone Museum (*Telefónia Múzeum*)

Map 5, C2. I, Úri utca 49.

Tues–Sun 10am–6pm.

A hands-on museum, which is a rarity in Budapest. You can send faxes and call one another on vintage phones.

THEATRE, DANCE AND OTHER ACTIVITIES

Folk dancing

Kids brave enough to try their steps at Hungarian folk dancing can go to one the children's *táncház*. The same top musicians who play for the adults play for the children too – which says a lot about attitudes to folk dancing. The venues are Belvárosi Művelődési Ház at V, Molnár utca 9 for **Kalamajka dance house** (Map 6, B7; Sat 5–6pm); and Fővárosi Művelődési Ház near Móricz Zsigmond körtér at XI, Fehérvári út 47 (Map 2, E7) for **Muzsikás dance house** (Tues 5.30–6.30pm) and **Téka dance house** (Fri 5.30–6.30pm).

"Kidstown" (*Kölyökvár*)

Map 4, G7. VII, Almássy tér Leisure Centre, Almássy tér 6 ©267-8709.

Mid-Oct to April Sun 10am–1pm.

A play and activity centre offering all sorts of activities from face-painting to model-building – plus films, music and drama.

Puppet theatre (*Bábszínház*)

Puppetry has a long tradition in Hungary, and there are some excellent performances. Mornings and matinées are for kids, while the evening's occasional masked grotesqueries or renditions of Bartók's *The Wooden Prince* and *The Miraculous Mandarin* are intended for adults. Tickets are available from the puppet theatres: the Bábszínház at VI, Andrássy út 69 (©342-2702) and the Kolibri at VI, Jókai tér 10 (©311-0870), which also organizes shows at Andrássy út 74 and 77.

PUBLIC TRANSPORT

A cheap and reliable form of amusement are the different forms of **public transport** in the city, and children under six travel free. **Trams** are an endless source of fun, the best ride being along the embankment in tram #2. Across the water, the **Sikló** (see p.49) is a great experience, running up from the Lánchíd to the Royal Palace, with the view of Pest suddenly appearing before your eyes. A popular way to spend an afternoon in the Buda Hills is to go on the "**railway circuit**" – the Cogwheel Railway, the Children's Railway and the chairlift (see p.61). In the summer (April–Oct) there's the added thrill of **boat rides** on the Danube – either short tours of the city up to Margit sziget and back, or further afield to Szentendre and on to Esztergom. The only problem with these is that if your child gets bored, you will be trapped on the boat with no escape. Another summer-time source of delight are the **steam trains** that run from Nyugati Station up to Vác. A simple all-year-round amusement are the **lifts** at the Astoria junction in the modern East-West Business Centre. Here lift-lovers can churn up their stomachs riding down in the glass lifts on the exterior of the building from the New York bagel outlet on the eighth floor.

Shopping

In recent years Western trends and Western money have started to infiltrate Budapest's shops. Familiar names like Benetton, Estée Lauder and Marks & Spencer have appeared, and shops have taken on a brighter, more customer-friendly style, with better lighting, more self-service, and fewer queues.

The **main shopping area** is located to the south of Vörösmarty tér in central Pest, in particular around Petőfi Sándor utca and the pedestrianized Váci utca, which have the biggest concentration of glamorous and expensive shops. The broader streets radiating out from the centre – Bajcsy-Zsilinszky, Andrássy and Rákóczi út – are also lined with shops, as are the two ring boulevards, the Nagykörút (especially from Margit híd to Blaha Lujza tér) and the Kiskörút, while some of the old craftsmen and workshops are still operating in the backstreets inside the Nagykörút. Shops in the Várhegy are almost exclusively given over to providing foreign tourists with folksy souvenirs such as embroidered tablecloths, hussar pots and fancy bottles of Tokaji wine.

Falk Miksa utca, running south off Szent István körút, near the Pest end of the Margit híd (Map 4, A3), is known as Budapest's "Street of Antiques", and is where you'll find the biggest collection of **antique stores** and galleries. Kossuth Lajos utca between Ferenciek tere and the *Astoria*

Hotel also has a couple of shops. If it's books and prints you want, head for Múzeum körút, where there are several **secondhand bookshops** (*antikvárium*) clustered opposite the Hungarian National Museum. Most shops should be able to advise on what you can export from the country and how to go about it. Several shops organize **auctions**; the best months for these are April, May, September and December – check the monthly free magazine *Where Budapest* (see p.9) for dates. Another great source of antiques are the flea markets listed on p.244, though you'll need to be wary about parting with large sums of money as stallholders can charge hugely inflated prices.

Budapest also has a set of distinguished **market halls** (*vásárcsarnok*) dating from the late nineteenth century, some of which still function as general markets, and some of which have been turned into supermarkets, although you can still admire their structure. There are also some outdoor markets (*piac*), which are a more lively proposition, with old folk coming into town to sell their produce. Most of the markets are busy, crowded places, so you should mind your pockets and bags at all times.

Unless otherwise stated, opening hours are Mon–Fri 10am–6pm, Sat 10am–1pm. Most shops in Budapest accept credit and charge cards.

ANTIQUES AND SECONDHAND BOOKS

BÁV

Map 6, C3, V, Bécsi utca 1–3 (for paintings); Map 6 C5, VI, Andrássy út 27 (for *objets d'art*); Map 4, D7, V, Ferenciek tere 10 (for carpets).
Mon–Fri 10am–6pm, Sat 10am–2pm.
There are eighteen outlets, including the three above, in this

large chain of assorted antique shops, which also holds regular auctions at Lonyai utca 30–32.

Forgács

Map 6, D3. Kempinski Corvinus Hotel, V, Erzsébet tér 7–8 ©266-1000 ext 898.

Mon–Fri 1–8pm, Sat 2–7pm.

A good range of old books, prints and antiques from a friendly dealer.

Honterus

Map 6, E8. V, Múzeum körút 35 ©317-3270.

Engravings, postcards and secondhand books, opposite the National Museum.

Központi Antikvárium (Central Antiquarian Bookshop)

Map 6, E7. V, Múzeum körút 17.

Mon–Fri 10am–6pm, Sat 10am–1pm.

Large secondhand bookshop opposite the Hungarian National Museum, with some antiquarian books and prints too.

Pless & Fox

Map 4, B3. XIII, Szent István körút 18 ©312-1238.

Old jewellery and rare metals, just down the road from the Margit híd.

Sóos

Map 6, D2. V, József Attila utca 22.

Mon–Fri 9am–5pm, Sat 10am–1pm.

An excellent place to pick up secondhand photographic goods at bargain rates, as well as assorted junk.

Stúdió Antikvárium

Map 4, E5. VI, Jókai tér 7 ©312-6294.

Five minutes' walk from the Oktogon, selling rare foreign books and prints and a good stock of art books.

ART AND PHOTOGRAPHY GALLERIES

Dovin

Map 6, B5. V, Galamb utca 6 ©318-3659.

Mon–Fri noon–6pm, Sat 11am–2pm.

Elegant gallery in central Pest selling contemporary Hungarian art.

Illárium

Map 4, I9. VIII, Köztársaság tér 15 ©210-4883.

Mon–Fri 10am–4pm, Sat 10am–2pm.

Small gallery on the south side of the large square, behind the Erkel Theatre, showing work by young Hungarian artists.

Mai Manó

Map 4, D6. VI, Nagymező utca 20 ©302-4398.

Mon–Fri 2–6pm.

On the first floor of the former Arizona Club, now restored as the House of Hungarian Photography and selling contemporary and old Hungarian photographs.

Miró

Map 4, E6. VI, Teréz körút 11–13 ©322-4041 ext 38.

Mon–Fri 11am–6pm.

Displays of contemporary photography.

Várfok Galéria

Map 3, C5. I, Várfok utca 14 ©213-5155.

Tues–Sat 11am–6pm.

One of three small galleries just off Moszkva tér. Work by the younger generation of Hungarian artists is displayed.

BOOKS AND MAPS

Bestsellers

Map 4, B7. V, Október 6 utca 11 ©312-1295.

Mon–Fri 9am–6.30pm, Sat 10am–6pm, Sun 10am–4pm.

Excellent range of English books, with English and Hungarian literature, travel, and reference books. Friendly staff, who can order books for you.

Cártográfia

Map 4, C5. VI, Bajcsy-Zsilinszky út 37.

Mon–Wed 9am–5pm, Thurs 9am–6.30pm, Fri 9am–3.30pm.

A map shop with a good range, but it's not self-service – you have to ask for the maps you want from the stern staff, which makes browsing difficult.

Írók Boltja

Map 4, E6. VI, Andrássy út 45.

July & Aug Mon–Fri 10am–6pm; Sept–June Mon–Fri 10am–6pm, Sat 10am–1pm.

The "Writers' Bookshop" is on the premises of the prewar *Japán* coffee house. There's a wide range of English-language books at the back, and a good selection of photography, art and architecture books in the main part of the shop. You can drink coffee and read at the tables in the front of the shop.

Litea

Map 5, D3. I, Hess András tér 4 (Fortuna Passage).

Daily 10am–6pm.

Right opposite you as you walk into the courtyard, this well-lit shop has a good stock of English books on Hungary, some CDs and cassettes, and a coffee bar with tables.

Rhythm 'n' Books

Map 6, D8. V, Szerb utca 21–23.

Mon–Fri noon–7pm.

At the far end of the courtyard as you enter from the street, offering a good selection of new and secondhand English-language books as well as some some CDs and tapes.

Studium

Map 6, C5. V, Váci utca 22.

Mon–Fri 10am–6.30pm, Sat 10am–3pm.

There's a good range of English-language books on Hungary straight ahead as you walk in, with English and travel books at the back of the shop.

Térkép bolt (Map shop)

Map 4, F9. VII, Nyár utca 1.

Mon–Fri 9.30am–5.30pm, Sat 10am–1pm.

You can browse here and check out the maps of Budapest, Hungary and Hungarian towns and regions, as well as European maps. The entrance is on Dohány utca.

Térképkirály

Map 6, E2. V, Sas utca 1.

Mon–Fri 9am–5.30pm.

Range of maps and guidebooks near Deák tér.

CLOTHES AND SHOES

Ciankáli

Map 4, D12. IX, Vámház körút 9.

Stylish secondhand clothes are sold in this basement shop at the back of the courtyard.

Cipőszerviz

Map 4, D5. VI, Jókai utca 10.

Mon–Fri 8.30am–5pm.

Shoe repairs near the Oktogon.

Csángó

Map 6, C4. V, Szervita tér 4.
Signposted in through a courtyard in central Pest. Bags of all shapes in a shop that has been going for sixty years.

Emilia Anda

Map 6, C4. V, Váci utca 16/b, Fortuna Passage.
Mon–Fri 10am–6pm, Sat 10am–1pm.
Classy, well-designed day and evening wear for women, and a range of jewellery including chunky rings and beautiful pendants.

Fleischer Shirts

Map 4, D6. V, Paulay Ede utca 53.
Mon–Fri 10am–6pm, Sat 10am–1pm.
Old-fashioned shirt-maker selling handmade shirts at good prices. On the corner of Nagymező utca, five minutes' walk from the Opera House.

Kaláka

Map 6, C5. V, Haris köz 2.
Mon–Fri 10am–6pm, Sat 10am–1pm.
Women's clothes, shoes and accessories by Hungarian designers.

Manier

Map 6, B7. V, Váci utca 53.
Mon–Fri 10am–7pm, Sat 10am–5pm.
Zany but appealing clothes from young fashion designer Ágnes Németh. Rather incongruously, the shop also stocks some good Hungarian wine.

Marácz Kalapbolt

Map 4, F8. VII, Wesselényi utca 41.
Mon–Fri 11am–6pm.
Old-fashioned hat shop with steamers and other old equipment in the back room. Sells beautiful fedoras in black and grey.

Marks & Spencer

Map 6, C3. V, Váci utca 3 & 4.

Mon–Wed 10am–6pm, Thurs & Fri 10am–7pm, Sat 10am–2pm.

Just off Vörösmarty tér, one shop sells clothes and the other lingerie.

Paroka bolt

Map 6, C3. VII, Kazinczy utca 26.

Wig-makers in the heart of the old Jewish quarter. Wigs don't come much cheaper between here and Brooklyn.

Vass

Map 6, C5. V, Haris köz 2 ©318-2375.

Mon–Fri 10am–6pm, Sat 10am–1pm.

A traditional shoemaker, just behind Ferenciek tere, producing handmade shoes to order and ready-to-wear.

Zábrák

Map 6, D3. V, Kempinski Hotel Corvinus, Erzsébet tér 7/8 ©266-8175.

Daily 9am–6pm.

Handmade shoes, ready-to-wear and made-to-order, in a hotel boutique near Deák tér.

FOOD AND WINE

Bio ABC

Map 6, E7. V, Múzeum körút 19.

Mon–Fri 10am–7pm, Sat 10am–2pm.

Natural oils, organic fruits, juices, cheeses and snacks, opposite the Hungarian National Museum.

Budapest Wine Society

Map 3, C5. V, Batthyány utca 59 ©212-2569.

Mon–Fri 10am–8pm, Sat 10am–6pm.

In a basement just up the street from Moszkva tér, offering some of Hungary's best wines from private producers across the country, good advice in English, and free tastings on Saturday afternoons.

Calendula Natura

Map 6, D4. V, Bárczy István utca 1–3

Oils, soaps and foodstuffs, a minute's walk from Deák tér.

La Boutique des Vins

Map 6, D1. V, József Attila utca 12 ©117-5919.

Mon–Fri 10am–6pm, Sat 10am–3pm.

Founded by the former *sommelier* of the *Gundel* restaurant, who now has a vineyard of his own. Strongest in wines from Villány and Tokaj.

Lekvárium

Map 4, E9. VII, Dohány utca 39

Mon–Fri 10am–6pm.

Hungarians have a strong tradition of pickling and preserving, with most families laying up jars of plum and apricot jam (*lekvár*), pickled cucumbers and peppers for the winter. This shop also sells some more interesting varieties, like quince compote and tobacco flower honey.

Rothschild

Map 6, G4. VII, Dob utca 12.

Mon–Thurs 8.30am–6pm, Fri 8.30am–2pm.

On the edge of the Jewish quarter, a couple of minutes' walk from the Dohány utca synagogue, this is one of the few shops in Budapest selling kosher Hungarian and imported wines and foods.

GIFTS, CRAFTS AND CHINA

Haas & Czjzek

Map 4, C6. VI, Bajcsy-Zsilinszky út 23 ©311-4094.

Full selection of Hungarian porcelain, including Hollóháza, Alföld and Zsolnay, and some glassware. The shop dates back to 1792, as the small display at the back of the shop documents.

Hephaistos

Map 6, B8. V, Molnár utca 27.

Mon–Fri 11am–6pm, Sat 10am–2pm.

Sells all kinds of wrought-iron objects from candlesticks to bookshelves. The latter might present transport difficulties, but the smaller items make great gifts. All goods are made in their Szentendre foundry.

Herend

Map 6, D2. V, József nádor tér 11 ©317-2622.

Very fancy – some would say twee – and expensive porcelain from the Herend factory in western Hungary, collected by the likes of Queen Victoria.

Holló Folk Art Gallery

Map 6, E5. V, Vitkovics Mihály utca 10 ©317-8103.

This beautiful early nineteenth-century shop near the Astoria is a very pleasant place to browse in, and you can also buy good presents, such as wooden furniture, boxes, eggs and candlesticks all hand-painted with bird, tulip and heart folk motifs, and intricately iced gingerbread figures.

Zsolnay

Map 6, C5. V, Kigyó utca 4 and Ferenciek tere 11.

Mon–Fri 10am–6pm, Sat 10am–1pm.

Art Nouveau-style porcelain that is less kitsch that some other Hungarian porcelains. Made at the factory in Pécs in southern Hungary that made its name designing the tiles on buildings such as the Applied Arts Museum.

MARKET HALLS AND FLEA MARKETS

Ecseri piac

Map 2, H8. XIX, Nagykörösi út, on the southeast edge of the city. Access by bus #54 (red) from the Határ út metro stop on the blue line, or bus #54 (black) from Boráros tér by Petőfi Bridge.

Mon–Fri 8am–4pm, Sat 8am–noon.

This flea market has become a well-known spot for tourists – and for ripping them off. Stalls sell everything from bike parts and jackboots to nineteenth-century peasant clothing and hand-carved pipes, with a few genuine antiques in amongst the tat. You'll need to bargain hard.

Hold utca

Map 4, B5. V, Hold utca.

Mon–Fri 6am–5pm, Sat 6am–1pm.

Right behind the American Embassy, this is one of the old market halls. Worth going into for the architecture alone.

István tér

Map 2, F3. IV, István tér.

Mon–Fri 7am–5pm, Sat 7am–1pm.

Large market in the square behind the town hall in the northern suburb of Újpest, at the northern end of the blue metro line (M3). It attracts a large number of farmers from the countryside, making it one of the most atmospheric markets in the city.

Klauzál tér

Map 4, E8. VII, Klauzál tér.

Mon–Fri 6am–5pm, Sat 6am–1pm.

A market hall in the heart of the old Jewish quarter, with a cheap supermarket and stalls. The fruit and veg stands have now been squeezed out into the entrance to the square.

Lehel tér

Map 4, D1. XIII, Lehel tér (M3).

Mon–Fri 6am–5pm, Sat 6am–1pm, Sun 6am–noon.

Large, popular market that's one of the cheapest in town, with crowds milling round its tightly packed rows of peasants selling fruit and strings of paprika, and Roma selling baskets and pans. The typical market snack is *lángos*, fried dough which you eat with cheese, sour cream, or garlic, or all three together.

Main Market Hall

Map 6, B9. IX, Vámház körút 2.

Mon 6am–4pm, Tues–Fri 6am–6pm, Sat 6am–2pm.

By the Szabadság híd at the bottom end of Váci utca, the *Nagycsarnok* is the largest and finest market hall of them all, as well as being the most expensive. It also has good stalls upstairs, amidst the touristy embroideries and tat.

Petőfi Csarnok

Map 2, F5. XIV, Zichy Mihály utca 14.

Sun 8am–2pm

Sunday flea market in and around the ugly cultural centre in the Városliget. Smaller than Ecseri, and less established, with stallholders laying out their wares every week. Lots of junk but some good bargains too. Small entry fee.

PHOTOGRAPHY

Fotólabor

Map 4, F10. VIII, Gyulai Pál utca 14.

Mon–Fri 8am–6pm.

Top quality black and white prints done very cheaply, and photos developed and enlarged.

Fotolux

Map 6, E4. VII, Károly körút 21.

Mon–Fri 9am–9pm, Sat 9am–7pm.

Good quality photographic developing and printing.

RECORDS AND CDs

Amadeus

Map 6. B2. V, Szende Pál utca 1.

Daily 9am–9pm.

Good store for classical and jazz music, which also stocks bargain Hungaroton CDs. Entrance from the Danube promenade. No credit cards.

CD Bar

Map 4, F11. VIII, Krúdy Gyula utca 6 ©338-4281.

Mon–Fri 10am–8pm, Sat 10am–4pm.

Classical and jazz records in this basement shop in an increasingly fashionable backstreet a couple of streets behind the Hungarian National Museum.

Fonó

Map 2, E7. XI, Sztregova utca 3 ©206-5300.

Sun–Fri 10am–11pm, Sat 6–11pm.

It's a twenty-minute tram ride from Deák tér on #47 to get to the shop in the bar of this folk club, but it's worth it for the range of jazz, ethno-jazz blues and world music, and, above all, Hungarian folk music CDs. Stays open into the evening during concerts.

Kodály Zoltán Zeneműbolt

Map 6, E7. V, Múzeum körút 17 & 21.

Scores and secondhand records, tapes and CDs, opposite the Hungarian National Museum.

Rózsavölgyi Zeneműbolt

Map 6, C4. V, Szervita tér 5.

Mon, Tues, Thurs & Fri 9.30am–7pm, Wed 10am–7pm, Sat 10am–5pm, Sun 11am–6pm.

Established record shop with a knowledgeable staff, near

Vörösmarty tér. Classical music on the ground floor, rock and folk downstairs. Good for sheet music as well.

TOYS

Fakopáncs

Map 4, F12. VIII, Baross utca 50 and József körút 50 ©337-0992.
Mon–Fri 9am–7pm, Sat 9am–4pm, Sun 9am–2pm.
A massive array of wooden puzzles and toys are crammed into the two "Woodpecker" shops, both at the junction of Baross utca and the Nagykörút.

Gondolkodó Logikai Játékok

Map 4, D7. VII, Király utca 25.
Mon–Fri 10am–6pm, Sat 10am–1pm.
"Thinking Logical Games" is the wordy name of the shop, so naturally it has puzzles, Rubik's cubes, chess sets, logic games and other toys to make you think. You can also get the Hungarian version of Monopoly.

Játékszerek anno

Map 4, D4. VI, Teréz körút 54.
Mon–Fri 10am–6pm, Sat 9am–1pm.
Beautifully made reproductions of turn-of-the-century toys and games including wooden tops, kaleidoscopes, and a spectacular wind-up duck on a bicycle.

Puppet Store

Map 6, C5. V, Párizsi utca 3.
Mon–Fri 10am–6pm, Sat 10am–1pm.
A handful of dragons and a nestful of birds are just two of the hand puppets available here. The shop assistants often go onto the street to demonstrate their "pets".

Directory

AIRLINES Aeroflot, V, Váci utca 4 ©318-5955; Air France, V, Kristóf tér 6 ©318-0411; Alitalia, East-West Business Centre, VIII, Rákóczi út 1–3 ©373-7782; Balkan, V, Párizsi utca 7 ©317-1818; British Airways, East-West Business Centre, VIII, Rákóczi út 1–3 ©266-6699; CSA, V, Vörösmarty tér 2 ©318-3045; KLM, VIII, Rákóczi út 1–3 ©373-7737; Lufthansa, V, Váci utca 19–21 ©266-4511; Malév, V, Roosevelt tér 2 ©266-5913; Sabena, V, Váci utca 1–3 ©318-4111; SAS, V, Váci utca 1–3 ©266-2633; Swissair, V, Kristóf ter 7–8 ©328-5000; TAROM, Ferihegy airport, Terminal 2B ©296-8661.

AIRPORT INFORMATION Terminal 2A: departures ©296-6059, arrivals ©296-8721; Terminal 2B: departures ©296-5882, arrivals ©296-58051. The Airport Minibus service can take you directly to your destination. Tickets (1200Ft) can be purchased while waiting in the luggage hall or when you come out into the main concourse. You can also return to the airport on the minibus – call a day in advance if you're on an early flight, and allow a couple of hours to get there.

BANKS AND EXCHANGE ATMs can be found across the city. The best places for changing money are the larger banks: the Magyar Külkereskedelmí Bank at Türr István utca 9, by the top of Váci utca, or the small Gönc és vidéke Bank at Rákóczi út 5 offer the best rates, while the exchange offices around

Vörösmarty tér have the worst ones. There is a 24-hour exchange service at V, Apáczai Csere János utca 1. You can transfer money from abroad through the Magyar Külkereskedelmí Bank, V, Szent István tér 11 and through the American Express Moneygram service (minimum $100), V, Deák utca 10 ©267-8680. The Magyar Külkereskedelmí Bank also has safe deposit boxes for storing valuables.

BIKE RENTAL Try Nella Bikes off Bajcsy-Zsilinszky út at V, Kálmán Imre utca 23 ©331-3184; or Tura Mobil at VI, Nagymező utca 43 ©312-5073. For repairs, go to Kerékvár at I, Hunyadi János utca 4, at the Buda end of the Lánchíd ©201-0713; or Probike at II, Zőldlomb utca 36-38 ©325-5406. Both of these sell bikes, and opening times are usually Mon–Fri 10am–6pm, Sat 10–1pm.

BRITISH COUNCIL, VI, Benczúr utca 26 ©321-4039. Library, newspapers and a noticeboard. Mon–Thurs 11am–6pm, Fri 11am–5pm. Closed Aug.

CAR RENTAL Budget at the *Hotel Mercure Buda*, I, Krisztina körút 41–43 ©214-0420; Főtaxi at VII, Kertész utca 24–28 ©322-1471; Eurodollar, XI, Prielle Kornélia utca 45 ©204-2993 or 204-2994; and Hertz at V, Aranykéz utca 4–8 ©296-0999.

CYBERCAFÉS *Eckermann Café*, VI, Andrássy út 24, near the Opera House (Mon–Fri 2–10pm, Sat 10am–10pm), offers access to the Internet at no charge. Other cybercafés include *Kommunikációs Szaküzlet Internet Rock Café*, IX, Mester utca 57 (*www.comfort.hu/*); *Internext Studio*, VIII, Horánszky utca 26 (*www.inext.hu/*); *Matávnet*, V, Petőfi Sándor utca 17-19 (Mon–Fri 8am–8pm, Sat 9am–3pm; © 318-1897), which is a cyber office rather than café; and the *Teleport Internet Café*, VIII, Vas utca 7 (Mon–Sat noon–10pm; ©267-6361), a café with snacks, just off Rákóczi út, which has the advantage of the use of a printer.

ELECTRIC POWER 220 volts. Round two-pin plugs are used. Bring an adaptor.

EMBASSIES Australia, XII, Királyhágó tér 8–9 ✆201-8899; Austria, VI, Benczúr utca 16 ✆269-6700; Bulgaria, VI, Andrássy út 115 ✆322-0824; Canada, XII, Budakeszi út 32 ✆275-1200; Czech Republic, VI, Rózsa utca 6 ✆351-0539; Germany, XIV, Stefánia út 101–3 ✆467-3500; Israel, II, Fullánk utca 8 ✆200-0781; Netherlands, II Füge utca 5-7 ✆326-5301; Romania, XIV, Thököly út 72 ✆352-0271; Russian Federation, Bajza utca 35 ✆302-5230; Slovakia, XIV, Stefánia út 22 ✆251-1700; Slovenia, II Cseppkő utca 68 ✆325-9202; UK, V, Harmincad utca 6 ✆266-2888; USA, V, Szabadság tér 12 ✆267-4400.

EMERGENCIES Ambulance ✆104; Police ✆107; Fire service ✆105.

HOSPITALS AND DENTISTRY There are 24-hour emergency departments at V, Hold utca 19, behind the US embassy (✆311-6816), and at II, Ganz utca 13–15 (✆202-1370). The Országos Baleseti Intézet, VIII, Fiumei út 17 (✆333-7599), specializes in broken limbs and accidents. Profident, VII, Károly körút 1, is a round-the-clock dentist where they speak English. Private clinics with English-speaking personnel include the IMS (International Medical Services) at XIII, Váci út 202 (Mon–Fri 7.30am–8pm; ✆329-8423) and at III, Vihar utca 29 (8pm–8am; ✆250-3829 or 250-1899); and the R-Klinika at II, Felsőzöldmáli út 13 (✆325-9999 or 325-8942). Embassies can also recommend private, foreign-language-speaking doctors and dentists.

INTERNATIONAL BUSES AND TRAINS International train tickets should be purchased 24–36hr in advance, at the stations or the MÁV booking office, VI, Andrássy út 35 (Mon–Fri 9am–5pm; ✆322-0856). Bookings are required on all international train routes. The Vienna-bound *Wiener Waltzer* often runs late, so you should reserve sleepers on from Austria in Budapest. Bring drinks too, as the buffet staff overcharge shamelessly. Tickets for international buses must be purchased at the bus stations 24hr in advance.

LOST PROPERTY For items left on public transport, go to the BKV office at VII, Akácfa utca 18 (Mon, Tues & Thurs 7.30am–3pm, Wed 7.30am–7pm, Fri 7.30am–2pm; ©322-6613). Lost or stolen passports should be reported to the police station in the district where they were lost. Any found are handed to the relevant embassy.

NAMES Surnames precede forenames in Hungary, to the confusion of foreigners. In this book, the names of historical personages are rendered in the Western fashion, for instance, Lajos Kossuth rather than Kossuth Lajos (Hungarian-style), except when referring to the names of buildings, streets, etc.

NEWSPAPERS British papers (in their international editions) and the *International Herald Tribune* are on sale in many places in the centre of town, including stalls on Vörösmarty tér and the newspaper shop at Petőfi Sándor utca 17.

PHARMACIES The following are all open 24hr: II, Frankel Leó út 22 ©212-4406; VI, Teréz körút 41 ©311-4439; VII, Rákóczi út 86, at Baross tér ©322-9613; XI, Kosztolányi Dezső, tér 11 ©466-6494; XII, Alkotás utca lB, opposite Déli Station ©355-4691; XIV, Bosnyák utca l/A ©383-0391. For herbal remedies try Herbária, VIII, Rákóczi út 49, and V, Bajcsy-Zsilinszky út 58.

PHOTOCOPYING Copy General, V, Semmelweis utca 4 (Mon–Fri 7am–10pm, Sat 9am–6pm) provides a photocopying service right in the centre of the city. Their branch at Lonyay utca 13, south of Kálvin tér, is open 24 hours.

POST OFFICES Main office with poste restante is at V, Petőfi utca 13 (Mon–Fri 8am–8pm, Sat 8am–2pm); letters should be sent to Poste restante, Magyar Posta, 1364, Budapest. There's a late-opening post office at VII, Baross tér 11C by Keleti Station (daily 7am–9pm).

TAXIS English-speaking taxi companies include: Buda-taxi ©233-3333, Citytaxi ©211-1111, Főtaxi ©222-2222, Tele-5-taxi ©355-5555 and Volántaxi ©466-6666.

TELEPHONES International calls can be made from the

Telephone and Telegram Bureau, V, Petőfi utca 17–19 (Mon–Fri 8am–8pm, Sat 10am–4pm) or from any phone booth on the street. The international operator can be reached on ✆199, though it can be a long wait to get the number you want.

TICKET OFFICES (*jegyiroda*) Filharmonia Budapest, V, Mérleg utca 10 (Mon–Fri 10am–6pm; ✆318-0281); Központi Jegyiroda (Central Ticket Office), VI, Andrássy út 18 (Mon–Thurs 9am–6pm, Fri 9am–5pm; ✆312-0000); Music Mix, V, Váci utca 33 (Mon–Fri 10am–6pm, Sat 10am–2pm; ✆338-2237); Publika, V, Károly körút 9 (Mon–Fri 10am–5pm; ✆322-2010); and Vigadó Jegyiroda, V, Vörösmarty tér 1 (Mon–Fri 9am–7pm, Sat & Sun 10am–3pm; ✆327-4322).

TIME Hungary is one hour ahead of GMT, six hours ahead of Eastern Standard Time and nine ahead of Pacific Standard Time in North America. A word of caution: Hungarians express time in a way that might confuse the anglophone traveller. For example, 10.30am is expressed as "half eleven" (written 1/2 11 or f11), 10.45am is "three-quarter-eleven" (3/4 11 or h11), and 10.15am is "a quarter of eleven" (1/4 11 or n11).

CONTEXTS

History

Although Budapest has only formally existed since 1873, when the twin cities of Buda and Pest were united in a single municipality together with the smaller Óbuda, the locality has been settled since **prehistory**. *Homo sapiens* appeared here around 8000 BC, and a succession of peoples overran the region during the first Age of Migrations, the most important of whom were the Celtic Eravisci who settled on Gellért-hegy in about 400 BC.

In 35 BC the Danube Basin was conquered by the **Romans** and subsequently incorporated within their empire as the province of Pannonia, whose northern half was governed from the town of **Aquincum** on the west bank of the Danube. Ruins of a camp, villas, baths and an amphitheatre can still be seen today in Óbuda and Római-Fürdő. Roman rule lasted until 430 AD, when Pannonia was ceded to **Attila the Hun**. Attila's planned assault on Rome was averted by his death on his wedding night, and thereafter Pannonia was carved up by Germanic tribes until they were ousted by the Turkic-speaking Avars, who were in turn assailed by the Bulgars, another warlike race from the Eurasian steppes.

The coming of the Magyars

The most significant of the invaders from the east were the **Magyars**, who stamped their language and identity on Hungary. Their original homeland was between the Volga and the Urals, where today two Siberian peoples still speak languages that are the closest linguistic relatives to Hungarian; along with Finnish, Turkish and Mongolian, these languages make up the Altaic family. Many of these Magyars migrated south, where they eventually became vassals of the Khazar empire and mingled with the Bulgars as both peoples moved westwards to escape the marauding Petchenegs.

In 895 or 896 AD, seven Magyar tribes led by Árpád entered the Carpathian Basin and spread out across the plain, in what Hungarians call the "**landtaking**" (*honfoglalás*). They settled here, though they remained raiders for the next seventy years, striking terror as far afield as France (where people thought them to be Huns), until a series of defeats persuaded them to settle for assimilating their gains. According to the medieval chronicler, known as Anonymous, the clan of Árpád settled on Csepel sziget, and it was Árpád's brother, Buda, who purportedly gave his name to the west bank of the new settlement.

The Árpád dynasty

Civilization developed gradually after Árpád's great-grandson **Prince Géza** established links with Bavaria and invited Catholic missionaries to Hungary. His son **Stephen** took the decisive step of applying to Pope Sylvester for recognition, and on Christmas Day in the year 1000 AD was crowned as a Christian king. With the help of Bishop Gellért, he then set about converting his pagan subjects. Stephen was subsequently credited with the **foundation of Hungary** and canonized after his death in 1038. His mummified hand and the crown of St Stephen have since been revered as both holy and national relics, and are some of Budapest's most popular tourist attractions today.

Despite succession struggles after Stephen's death, a lack of external threats during the eleventh and twelfth centuries enabled the **development of Buda and Pest** to begin in earnest, largely thanks to French, Walloon and German settlers who worked and traded here under royal protection. However, the growth in royal power caused tribal leaders to rebel in 1222 AD, and Andrew II was forced to recognize the noble status and rights of the **natio** – landed freemen ·mpt from taxation – in the Golden Bull, a kind of ·arian Magna Carta.

Andrew's son **Béla IV** tried to restore royal authority, but the **Mongol invasion** of 1241 devastated the country and left even the royal palace of Esztergom in ruins. Only the timely death of Ghengis Khan spared Hungary from further ravages. Mindful of a return visit, Béla selected **Várhegy** as a more defensible seat and encouraged foreign artisans to rebuild Buda, which German colonists called "*Ofen*" after its numerous lime-kilns (the name Pest, which is of Slav origin, also means "oven").

Renaissance and decline

After the Árpád dynasty expired in 1301, foreign powers advanced their own claims to the throne and for a while there were three competing kings, all duly crowned. Eventually **Charles Robert** of the French Angevin (or Anjou) dynasty triumped. Peacetime gave him the opportunity to develop the gold mines of Transylvania and northern Hungary – the richest in Europe – and Charles bequeathed a robust exchequer to his son **Louis the Great**, whose reign saw the population of Hungary rise to three million, and the crown territories expanded to include much of what are now Croatia and Poland. The oldest extant strata of the Buda Palace on Várhegy date from this time.

After Louis's demise, the throne was claimed by **Sigismund of Luxembourg**, Prince of Bohemia, whom the nobility despised as the "Czech swine". His failure to check the advance of the Turks through the Balkans was only redeemed by the Transylvanian warlord **János Hunyadi**, whose lifting of the siege of Belgrade caused rejoicing throughout Christendom. Vajdahunyad Castle in the Városliget is a romantic nineteenth-century replica of Hunyadi's ancestral seat in Transylvania.

Hunyadi's nephew, **Mátyás Corvinus**, is remembered as the **Renaissance king**, who, together with his second wife

Beatrice of Naples, lured humanists and artists from Italy to their court. Mátyás was an enlightened despot, renowned for his fairness, but when he died in 1490 leaving no legitimate heir the nobles took control, choosing a pliable successor and exploiting the peasantry. However, in 1514 the peasants, led by **György Dósza**, rebelled against the oppression. The savage repression of this **revolt** (over 70,000 peasants were killed and Dózsa was roasted alive) and subsequent laws imposing "perpetual serfdom" alienated the mass of the population – a situation hardly improved by the coronation of the 9-year-old **Louis II**, who was barely 16 when he had to face the full might of the Turks under Sultan Süleyman "the Magnificent".

The Turkish conquest: Hungary divided

The battle of **Mohács** in 1526 was a shattering defeat for the Hungarians. After sacking Buda, the Turks withdrew to muster forces for their real objective, Vienna. To forestall this, Ferdinand of Habsburg proclaimed himself king of Hungary and occupied western Hungary, while in Buda the nobles put János Zápolyai on the throne. Following Zápolyai's death in 1541, Ferdinand claimed full sovereignty, but the Sultan occupied Buda and central Hungary and made Zápolyai's son ruler of Transylvania, which henceforth became a semi-autonomous principality – a **tripartite division** formally recognized in 1568. Despite various truces, warfare became a fact of life for the next 150 years, and national independence was not to be recovered for centuries afterwards.

Turkish-occupied Hungary was ruled by a Pasha in Buda, with much of the land either deeded to the Sultan's soldiers and officials, or run directly as a state fief. The owns, however, enjoyed some rights and were encouraged rade, and the Turks were largely indifferent to the sec- bigotry practised in Habsburg-ruled Hungary. The

Habsburg **liberation of Buda** in 1686 was actually a disaster for its inhabitants, as the victors massacred Jews, pillaged at will and reduced Buda and Pest to rubble. The city's Turkish baths and the tomb of Gül Baba were almost the only surviving buildings.

Habsburg rule

Habsburg rule was a bitter pill, which the Hungarians attempted to reject in the **War of Independence** of 1703–11, led by **Ferenc Rákóczi II**. Though it was unsuccessful, the Habsburgs began to soften their autocracy with paternalism as a result. The revival of towns and villages during this time owed much to settlers from all over the empire, hence the Serb and Greek churches that remain in Pest and Szentendre. Yet while the aristocracy commissioned over two hundred palaces, and Baroque town centres and orchestras flourished, the masses remained all but serfs, mired in isolated villages.

Such contradictions impelled the **Reform movement** led by Count **István Széchenyi**. His vision of progress was embodied in the construction of the **Lánchíd** (Chain Bridge) between Buda and Pest, which proved an enormous spur to the development of the two districts. The National Museum, the Academy of Sciences and many other institutions were founded at this time, while the coffee houses of Pest became a hotbed of radical politics.

When the empire was shaken by revolutions which broke out across Europe in **March 1848**, local radicals seized the moment. **Lajos Kossuth** dominated parliament, while **Sándor Petőfi** mobilized crowds on the streets of Pest. A second war of independence followed, which again ended in defeat and Habsburg repression, epitomized by the execution of Prime Minister Batthyány in 1849, and the Citadella atop Gellért-hegy, built to intimidate citizens with its guns.

Budapest's Belle Époque

Following the historic Compromise of 1867, which established the **Dual Monarchy** of Austria-Hungary, Buda and Pest underwent rapid **expansion** and formally merged. Pest was extensively remodelled, acquiring the Nagykörút (Great Boulevard) and Andrássy út, a grand approach to the Városliget, where Hungary's **millennial anniversary celebrations** were staged in 1896. New suburbs were created to house the burgeoning population, which was by now predominantly Magyar, though there were still large German and Jewish communities. Both elegance and squalor abounded, café society reached its apogee, and Budapest experienced a **cultural efflorescence** in the early years of the twentieth century to rival that of Vienna. Today, the most tangible reminders are the remarkable buildings by Ödön Lechner, Béla Lajtha and other masters of Art Nouveau and National Romanticism – the styles that characterized the era.

The Horthy years

With the collapse of the Dual Monarchy at the end of **World War I**, the liberal Count Károlyi was rapidly superseded by a revolutionary **Republic of Councils** that terrified the landowning classes. The Republic collapsed in 1919 after the Romanian army routed it on the battlefield and occupied Budapest, whereupon the status quo ante was restored by **Admiral Horthy**, self-appointed regent for Karl IV, who had been exiled by the Western allies ("the Admiral without a fleet, for the king without a kingdom"). His regency was characterized by gala balls and hunger marches, revanchism and anti-Semitism. Yet Horthy was a moderate compared to the **Arrow Cross** Fascists waiting in ·e wings, whose power grew as **World War II** raged.

nticipating Horthy's defection from the Axis in ·er 1944, Nazi Germany staged a coup, installing an

Arrow Cross government, which enabled them to begin the massacre of the **Jews** of Budapest. It was only thanks to the valiant efforts of foreign diplomats like Wallenberg and Lutz that half of them survived, when ninety percent of Hungary's provincial Jews perished. In the same year, the five-month-long **siege of Budapest** was a time of awful hardships for the city's inhabitants, during which the Danube bridges were blown up and Várhegy reduced to rubble, as the Red Army battered the *Wehrmacht* into submission.

The Communist takeover and the 1956 Uprising

As Budapesters struggled to rebuild their lives after the war, the Soviet-backed **Communists** took control by "salami tactics" – stealthily reducing the power of other forces in society, and using the threat of the Red Army and the ÁVO secret police, who took over the former Arrow Cross torture chambers on Andrássy út. By 1948 their hold on Hungary was total, symbolized by the red stars that replaced the crown of St Stephen everywhere, and a huge statue of Stalin beside the Városliget, where citizens were obliged to parade before Hungary's "Little Stalin", **Mátyás Rákosi**.

As elsewhere in Eastern Europe, the Communist Party was racked by power struggles, and after the death of Stalin in 1953 Rákosi was replaced by **Imre Nagy**. Nagy's "New Course" allowed Hungarians an easier life before Rákosi struck back by expelling him from the Party for "deviationism". However, society had taken heart from the respite and intellectuals held increasingly outspoken public debates during the summer of 1956. The mood came to a head in October, when 200,000 people attended the funeral of László Rajk, a victim of the show trials in 1949, in Kerepesi Cemetery, and Budapest's students decided to march to the General Bem statue near the Margit híd.

On October 23 demonstrators chanting anti-Rákosi slogans crossed the Danube to mass outside Parliament. As dusk fell, students demanding access to the Radio Building were fired upon by the ÁVO, and a spontaneous **Uprising** began that rapidly took hold throughout Budapest and spread across Hungary. The newly restored Nagy found himself in a maelstrom, as popular demands were irreconcilable with realpolitik. It was Hungary's misfortune that the UN was preoccupied with the Suez Crisis when the Soviets reinvaded and crushed the Uprising, causing 200,000 Hungarians to flee abroad.

"Goulash socialism" and the end of Communism

After Soviet power had been bloodily restored, **János Kádár** gradually normalized conditions, embarking on cautious reforms to create a "**goulash socialism**" that made Hungary the envy of its Warsaw Pact neighbours and the West's favourite Communist state in the late 1970s. Though everyone knew the limits of the "Hungarian condition", there was enough freedom and consumer goods to keep the majority content. During the 1980s, however, it became apparent that the attempt to reconcile a command economy and one-party rule with market forces was unsustainable. Dissidents tested the limits of criticism, and even within the Party there were those who realized that changes were needed. Happily, this coincided with the advent of Gorbachev, which made it much easier for the reform Communists to shunt Kádár aside in 1988.

The **end of Communism** was heralded by two events the following summer: the ceremonial reburial of Nagy, and the dismantling of the barbed wire along the border ith Austria, which enabled thousands of East Germans to be while "on holiday". In October 1989, the govern- announced the legalization of other parties as a prelude to free elections, and the People's Republic was renamed the Republic of Hungary in a ceremony broadcast live on national television. Two weeks later this watershed was eclipsed by the fall of the Berlin Wall, closely followed by the Velvet Revolution in Czechoslovakia and the overthrow of Ceauşescu in Romania.

Budapest today: the post-Communist era

After such events, Hungary's first **free elections** in the spring of 1990 seemed an anti-climax, despite resulting in a rejection of the Socialists (reform Communists), and a centre-right coalition dominated by the **Hungarian Democratic Forum** (**MDF**) under Premier **József Antall**. The MDF aimed to restore the traditions and hierarchies of prewar Hungary. However, not everyone wanted the Catholic Church to regain its former power, and the MDF's desire to restore the Hungarian nation to its former position sounded to Hungary's neighbours like a revanchist claim on the lost lands of Trianon.

After Antall's death in 1993, his successor was unable to turn the economy around, and the 1994 elections saw the **Socialists return to power**, assisted by sympathetic media. To guard against accusations of abusing power like their predecessors, they included the **Free Democrats** (**SzDSz**) in government and reassured Hungary's creditors with austerity measures that disillusioned voters who had hoped that the Socialists would reverse the growing inequalities in society. The emergence of a brash new entrepreneurial class and consumer culture, rising crime, unemployment and homelessness were deeply unsettling to many, especially the older generation – yet there seemed no alternative to the onward march of capitalism.

Widespread corruption among the Socialists led to their defeat in the **1998 election**, which was narrowly won by the **Fidesz-Hungarian Civic Party** of **Viktor Orbán**. Like

Britain's Tony Blair, whose style of leadership he emulates, Orbán managed to reposition his party to the right by talking about the need to revive national culture and using the buzzword *polgári* (meaning "civic", but redolent of bourgeois middle-class values) to appeal to a broad constituency.

A decade after the historic "change of systems" (*rendszerváltas*), Hungary is settling down as a capitalist democracy, set to **join the EU** in 2002 – a move that most Hungarians support, believing that they will benefit from being under Europe's protective mantle. At the same time, most also wish to limit foreign ownership – contrary to EU directives – and many are uneasy about the erosion of their national identity by global capitalism and multi-culturalism. Even joining NATO, which was widely supported, may be cause for second thoughts since the conflict with Serbia began.

There is also tension between Orbán's government and the Mayor of Budapest, Gábor Demszky, who escaped the fate of his party SzDSz by being re-elected for a third term in 1998. In an effort to undermine Demszky's position, Orbán halted the building of the National Theatre whose foundations had already been laid at vast expense (see p.207), and cancelled the city's planned fourth metro line. Besides personal animosity between former political allies, the feud reflects an older conflict between Budapest and the provinces, where the capital has long been viewed with suspicion as too cosmopolitan and alien to true Hungarian values - a constituency that Orbán seems happy to champion.

Books

There is quite a range of books on Budapest available in the city, particularly books on architecture and translations of Hungarian literature. The Hungarian publisher Corvina publishes a number of books covering Hungary's folk traditions and artistic treasures, mostly translated into English or German, which can be bought fairly cheaply in Budapest.

Publishers are detailed below in the form of British publisher/American publisher, where both exist. Where books are published in one country only, UK or US follows the publisher's name. Out-of-print books are designated o/p.

See p.238 for details of bookshops in Budapest.

Art and architecture

Our Budapest (Budapest City Hall). A very informative series of pocket-size books available from the English-language bookshops listed on p.238. Written in Hungarian, English and other languages by experts in their fields, they cover the city's architecture, baths, and parks, and cost a mere 300Ft or so each, though unfortunately the standard of English varies.

Györgyi Éri et al, *A Golden Age: Art and Society in Hungary 1896–1914* (Corvina). Hungary's Art Nouveau age captured in a beautifully illustrated coffee-table volume.

János Gerle et al, *Budapest: An Architectural Guide* (6 BT, Budapest). The best of the small new guides to the city's twentieth-century architecture, covering almost 300 buildings, with brief descriptions in Hungarian and English.

Ruth Gruber, *Jewish Heritage Travel: A Guide to Central and Eastern Europe* (John Wiley o/p). The most comprehensive guide to Jewish sights in Budapest and elsewhere.

Edwin Heathcote, *Budapest: A Guide to Twentieth-Century Architecture* (Ellipsis, UK). A useful and informative pocket guide to the city, though with some curious omissions.

Tamás Hofer et al, *Hungarian Peasant Art* (Constable/International Publications Service o/p). An excellently produced examination of Hungarian folk art, with lots of good photos.

Imre Móra, *Budapest Then and Now* (New World Publishing, Budapest). A personal and very informative set of accounts of life in the capital, past and present.

Tamás Révész, *Budapest: A City before the Millennium* (Herald, Budapest). Excellent collection of black and white photographs of the city, though the text can be irritating.

History, politics and society

Robert Bideleux, Ian Jeffries, *A History of Eastern Europe: Crisis and Change* (Routledge, UK). An excellent and wide-ranging history of the region.

Judit Frigyesi, *Béla Bartók and Turn-of-the-century Budapest* (University of California Press). Placing Bartók in his cultural milieu, this is an excellent account of the Hungarian intellectual world at the beginning of the century.

Jörg K Hoensch, *A History of Modern Hungary 1867–1994* (Longman/Addison-Wesley). An authoritative history of the country.

Bill Lomax, *Hungary 1956* (Allison & Busby/St Martin's Press o/p). Still probably the best – and shortest – book on the Uprising, by an acknowledged expert on modern Hungary. Lomax also edited *Eyewitness in Hungary* (Spokesman, UK), an anthology of accounts by foreign Communists (most of whom were sympathetic to the Uprising) that vividly depicts elation, confusion and tragedy of the events of October

John Lukács, *Budapest 1900* (Weidenfeld/Grove Press). Excellent and very readable account of the politics and society of Budapest at the turn of the century, during a golden age that was shortly to come to an end.

George Schöpflin, *Politics in Eastern Europe 1945–92* (Blackwell). An excellent overview of the region in the last fifty years by one of the acknowledged experts.

Michael Stewart, *The Time of the Gypsies* (Westview Press). This superb book on gypsy culture is based on anthropological research in a gypsy community in Hungary.

Peter Sugar (ed), *A History of Hungary* (I B Tauris). A useful, not too academic, survey of Hungarian history from pre-Conquest times to the close of the Kádár era, with a brief epilogue on the transition to democracy.

Nigel Swain, *Hungary: The Rise and Fall of Feasible Socialism* (Verso/Routledge Chapman & Hall). Analyses the "Hungarian model" of socialism in decline, and the prospects for a market economy in the 1990s, now that capitalism is showing little sign of delivering prosperity and social justice.

Biography and travel writing

Magda Dénes, *Castles Burning: A Child's Life in War* (Anchor/Touchstone Books). A moving biographical account of the Budapest ghetto and postwar escape to France, Cuba, and the United States, seen through the eyes of a Jewish girl. The author died in December 1966, shortly before the book she always wanted to write was published.

Patrick Leigh Fermor, *A Time of Gifts* (Penguin); *Between the Woods and the Water* (Penguin). In 1934 the young Leigh Fermor started walking from Holland to Turkey, reaching Hungary in the closing chapter of *A Time of Gifts*. In *Between the Woods and the Water* the inhabitants of the Great Plain and Transylvania –

both gypsies and aristocrats –are superbly evoked. Lyrical and erudite.

George Mikes, *Any Souvenirs?* (Penguin/Harvard Common Press o/p). Born in Siklós in southern Hungary, Mikes fled the country in 1956 and made a new life in Britain as a humorist. This wry account relates his first visit home in fifteen years.

John Paget, *Hungary and Transylvania* (Ayer, US). Paget's massive book attempted to explain nineteenth-century Hungary to the English middle class, and, within its aristocratic limitations, succeeded. Occasionally found in secondhand bookshops.

Walter Starkie, *Raggle-Taggle* (John Murray o/p/Transatlantic Arts o/p). The wanderings of a Dublin professor with a fiddle, who bummed around Budapest and the Plain in search of gypsy music in the 1920s. First published in 1933 and last issued in 1964; a secondhand bookshop perennial.

Ernő Szép, *The Smell of Humans* (Central European University Press, Budapest/Arrow, UK). A superb and harrowing memoir of the Holocaust in Hungary.

Literature

Access to Hungarian literature has greatly improved in recent years, and authors like Péter Nádas and Péter Esterházy, whose dense and very Hungarian style had long been inaccessible to English readers, are now appearing in translation. There are numerous collections of short stories published by Corvina in Budapest, though the quality of translations varies from the sublime to the ridiculous. Works by nineteenth-century authors such as Mór Jókai are most likely found in secondhand bookshops (see

ANTHOLOGIES

Loránt Czigány (ed), *The Oxford History of Hungarian Literature from the Earliest Times to the Present* (Oxford University Press). Probably the most comprehensive collection in print to date. In chronological order, with good coverage of the political and social background.

György Gömöri (ed), *Colonnade of Teeth* (Bloodaxe/Dufour). In spite of its strange title, this is a good introduction to the work of young Hungarian poets.

Michael March (ed), *Description of a Struggle* (Picador/Vintage). A collection of contemporary Eastern European prose, featuring four pieces by Hungarian writers including Nádas and Esterházy.

POETRY

Endre Ady, *Poems of Endre Ady* (University Press of America). Regarded by many as the finest Hungarian poet of the twentieth century, Ady's allusive verses are notoriously difficult to translate.

George Faludy, *Selected Poems 1933–80* (McClelland & Stewart/University of Georgia Press o/p). Fiery, lyrical poetry by a victim of both Nazi and Soviet repression. Themes of political defiance, the nobility of the human spirit, and the struggle to preserve human values in the face of oppression predominate.

Miklós Radnóti, *Under Gemini: the Selected Poems of Miklós Radnóti, with a Prose Memoir* (Ohio University Press, US); *Foamy Sky: the Major Poems* (Princeton University Press, US). The two best collections of Radnóti's sparse, anguished poetry. His final poems, found in his coat pocket after he had been shot on a forced march to a labour camp, are especially moving.

FICTION

Géza Csáth, *The Magician's Garden and Other Stories* (Penguin/Columbia University Press o/p); *Opium and Other Stories* (Penguin o/p). Disturbing short stories written in the magic realist genre. The author was tormented by insanity and opium addiction, killing his wife and then himself in 1918.

Tibor Dery, *The Portuguese Princess* (Calder/Northwestern University Press o/p). Short stories by a once-committed Communist, who was jailed for three years after the Uprising and died in 1977.

Peter Esterházy, *The Glance of Countess Hahn-Hahn, Down the Danube* (Quartet/Grove). Surreal story by a playful wordsmith. *Helping Verbs of the Heart*, *A Little Hungarian Pornography* and *She Loves Me* are three more works by this descendant of the famous aristocratic family.

Tibor Fischer, *Under the Frog, A Black Comedy* (Penguin/New Press). A fictional account of the 1956 revolution by the son of Hungarian survivor emigrés. Witty and enjoyable.

Agnes Hankiss, *A Hungarian Romance* (Readers International). A lyrical first novel by "Hungary's new feminist voice", dealing with a woman's quest for self-identity during the sixteenth century and the timeless conflict between personal and public interests. Translated by Emma Roper-Evans.

Dezső Kosztolányi, *Skylark* (Central European University Press, Budapest). A short and tragic story of an old couple and their beloved child by one of Hungary's top writers of the twentieth century, in a masterly translation by Richard Aczél.

Gyula Krúdy, *Adventures of Sinbad* (Central European University Press, Budapest/Random House). Stories about a gourmand and womanizer by a popular Hungarian author with similar interests to his hero.

igmond Móricz, *Be Faithful Unto Death* (Penguin). This novel a major late nineteenth-century Hungarian author sheds n how Hungarians see themselves – both then and

Péter Nádas, *A Book of Memories* (Vintage/Overlook Press). This translation of a novel about a novelist writing about a novel caused a sensation when it appeared in 1998. A Proustian account of bisexual relationships, Stalinist repression, and modern-day Hungary in a brilliant translation by Iván Sanders.

Giorgio and Nicola Pressburger, *Homage to the Eighth District* (Readers International). Evocative short stories about Jewish life in Budapest, before, during and after World War II, by twin brothers who fled Hungary in 1956.

Food and wine

Lesley Chamberlain, *The Food and Cooking of Eastern Europe* (Penguin o/p). A great compendium of recipes, nostrums and gastronomical history, guaranteed to have you experimenting in the kitchen.

Susan Derecskey, *The Hungarian Cookbook* (HarperCollins, US). A good, easy-to-follow selection of traditional and modern recipes.

Stephen Kirkland, *The Wine and Vines of Hungary* (New World Publishing, Budapest). Authoritative and accessible guide with tips on what to order. Covers the different wines of the country's regions, and their winemakers too.

George Lang, *The Cuisine of Hungary* (Penguin/Random House). A well-written and beautifully illustrated work, telling you everything you need to know about Hungarian cooking, its history and how to do it yourself.

Glossary of Hungarian terms

ÁFA Goods tax, equivalent to VAT.
Állatkert Zoo.
Áruház Department store.
ÁVO The dreaded secret police of the Rákosi era, renamed the *ÁVH* in 1949.
Barlang Cave.
Borkostoló Wine tasting.
Borozó Wine bar.
Botanikuskert Botanical garden.
Büfé Snack bar.
Cigány Gypsy (can be abusive).
Cigánytelep Gypsy settlement.
Cigányzene Gypsy music.
Csárda Inn; nowadays, a restaurant with rustic decor.
Csárdás Traditional wild dance to violin music.
Cukrászda Cake shop.
Díszterem Ceremonial hall.
Domb Hill.
Duna River Danube.
Egyetem University.
Erdő Forest, wood.
Étterem Restaurant.
Fogadó Inn.
Folyó River.
Forrás Natural spring.
Fürdő Public baths.
Gyógyfürdő Mineral baths fed by thermal springs with therapeutic properties.
Hajó Boat.
Hajóállomás Boat landing stage.
ászcsárda/halászkert Fish restaurant.
ouse.
ill or low mountain.

HÉV Commuter train running between Budapest and Szentendre.
Híd Bridge.
Honvéd Hungarian army.
Ifjúsági szálló Youth hostel.
Iskola School.
Kápolna Chapel.
Kapu Gate.
Kert Garden, park.
Kerület (ker.) District.
Kiállítás Exhibition.
Kincstár Treasury.
Kollégium Student hostel.
Komp Ferry.
Körút *(krt.)* Literally, ring road, but in Budapest refers to the main boulevards surrounding the Belváros.
Köz Alley, lane; also used to define narrow geographical regions.
Kulcs Key.
Kút Well or fountain.
Lakótelep High-rise housing estate.
Lépcső Flight of steps.
Liget Park, grove or wood.
Lovarda Riding school.
Magyar Hungarian (pronounced "*mod*-yor").
Magyarország Hungary.
Malév Hungarian national airline.
MÁV Hungarian national railways.
Megálló Railway station or bus stop.
Megye County; the county system was originally established by King Stephen to extend his authority over the Magyar tribes.
Mozi Cinema.
Műemlék Historic monument, protected building.
Művelődési ház/központ Arts centre.

Nyilas "Arrow Cross"; Hungarian Fascist movement.
Palota Palace; *püspök-palota*, a bishop's residence.
Pályaudvar (*pu.*) Rail terminus.
Panzió Pension.
Patak Stream.
Pénz Money.
Piac Outdoor market.
Pince Cellar.
Rakpart Embankment or quay.
Református The reformed church, which in Hungary means the Calvinist faith.
Rendőrség Police.
Repülőtér Airport.
Rév Ferry.
Rom Ruined building; sometimes set in a *romkert*, a garden with stonework finds.
Roma The romany word for gypsy, preferred by many Roma in Hungary.
Sétány "Walk" or promenade.
Söröző Beer hall.
Strand Beach, or any area for sunbathing or swimming.
Szabadtér Open-air.
Szálló or **szálloda** Hotel.
Szent Saint.
Sziget Island.
Szoba kiadó Room to let.
Tájház Old peasant house turned into a museum, often illustrating the folk traditions of a region or ethnic group.
Táncház Venue for Hungarian folk music and dance.
Temető Cemetery.
Templom Church.
ér Square; *tere* in the possessive case.
m Hall.
orbidden; *tilos a dohányzás* means "smoking is forbid-

Tó Lake.
Torony Tower.
Türbe Tomb or mausoleum of a Muslim dignitary.
Turista térkép Hiking map.
Udvar Courtyard.
Út Road; in the possessive case, *útja*.
Utca (*u.*) Street.
Vár Castle.
Város Town.
Városháza Town hall.
Vásár Market.
Vásárcsarnok Market hall.
Vasútállomás Train station.
Vendéglő Restaurant.
Völgy Valley.
Zsidó Jew or Jewish.
Zsinagóga Synagogue.

INDEX

M

N

O

P

R

S

T

U

V

Z

NOTES

NOTES

NOTES

NOTES

NOTES

NOTES

NOTES

NOTES

ROUGH GUIDES: Mini Guides, Travel Specials and Phrasebooks

MINI GUIDES

Antigua
Bangkok
Barbados
Big Island of Hawaii
Boston
Brussels
Budapest
Dublin
Edinburgh
Florence
Honolulu
Lisbon
London Restaurants
Madrid
Maui
Melbourne
New Orleans
St Lucia
Seattle
Sydney
Tokyo
Toronto

TRAVEL SPECIALS

First-Time Asia
First-Time Europe
More Women Travel

PHRASEBOOKS

Czech
Dutch
Egyptian Arabic
European
French
German
Greek
Hindi & Urdu
Hungarian
Indonesian
Italian
Japanese
Mandarin Chinese
Mexican Spanish
Polish
Portuguese
Russian
Spanish
Swahili
Thai
Turkish
Vietnamese

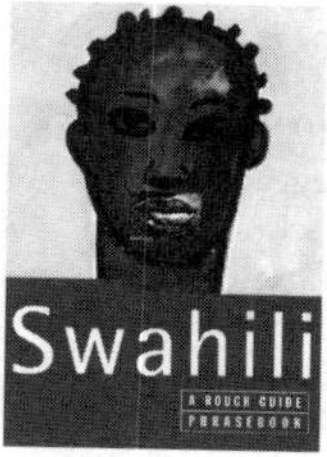

AVAILABLE AT ALL GOOD BOOKSHOPS

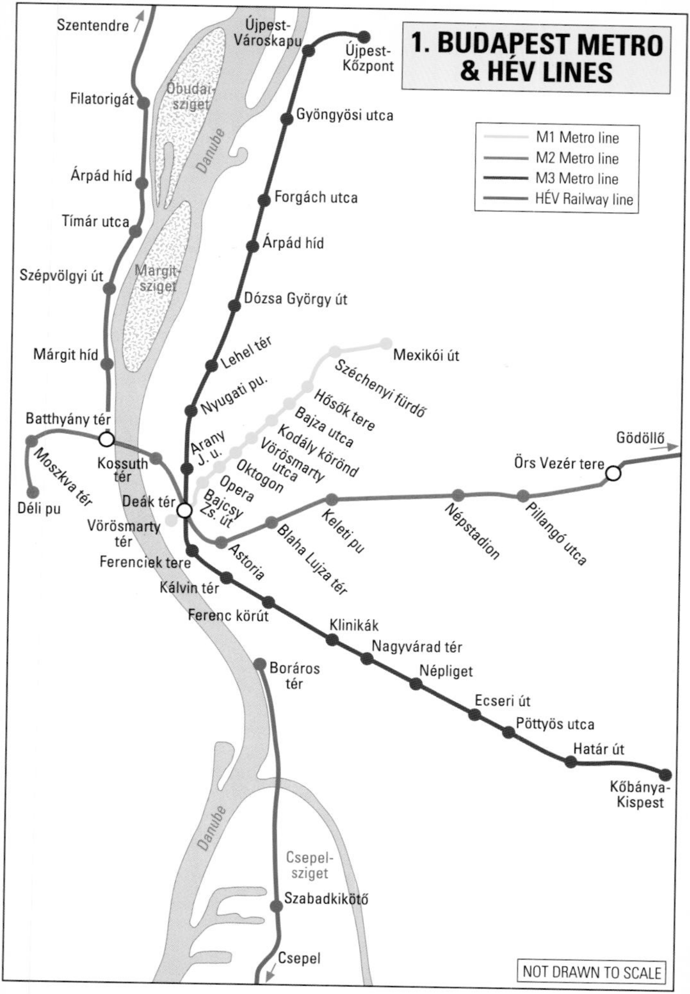
1. BUDAPEST METRO & HÉV LINES
M1 Metro line
M2 Metro line
M3 Metro line
HÉV Railway line
Szentendre
Filatorigát
Árpád híd
Tímár utca
Szépvölgyi út
Márgit híd
Batthyány tér
Moszkva tér
Déli pu
Kossuth tér
Deák tér
Vörösmarty tér
Ferenciek tere
Kálvin tér
Ferenc körút
Óbudai-sziget
Margit-sziget
Danube
Újpest-Városkapu
Újpest-Központ
Gyöngyösi utca
Forgách utca
Árpád híd
Dózsa György út
Lehel tér
Nyugati pu.
Arany J. u.
Bajcsy Zs. út
Opera
Oktogon
Vörösmarty utca
Kodály körönd
Bajza utca
Hősök tere
Széchenyi fürdő
Mexikói út
Astoria
Blaha Lujza tér
Keleti pu
Népstadion
Pillangó utca
Örs Vezér tere
Gödöllő
Klinikák
Nagyvárad tér
Népliget
Ecseri út
Pöttyös utca
Határ út
Kőbánya-Kispest
Boráros tér
Danube
Csepel-sziget
Szabadkikötő
Csepel
NOT DRAWN TO SCALE

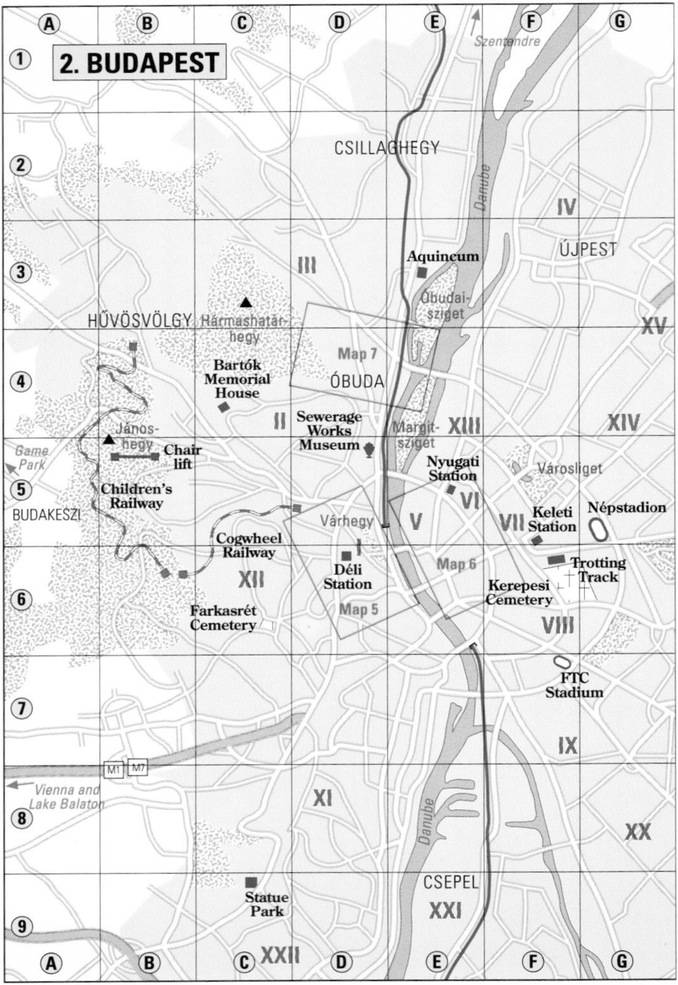
2. BUDAPEST
A
B
C
D
E
F
G
1
2
3
4
5
6
7
8
9
Szentendre
CSILLAGHEGY
Danube
IV
ÚJPEST
III
Aquincum
Óbudai-sziget
HŰVÖSVÖLGY
Hármashatár-hegy
XV
Map 7
Bartók Memorial House
ÓBUDA
II
Sewerage Works Museum
Margit-sziget
XIII
XIV
János-hegy
Chair lift
Game Park
Nyugati Station
Városliget
Children's Railway
VI
Népstadion
BUDAKESZI
Várhegy
V
VII
Keleti Station
Cogwheel Railway
Déli Station
Map 6
Trotting Track
XII
Kerepesi Cemetery
Map 5
Farkasrét Cemetery
VIII
FTC Stadium
IX
M1
M7
Vienna and Lake Balaton
XI
XX
CSEPEL
Statue Park
XXI
XXII

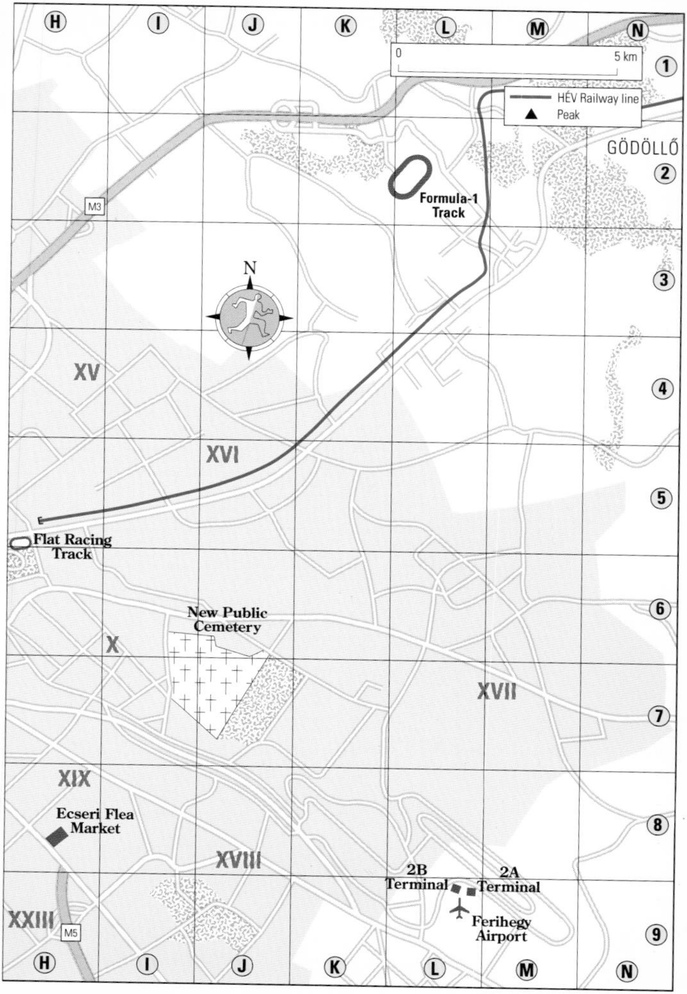
H
I
J
K
L
M
N
0
5 km
1
2
3
4
5
6
7
8
9
HÉV Railway line
Peak
GÖDÖLLŐ
M3
Formula-1 Track
N
XV
XVI
Flat Racing Track
New Public Cemetery
X
XVII
XIX
Ecseri Flea Market
XVIII
2B Terminal
2A Terminal
Ferihegy Airport
XXIII
M5

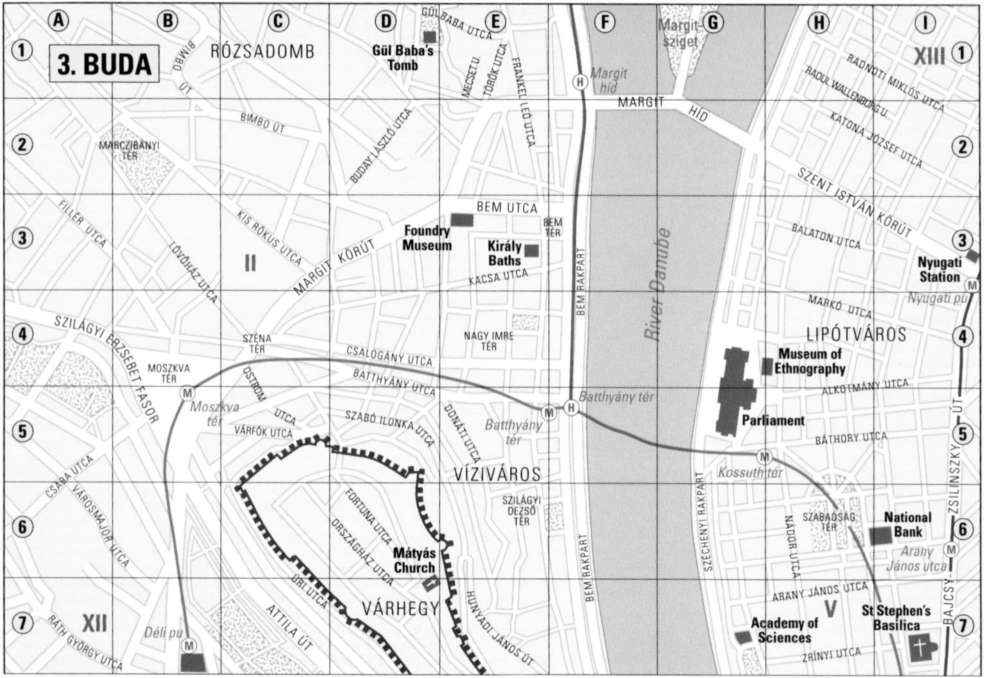
3. BUDA
RÓZSADOMB
Gül Baba's Tomb
GÜL BABA UTCA
MECSET U.
TÖRÖK UTCA
FRANKEL LEÓ UTCA
Margit híd
Margit-sziget
MARGIT HÍD
RADNÓTI MIKLÓS UTCA
RAOUL WALLENBURG U.
KATONA JÓZSEF UTCA
XIII
BIMBÓ ÚT
MARCZIBÁNYI TÉR
BUDAY LÁSZLÓ UTCA
SZENT ISTVÁN KÖRÚT
FILLÉR UTCA
LÖVŐHÁZ UTCA
KIS RÓKUS UTCA
II
MARGIT KÖRÚT
BEM UTCA
BEM TÉR
Foundry Museum
Király Baths
KACSA UTCA
BEM RAKPART
River Danube
BALATON UTCA
Nyugati Station
Nyugati pu
MARKÓ UTCA
LIPÓTVÁROS
SZILÁGYI ERZSÉBET FASOR
SZÉNA TÉR
NAGY IMRE TÉR
MOSZKVA TÉR
CSALOGÁNY UTCA
BATTHYÁNY UTCA
Museum of Ethnography
ALKOTMÁNY UTCA
Moszkva tér
OSTROM UTCA
VÁRFOK UTCA
SZABÓ ILONKA UTCA
DONÁTI UTCA
Batthyány tér
Parliament
BÁTHORY UTCA
ZSILINSZKY ÚT
VÍZIVÁROS
Kossuth tér
CSABA UTCA
VÁROSMAJOR UTCA
FORTUNA UTCA
ORSZÁGHÁZ UTCA
SZILÁGYI DEZSŐ TÉR
SZÉCHENYI RAKPART
NÁDOR UTCA
SZABADSÁG TÉR
National Bank
Arany János utca
Mátyás Church
ÚRI UTCA
ARANY JÁNOS UTCA
XII
RÁTH GYÖRGY UTCA
Déli pu
ATTILA ÚT
VÁRHEGY
HUNYADI JÁNOS ÚT
V
Academy of Sciences
St Stephen's Basilica
ZRÍNYI UTCA
BAJCSY-

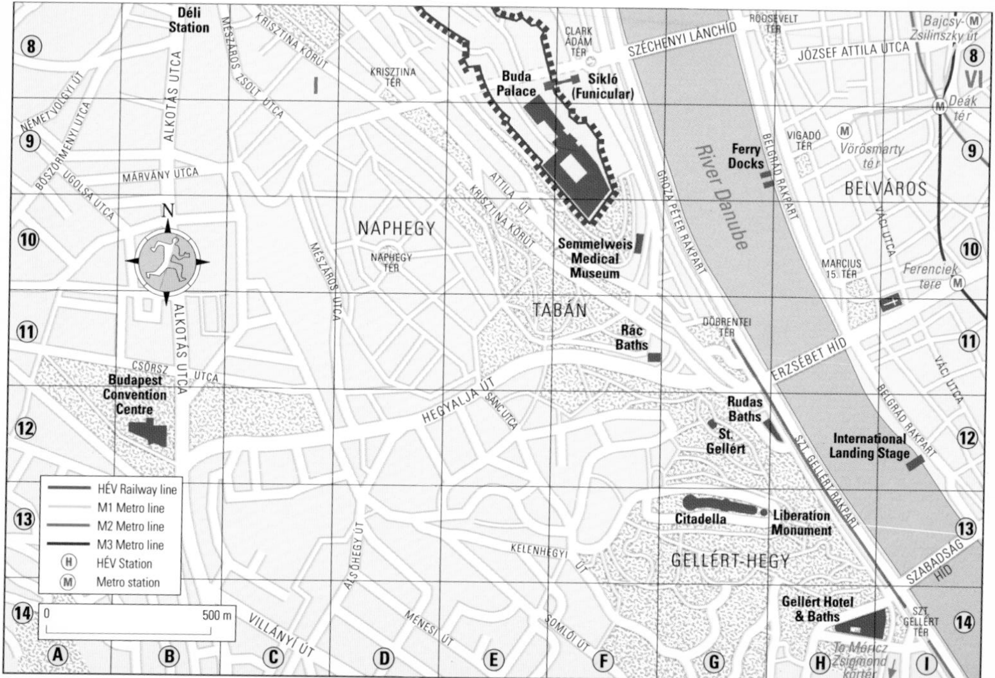

Déli Station
Buda Palace
Sikló (Funicular)
Semmelweis Medical Museum
Rác Baths
Rudas Baths
St. Gellért
Ferry Docks
River Danube
International Landing Stage
Citadella
Liberation Monument
Gellért Hotel & Baths
Budapest Convention Centre
NAPHEGY
TABÁN
BELVÁROS
GELLÉRT-HEGY
VI
KRISZTINA TÉR
NAPHEGY TÉR
CLARK ÁDÁM TÉR
ROOSEVELT TÉR
VIGADÓ TÉR
Vörösmarty tér
MARCIUS 15. TÉR
Ferenciek tere
Deák tér
Bajcsy-Zsilinszky út
DÖBRENTEI TÉR
SZT. GELLÉRT TÉR
To Móricz Zsigmond körtér
SZÉCHENYI LÁNCHÍD
ERZSÉBET HÍD
SZABADSÁG HÍD
JÓZSEF ATTILA UTCA
VÁCI UTCA
BELGRÁD RAKPART
GROZA PÉTER RAKPART
SZT. GELLÉRT RAKPART
KRISZTINA KÖRÚT
ATTILA ÚT
MÉSZÁROS ZSOLT UTCA
MÉSZÁROS UTCA
ALKOTÁS UTCA
MÁRVÁNY UTCA
NÉMETVÖLGYI ÚT
BÖSZÖRMÉNYI UTCA
UGOLSA UTCA
CSÖRSZ UTCA
HEGYALJA ÚT
SÁNC UTCA
KELENHEGYI ÚT
ALSÓHEGY ÚT
MÉNESI ÚT
SOMLÓI ÚT
VILLÁNYI ÚT
N
HÉV Railway line
M1 Metro line
M2 Metro line
M3 Metro line
HÉV Station
Metro station
0
500 m
A
B
C
D
E
F
G
H
I
8
9
10
11
12
13
14

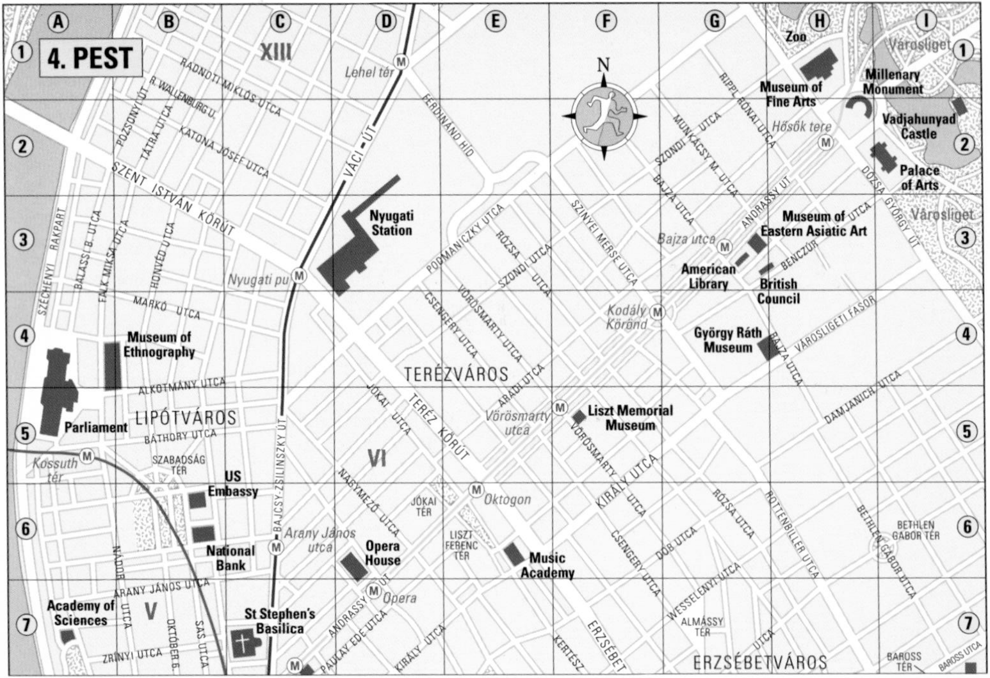
4. PEST
A
B
C
D
E
F
G
H
I
1
2
3
4
5
6
7
N
XIII
VI
V
Lehel tér
Nyugati pu
Váci út
Radnoti Miklós utca
R. Wallenburg u.
Pozsonyi út
Tátra utca
Katona József utca
Szent István körút
Széchenyi rakpart
Balassi B. utca
Falk Miksa utca
Honvéd utca
Markó utca
Alkotmány utca
Báthory utca
Szabadság tér
Kossuth tér
Nádor utca
Arany János utca
Október 6.
Sas utca
Zrínyi utca
Bajcsy-Zsilinszky út
Arany János utca
Ferdinánd híd
Podmaniczky utca
Rózsa utca
Szondi utca
Csengery utca
Vörösmarty utca
Aradi utca
Jókai utca
Teréz körút
Nagymező utca
Jókai tér
Liszt Ferenc tér
Oktogon
Vörösmarty utca
Andrássy út
Opera
Paulay Ede utca
Király utca
Kertész
Erzsébet
Szinyei Merse utca
Kodály Körönd
Bajza utca
Munkácsy M. utca
Rippl Rónai utca
Hősök tere
Benczúr
Városligeti fasor
Damjanich utca
Rottenbiller utca
Rózsa utca
Dob utca
Wesselényi utca
Almássy tér
Bethlen Gábor tér
Bethlen Gábor utca
Dózsa György út
Városliget
Baross tér
Baross utca
Terézváros
Lipótváros
Erzsébetváros
Zoo
Museum of Fine Arts
Millenary Monument
Vadjahunyad Castle
Palace of Arts
Museum of Eastern Asiatic Art
American Library
British Council
György Ráth Museum
Liszt Memorial Museum
Nyugati Station
Museum of Ethnography
Parliament
US Embassy
National Bank
Opera House
Music Academy
St Stephen's Basilica
Academy of Sciences

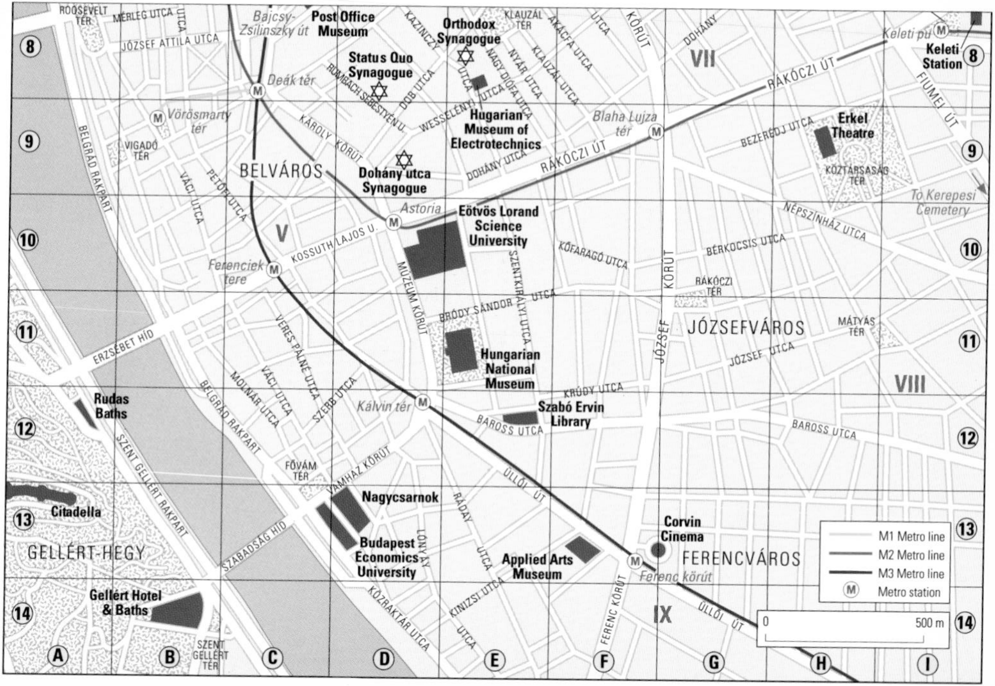
Post Office Museum
Status Quo Synagogue
Orthodox Synagogue
Hugarian Museum of Electrotechnics
Dohány utca Synagogue
Eötvös Lorand Science University
Erkel Theatre
Keleti Station
Hungarian National Museum
Szabó Ervin Library
Rudas Baths
Citadella
Gellért Hotel & Baths
Nagycsarnok
Budapest Economics University
Applied Arts Museum
Corvin Cinema
BELVÁROS
JÓZSEFVÁROS
FERENCVÁROS
GELLÉRT-HEGY
V
VII
VIII
IX
Deák tér
Bajcsy-Zsilinszky út
Vörösmarty tér
Astoria
Ferenciek tere
Kálvin tér
Blaha Lujza tér
Keleti pu
Ferenc körút
To Kerepesi Cemetery
ROOSEVELT TÉR
MÉRLEG UTCA
JÓZSEF ATTILA UTCA
VIGADÓ TÉR
BELGRÁD RAKPART
VÁCI UTCA
PETŐFI UTCA
KÁROLY KÖRÚT
RUMBACH SEBESTYÉN U.
DOB UTCA
KAZINCZY UTCA
WESSELÉNYI UTCA
NAGY DIÓFA UTCA
NYÁR UTCA
KLAUZÁL TÉR
KLAUZÁL UTCA
AKÁCFA UTCA
DOHÁNY UTCA
KÖRÚT
RÁKÓCZI ÚT
BEZERÉDJ UTCA
KÖZTÁRSASÁG TÉR
FIUMEI ÚT
NÉPSZÍNHÁZ UTCA
BÉRKOCSIS UTCA
RÁKÓCZI TÉR
MÁTYÁS TÉR
JÓZSEF UTCA
JÓZSEF KÖRÚT
KŐFARAGÓ UTCA
SZENTKIRÁLYI UTCA
BRÓDY SÁNDOR UTCA
MÚZEUM KÖRÚT
KOSSUTH LAJOS U.
ERZSÉBET HÍD
VERES PÁLNÉ UTCA
MOLNÁR UTCA
SZERB UTCA
KRÚDY UTCA
BAROSS UTCA
FŐVÁM TÉR
VÁMHÁZ KÖRÚT
SZENT GELLÉRT RAKPART
SZABADSÁG HÍD
LÓNYAY UTCA
RÁDAY UTCA
ÜLLŐI ÚT
KINIZSI UTCA
KÖZRAKTÁR UTCA
FERENC KÖRÚT
SZENT GELLÉRT TÉR
M1 Metro line
M2 Metro line
M3 Metro line
Metro station
0
500 m
A
B
C
D
E
F
G
H
I
8
9
10
11
12
13
14

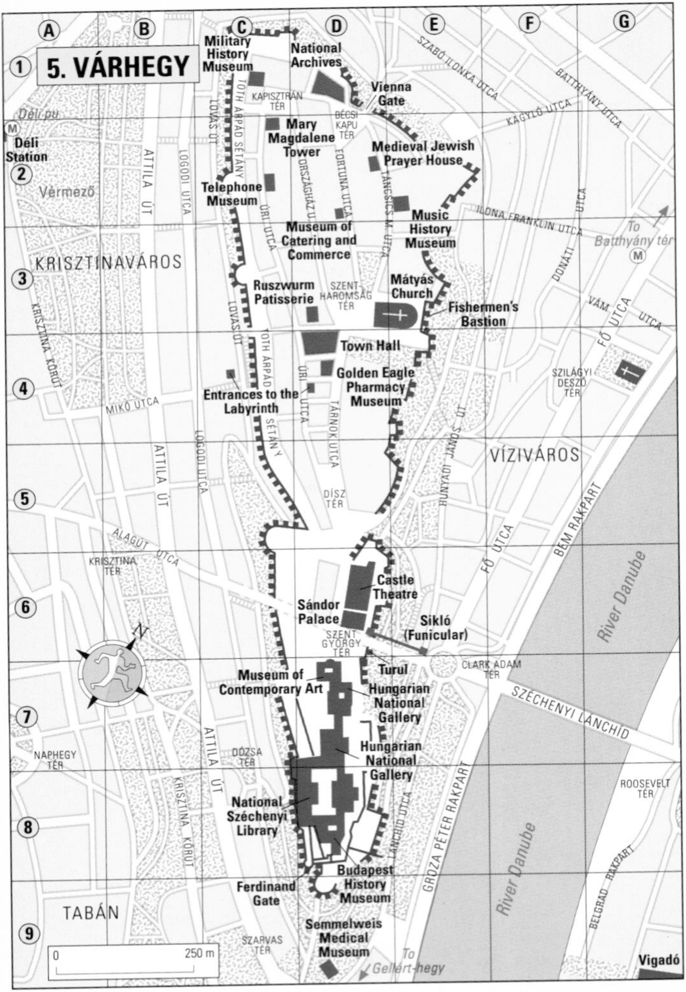
5. VÁRHEGY
Military History Museum
National Archives
Vienna Gate
Kapisztrán tér
Bécsi kapu tér
Mary Magdalene Tower
Medieval Jewish Prayer House
Telephone Museum
Music History Museum
Museum of Catering and Commerce
Ruszwurm Patisserie
Szentháromság tér
Mátyás Church
Fishermen's Bastion
Town Hall
Golden Eagle Pharmacy Museum
Entrances to the Labyrinth
Dísz tér
Castle Theatre
Sándor Palace
Sikló (Funicular)
Szent György tér
Turul
Museum of Contemporary Art
Hungarian National Gallery
Hungarian National Gallery
National Széchenyi Library
Budapest History Museum
Ferdinand Gate
Semmelweis Medical Museum
Déli pu
Déli Station
Vérmező
Krisztinaváros
Víziváros
Tabán
Szabó Ilonka utca
Batthyány utca
Kagyló utca
Ilona Franklin utca
Donáti utca
To Batthyány tér
Vám utca
Fő utca
Szilágyi Dezső tér
Bem rakpart
River Danube
Clark Ádám tér
Széchenyi Lánchíd
Groza Péter rakpart
Roosevelt tér
Belgrád rakpart
Vigadó
To Gellért-hegy
Lánchíd utca
Hunyadi János út
Tárnok utca
Úri utca
Országház u.
Fortuna utca
Táncsics M. utca
Tóth Árpád sétány
Lovas út
Attila út
Logodi utca
Krisztina körút
Mikó utca
Alagút utca
Krisztina tér
Naphegy tér
Dózsa tér
Szarvas tér
0
250 m
N

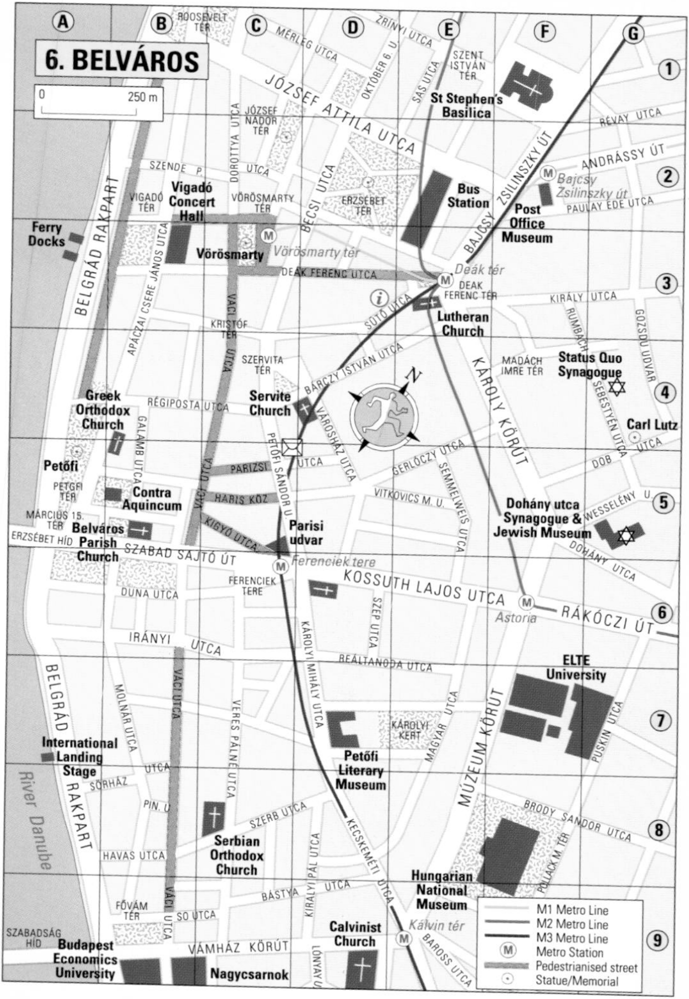
6. BELVÁROS
0 250 m
St Stephen's Basilica
Bus Station
Post Office Museum
Vigadó Concert Hall
Ferry Docks
Vörösmarty
Vörösmarty tér
Deák tér
Lutheran Church
Status Quo Synagogue
Carl Lutz
Greek Orthodox Church
Servite Church
Petőfi
Contra Aquincum
Belváros Parish Church
Parisi udvar
Ferenciek tere
Dohány utca Synagogue & Jewish Museum
Astoria
ELTE University
International Landing Stage
Petőfi Literary Museum
Serbian Orthodox Church
Hungarian National Museum
Calvinist Church
Kálvin tér
Budapest Economics University
Nagycsarnok
River Danube
JÓZSEF ATTILA UTCA
ANDRÁSSY ÚT
BAJCSY ZSILINSZKY ÚT
KÁROLY KÖRÚT
KOSSUTH LAJOS UTCA
RÁKÓCZI ÚT
MÚZEUM KÖRÚT
VÁMHÁZ KÖRÚT
BELGRÁD RAKPART
SZABAD SAJTÓ ÚT
VÁCI UTCA
M1 Metro Line
M2 Metro Line
M3 Metro Line
Metro Station
Pedestrianised street
Statue/Memorial

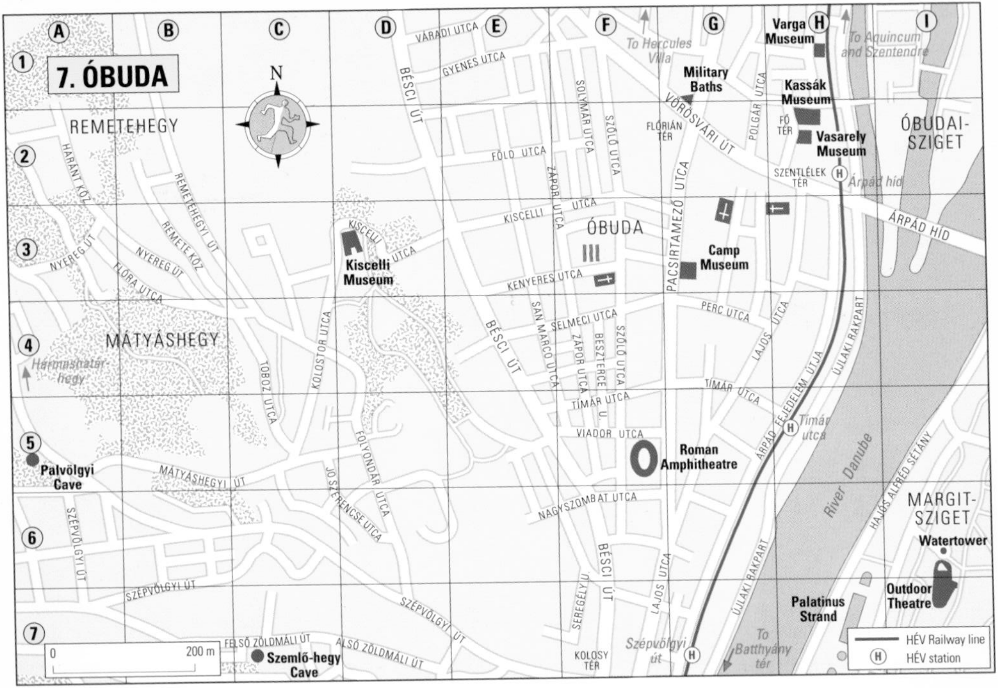
7. ÓBUDA
N
REMETEHEGY
MÁTYÁSHEGY
Hármashatár-hegy
Palvölgyi Cave
Szemlő-hegy Cave
Kiscelli Museum
Military Baths
Varga Museum
Kassák Museum
Vasarely Museum
Camp Museum
Roman Amphitheatre
Palatinus Strand
Outdoor Theatre
Watertower
ÓBUDA
ÓBUDAI-SZIGET
MARGIT-SZIGET
River Danube
To Hercules Villa
To Aquincum and Szentendre
To Batthyány tér
BÉCSI ÚT
VÁRADI UTCA
GYENES UTCA
FÖLD UTCA
SOLYMÁR UTCA
SZŐLŐ UTCA
ZÁPOR UTCA
KISCELLI UTCA
KENYERES UTCA
SAN MARCO UTCA
SELMECI UTCA
BESZTERCE U.
TÍMÁR UTCA
VIADOR UTCA
NAGYSZOMBAT UTCA
SEREGÉLY U.
KOLOSY TÉR
LAJOS UTCA
PERC UTCA
PACSIRTAMEZŐ UTCA
VÖRÖSVÁRI ÚT
FLÓRIÁN TÉR
POLGÁR UTCA
FŐ TÉR
SZENTLÉLEK TÉR
Árpád híd
ÁRPÁD HÍD
ÁRPÁD FEJEDELEM ÚTJA
Tímár utca
ÚJLAKI RAKPART
HAJÓS ALFRÉD SÉTÁNY
Szépvölgyi út
SZÉPVÖLGYI ÚT
FELSŐ ZÖLDMÁLI ÚT
ALSÓ ZÖLDMÁLI ÚT
JÓ SZERENCSE UTCA
FOLYONDÁR UTCA
KOLOSTOR UTCA
TOBOZ UTCA
MÁTYÁSHEGYI ÚT
HARANT KÖZ
REMETEHEGYI ÚT
REMETE KÖZ
NYEREG ÚT
FLÓRA UTCA
0 200 m
HÉV Railway line
HÉV station